MISSOURI
GOVERNMENT & CONSTITUTION
—— A Concise Survey & Study ——

By Dr. Richard R. Dohm
Professor Emeritus of Political Science
University of Missouri – Columbia

Edited by Brett Dufur & David Knauer

Pebble Publishing, Inc.
Rocheport, Missouri

Pebble Publishing, Inc.

ISBN 1-891708-03-1   24.95

Pebble Publishing, Inc., P.O. Box 2, Rocheport, MO 65279
Phone: 1 (800) 576-7322 • Fax: (573) 698-3108
Website: www.pebblepublishing.com
E-Mail: info@pebblepublishing.com

Editor & Publisher: Brett Dufur
Project Founder: William Higdon
Assistant Editors: Brian Beatte & David Knauer
Lead Photo Researcher: Laura Jolley, Missouri State Archives
Assistant Researchers: Angie Blume, Jed Clark, Matt Cook, Kathy Dufur, Neal Dufur, Tawnee Dufur & Derek Langendoerfer
Copy Editors: Alice Letsky & Pippa Letsky
Designers: Brian Beatte & Brett Dufur
Flowchart and map creation by Ted Twenter of Cartographic Works
Illustrator: Dennis Murphy
Cover Design: John Knight
Photo credits are listed in the back of the book.

Printed by Walsworth Publishing, Marceline, Missouri, USA

Acknowledgments

The unwavering support of William (Bill) Higdon's wife, Virginia, and the enthusiasm of Brett Dufur, editor and publisher at Pebble Publishing, Inc., have allowed Mr. Higdon's dream of a new Missouri government book to become a reality—and to become an important contribution to the Missouri curriculum.

A considerable debt of gratitude is owed to Warren Solomon, Education Consultant, Department of Elementary and Secondary Education; Laura Robinson Jolley of the Missouri State Archives for her assistance; Millie Aulbur, Field Director of Law-Related Education, The Missouri Bar Association, for providing reprint permission for the juvenile justice chapter; and Jack Wax, Media Relations Director for The Missouri Bar Association,

A heartfelt thanks is given to all of the teachers, advisors, government officials, photographers, illustrators and the dedicated staff at Pebble Publishing, Inc., who have assisted in the creation of this book.

Dedication

For All of the People of Missouri

This book is dedicated to the memory of William Higdon. Mr. Higdon taught social studies and geography at Ozark High School from 1956 to 1959 and at Hickman High School in Columbia, from 1959 to 1993. He served as Chairman of the Secondary Social Studies Department for Columbia Public Schools from 1959 to 1986. Honors received by Mr. Higdon include his appointment to the Educators to Africa Study Group in 1970, Outstanding Educator of the Year from The Guardians Inc., in 1974, and the prestigious recognition of being named Missouri State Teacher of the Year for 1974-1975.

Mr. Higdon was a member of the executive committee of the Missouri State Teachers Association and numerous other education-related organizations. He served as consultant and instructor for many institutes and workshops. Active in the community, Mr. Higdon served on the board of the Boone County Historical Museum, was vice chairman of the Columbia Bicentennial Commission and president of the Columbia Babe Ruth Baseball Association. Mr. Higdon was also a Marine and served in the Korean War.

After retiring from teaching, Mr. Higdon founded Missouri Gold Booksellers, a distributor of Missouri-related books and curriculum aids for Missouri schools and libraries. Mr. Higdon also developed much-needed curriculum aids.

The completion of this book and the continuation of Missouri Gold Booksellers as a division of Pebble Publishing, Inc., continue Mr. Higdon's efforts to enhance education in Missouri.

Preface

*M*issouri Government & Constitution: A Concise Survey & Study is designed to provide students with a knowledge of state and local governments, the reasons for their existence, the purposes they serve, and how they operate. It also demonstrates how Missouri government applies to the lives of each and every Missouri citizen.

This book has been organized to address the Show Me Standards and concepts developed by a special statewide committee of teachers (and a representative of the Missouri Department of Elementary and Secondary Education), in accordance with the Outstanding Schools Act of 1993. There are 73 Show Me Standards that define what students should know by the time they graduate from Missouri public high schools.

Students using this text should, upon completion, be able to respond favorably to the Show Me Standards pertaining to state government. This book focuses on government and political science, although certainly not in isolation. Other social studies insights and findings are integrated to provide further understanding.

"Educate and inform the whole mass of the people. Enable them to see that it is their interest to preserve peace and order, and they will preserve them. And it requires no very high degree of education to convince them of this. They are the only sure reliance for the preservation of our liberty."

— Thomas Jefferson

Contents

Chapter 1: Overview of Missouri:
    History, Politics & Progress **15**
    Introduction to Missouri 15
        How Missouri Became the Show Me State 15
        Early Explorers down the Mississippi 15
        French Influence & Ownership 16
        Territorial Legislatures 17
        Early Statehood 18
        The Civil War Divides Missouri 18
        New Constitutions 19
        Crossroads of a Nation 21
        Missouri at a Glance 22
        Commerce & Economic Development 24
    Summary & Conclusions 27
    End of Chapter Questions 28
    End of Chapter Activities 28

Chapter 2: The Foundations of Missouri Government 29
    Introduction to Governance Systems 31
    Introduction to the Federal Government 33
    Introduction to Missouri State Government 37
    State Representation in Washington, D.C.
        The Road from Missouri to the Federal Government 38
        U.S. Senators 40
        U.S. Representatives 42
    Federal Versus Local Government 44
    The Purposes that Governments Serve 44
    Governance Systems Address Human Needs 45
    How Geography Affects the Formation
        & Development of Governments 46
    How Missouri's Political Culture
        Affects Its Governance Systems 50
    How Governance Systems Serve Economic Functions 52
    How Economic Choices Confront Governments 53
    Summary & Conclusions 55
    A Few Words on Flag Etiquette 56
    End of Chapter Questions 57
    End of Chapter Activities 58
    Legal Point 58
    Out of Class Activity 58

Chapter 3: The Basis of Politics: Political Parties 59

Introduction to the Importance of Parties 61
Party Organization 63
    Primaries 63
    Committees 64
Funding 66
Campaign Finance Reform in Missouri 66
Reform Politics: Non-Partisan Elections 68
Patronage and Merit Systems 70
Party Strength in Missouri 71
Pick a Party 72
Registration and Mail-In Elections 74
Summary & Conclusions 76
End of Chapter Questions 77
End of Chapter Activities 78

Chapter 4: The Executive Branch:
Membership, Powers, Authority & Influence 79

Introduction to the Executive Branch 81
Governor's Office 83
    Qualifications for Governor 83
    The Governor's Terms of Office 85
    The Governor's Executive Powers 86
    The Governor's Appointment Authority 86
    The Governor's Role in Peace Keeping 87
    The Governor's Legislative Powers and Veto 88
    The Governor's Political Influence 91
    The Governor's Pardon Privilege 94
Other Elective Offices of the Executive Branch 96
    Lieutenant Governor's Office 96
    Secretary of State's Office 97
    State Auditor's Office 97
    State Treasurer's Office 98
    Attorney General's Office 98
The Non-Elective Executive Branch 99
    Executive Branch Departments 99
Summary & Conclusions 106
End of Chapter Questions 107
End of Chapter Activities 108
Out of Class Activity 108

Chapter 5: The Legislature:
Organization & Function 109

Introduction to the Legislative Branch 111
The Missouri Senate 112
The Missouri House of Representatives 117
Reapportionment & Redistricting 120
How a Bill Becomes a Law 122
The Legislative Process 123
Initiative & Referendum 125
The Role of Lobbyists 127
Legislative Intern Program 128
Summary & Conclusions 129
End of Chapter Questions 131
End of Chapter Activities 132
Out of Class Activities 132

Chapter 6: The Judicial System: Law & Order 135

Introduction to the Judicial Branch 135
    Organization of the Courts 135
Missouri Supreme Court 138
Court of Appeals 140
Circuit Courts 140
    Circuit Division 140
    Associate Division 143
    Municipal Division 143
Introduction to Small Claims Court 144
    How to Use Small Claims Court 146
Missouri Judges 149
    Qualifications & Terms 149
Election & Appointment 149
Non-Partisan Court Plan 151
Discipline & Removal 151
Automation 152
Significant Missouri Court Cases 154
Brief Overview of Select Missouri Lawsuits 155
Summary & Conclusions 159
End of Chapter Questions 161
End of Chapter Activities 162
Out of Class Activity 162

Chapter 7: Juvenile Justice in Missouri:
A Series of Lessons 165

Lesson 1 166
Lesson 2 173
Lesson 3 179
End of Chapter Questions 192

Chapter 8: Local Government:
Organization & Practice 193

Introduction to Local Government 195
Examples of Local Government 197
    Municipalities 197
    Villages 198
    Towns & Townships 198
    Cities 198
Forms of Government 201
Home Rule 205
Counties 206
Special Districts 209
Summary & Conclusions 211
End of Chapter Questions 215

Chapter 9: Overview of Jefferson City:
Missouri State Capital 216

History of the Missouri State Capitol 219
A Walking Tour of the Capitol Grounds 225
Tour Information 237
Other Places of Interest in Jefferson City 237

Chapter 10: Summary of the
Missouri State Constitution 239

Introduction to the Missouri Constitution 241
The Missouri Constitution 241
    Preamble 241
    Article I, Bill of Rights 241
    Articles II-XIV 246
Even with the Missouri Constitution, the Only Constant Is Change 246

Missouri Government: Online Resources 248
Recommended Reading & Bibliography 250
Index 252

Salus populi suprema lex esto

"The welfare of the people shall be the supreme law"

— Missouri State Motto

Chapter

Overview of Missouri: History, Politics & Progress

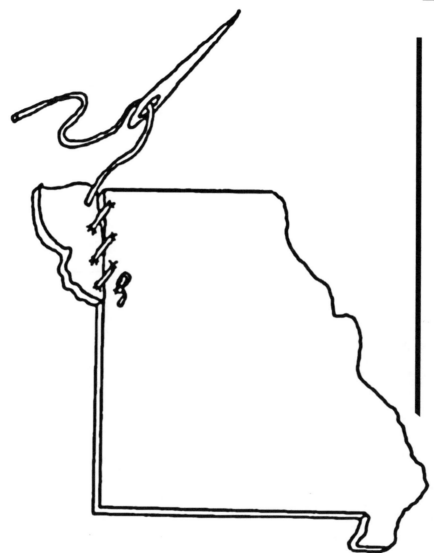

Although the original state boundary did not include the wedge-shaped area of northwest Missouri, whites settled there almost as soon as statehood was declared in 1820. In the 1830s, politicians bought the claims of the Iowa, Sac, Fox, Missouri, Omaha, Otoe, Yankton, Santee and other tribes who had been relocated there. The Platte Purchase area officially became part of Missouri in 1837.

Key Terms & Concepts

apportionment
cede
factions
government
political districts

Threshing crew near Corder, Missouri, in 1893.

Introduction to Missouri

M issouri gets its name from a tribe of Sioux Indians native to the state called the Missouris. The word "Missouri" has often been construed to mean "muddy water," but the Smithsonian Institution Bureau of Ethnology has stated that it means "town of the large canoes," and other authorities have said that the Indian syllables from which the word comes mean "wooden canoe people" or "he of the big canoe."

How Missouri Became the Show Me State

Missouri has been nicknamed several times, but the "Show Me State" is probably the most common. The saying gained favor in the 1890s, although its origin is unknown. Whatever its source, much of the credit for popularizing the expression goes to Congressman Willard D. Vandiver of Cape Girardeau County. During an 1899 speech in Philadelphia, the noted orator used the phrase, "I'm from Missouri. You've got to show me." The expression soon caught the public fancy, portraying Missourians as tough-minded skeptics.

Early Explorers down the Mississippi River

The first Europeans to visit Missouri may have been the remnants of the Spanish Conquistadores, but probably were French explorers from Canada. Father John Marquette and Louis Joliet, who descended the Mississippi from the north in 1673, supplied the first written accounts of exploration in Missouri. In 1682, the area was claimed for France by Robert Cavalier Sieur de la Salle.

A family and their covered wagon, near Hermann in 1913.

French Influence & Ownership

As part of the Louisiana Purchase Territory, Missouri had a complex history of ownership. France **ceded**, or transferred the title of, the area to Spain in 1762. Although Spain held it for 40 years, its influence was slight. The early culture of the region was determined mostly by the French.

It was the French who were responsible for the first permanent settlement in Missouri—Ste. Genevieve, in the mid-1730s. Numerous buildings from the 1700s still stand in that historic Mississippi River town. Ste. Genevieve stood alone in the huge upper Louisiana Territory until the establishment of St. Louis as a fur trading post in 1764. Because of its key location at the confluence of the Missouri and Mississippi Rivers, St. Louis quickly outgrew other area settlements and today is one of the nation's major cities.

By secret treaty in 1802, Spain returned the Louisiana Territory to the control of France. Napoleon Bonaparte, anxious to rid himself of the vast and troublesome frontier, sold it to the United States in 1803 for $15 million.

About this time, President Thomas Jefferson organized the Lewis and Clark Expedition, which was the first extensive exploration of the northwestern part of the new territory. The explorers left the St. Charles area in 1804. Their Missouri River route includes several sites still of interest to today's explorers. One is Fort Osage, just east of Kansas City—a reconstruction on the site of William Clark's original 1808 fort.

Territorial Legislatures

In 1804, the Territory was divided into two sections. The area that became Missouri was located in the District of Louisiana, part of the larger Territory of Indiana. In response to complaints that government officials were too far away, in 1805 the U.S. Congress changed the District of Louisiana to the Territory of Louisiana, with the capital at St. Louis. It was ranked as a first-class territory with a governor and three judges.

In 1812, the Territory of Louisiana was ranked second-class, allowing men in the region to vote and take part in their own **government**, or system of ruling power. Representatives were elected (one per every 500 free white male inhabitants) for a two-year term to the lower house of the legislature, the Territorial House of Representatives. The nine members of the upper house, the Legislative Council, were selected by the U.S. President from a list of 18 nominees suggested by the lower house. One non-voting representative chosen by the people was allowed in the U.S. House of Representatives. The area became the Territory of Missouri in 1812, and in 1816, it became a third-class territory, allowing both houses of the territorial legislature to be elected by the people.

The Meyer Homestead in Swiss, Missouri, circa 1900.

Early Statehood

The Missouri Compromise in 1820 allowed Missouri to enter the Union as a slave state, and the U.S. Congress authorized the people of Missouri to write a state constitution and form a state government. In June 1820, delegates were elected to a constitutional convention, where they wrote the Constitution of the State of Missouri in a little over a month. It was readily adopted. On August 28, 1820, the first state election was held and a governor, a congressman, and members of the two houses of the state legislature were chosen. The state legislature was responsible for selecting two members for the U.S. Senate. This method was used until 1913, when an amendment to the U.S. Constitution allowed for direct election of senators by the people.

The 1820 constitution stipulated that the Missouri General Assembly was to be made up of a house of representatives and a senate. House members would serve for two years and senators for four. Each county was to have at least one delegate in the house of representatives. A maximum number of 100 legislators was determined. The senate was to be smaller, with a membership of between 14 and 33 legislators, depending on the number of senatorial districts established in the state.

Missouri was admitted to the Union as the 24th state on August 10, 1821. It became the second state, after Louisiana, of the Louisiana Purchase to be admitted to the Union.

The Civil War Divides Missouri

Despite the 1820 Missouri Compromise, the state remained sharply divided between pro-Southern and Unionist **factions**, or groups of people working in a common cause against the main body. Before and during the Civil War, the tensions between these two factions led to both large-scale combat and frequent guerrilla skirmishes. The most important battle fought in Missouri was the Battle of Wilson's Creek near Springfield. Although the battle lasted little more than four hours, it was one of the bloodiest of the war. Today, the site is a National Battlefield, preserved by the National Park Service. Other important battles in Missouri were fought at Carthage, Lexington, Westport and Boonville. Missouri was the scene of 11 percent of the engagements in the war.

New Constitutions

In 1875, the constitution of Missouri was rewritten. A new formula for the representation of cities was introduced, allowing larger cities a bigger voice in state government. Many of the large cities were divided into **political districts**, where a geographic area is divided, normally based on population, for political reasons. The other components of representation remained unchanged.

In 1945, the constitution of Missouri was again rewritten, and again the basis for representation in the house of representatives was modified. Representation in the house had always been closely associated with geographic or political divisions of the state, with each county assured at least one delegate. A formula was developed to determine representation and to ensure that each county was represented fairly. It also allowed additional representatives for highly populated urban areas. The senate districts remained divided primarily on the basis of population, with a slight variation allowed.

In 1964, a special three-judge federal court in Kansas City ordered the 73rd General Assembly to pass legislation creating and establishing a system of redistricting and **apportionment.** This means to divide up an area into equal portions. This ensures equal

Meriwether Lewis (1774-1809)
Explorer, Louisiana Territorial Governor, 1807

A native Virginian, Lewis was an army officer and President Jefferson's private secretary from 1801 to 1804. He was captain of the Lewis and Clark Expedition from 1803 to 1806. After returning from the expedition, Lewis continued to have an impact on the Louisiana Purchase and the Missouri Territory. President Jefferson named Lewis governor of the Louisiana Territory as a reward for his successful expedition.

But Lewis was handicapped by his attempt to govern the territory from Washington, D.C. When Lewis finally arrived in St. Louis in 1808, he found the acting governor, Frederick Bates, well established and not happy to relinquish his power to Lewis. One of Lewis' first acts upon arrival was to request funding for an expedition to escort an Indian chief home, who had accompanied him on his expedition's return. Accusations of corruption arose when it was discovered that members of the Lewis circle of family and friends would participate in the mission to return the chief. Lewis' problems were compounded by the fact that Jefferson was no longer in the White House and Bates was undermining Lewis' authority in St. Louis. Lewis decided to return personally to Washington to clear up the misunderstanding. His personal, economic and political problems were great. He died of gunshot wounds during a stopover in Nashville, Tennessee, on the night of October 10, 1809. The debate continues as to whether he was killed or the wounds were self-inflicted.

representation for all Missourians in the house of representatives and the senate. Failure to reapportion would have resulted in a plan being imposed by the federal court.

The only practical solution was to abandon the system of using the county as a basis for representation. Instead, districts were created for house representation. The governor appointed a reapportionment committee and an amendment providing for the reapportionment was passed by the legislature and ratified by the people in time for the 1966 elections. This amendment also stipulated that reapportionment would thereafter follow each ten-year census, which has been the case since that time.

Claiborne Fox Jackson (1806-1862)
U.S. Senator
Missouri's Secessionist Governor, 1861

Claiborne Fox Jackson is one of the most outlandish figures of Missouri's colorful history. He arrived in Franklin in 1826 a poorly educated, but ambitious 20-year-old. The door to politics was opened for him by his three-time father-in-law, John S. Sappington, who introduced Jackson to Senator Thomas Hart Benton. While campaigning for Benton in 1842, Jackson was drawn back into the state legislature from which he had retired four years earlier. He eventually served as house speaker, though he broke with Benton over the elder statesman's opposition to the expansion of slavery. Jackson's support of slaveowners' rights helped lead to Benton's defeat in 1850 after 30 years in the U.S. Senate. Benton retaliated by using his influence to stop Jackson from being nominated to Congress in 1853 and 1855.

The last two years of Jackson's life made his an infamous name in the annals of Missouri history. He ran as a moderate Democrat for the office of governor and, despite showing his Southern sympathies, was elected in 1860, the year Abraham Lincoln was elected president. Jackson saw Lincoln as an enemy of the South and the slaveholder. Nevertheless, Jackson was too politically sharp to call for secession directly. He instead baited the federal government so severely over the first half of 1861 that when the federal government reacted, Jackson had his excuse to secede. Unfortunately for Jackson, the Union captain stationed at the St. Louis arsenal immediately launched an offensive, taking Jefferson City and forcing Jackson's secessionist government to flee. Jackson for a time kept the Confederate dream alive for his followers, but after a defeat at the Battle of Pea Ridge in Arkansas, he retreated. Soon after taking his family to live in Little Rock, Arkansas, Jackson died of cancer at the age of 56.

Crossroads of the Nation

Before and after the Civil War, Missouri was literally the crossroads of the nation. It was called the "Gateway to the West" since it was a popular starting point for settlers heading westward. Some settlers, of course, chose to stay in Missouri. From the lead-mining region of southeast Missouri to the German settlements along the Missouri River, a flood of immigrants made their home on the abundant Missouri frontier.

As the frontier moved farther west, pioneers passed through Arrow Rock, Independence, Kansas City and other towns. St. Joseph was assured its place in frontier history when the Pony Express began there in 1860. The old Pony Express stable is now a museum.

As the 1800s gave way to the 1900s, Missouri's history became increasingly entwined with international events. During World War I, Missouri provided 140,257 soldiers, one-third being volunteers. Notable leaders such as General John J. Pershing of Laclede, commander of the American Expeditionary Forces in Europe, came from Missouri.

During World War II, Missouri contributed more than 450,000 men and women to the various armed forces. Eighty-nine top officers were from Missouri, including General Omar N. Bradley and Lieutenant General James H. Doolittle.

The nation's leader during the last year of World War II was Lamar-born President Harry Truman. After assuming office upon the death of Franklin Roosevelt in 1945, Truman was elected to a full four-year term. Truman made the fateful decision to use the atom bomb. This hastened the Japanese surrender, which was signed on the deck of the battleship U.S.S. *Missouri* in Tokyo Bay.

World War II added an unusual page to Missouri's history as well, when Sir Winston Churchill came to Missouri in 1946 to speak at Fulton's Westminster College. During his speech, he introduced the term "Iron Curtain" into the world's lexicon. England's 17th century St. Mary Aldermanbury Church was later brought piece by piece from London and now stands in Fulton, along with a section of the Berlin Wall, as a memorial to Churchill.

In recent years, Missouri has moved rapidly into the space age, with Missouri companies providing vital components for exploration of this new frontier. From the rock carvings of ancient Missourians to the mysterious depths of space, Missouri's history is a wandering, but unbroken, chain of progress.

Wingo Family gathering in Seymour, Missouri, in 1914.

Over the past decade, Missouri has averaged 90 new manufacturers each year, while providing an average of 4,716 new jobs annually.

Since 1984, nearly $7.4 billion has been invested by new and expanding industries in Missouri.

More than 68 percent of Missouri's non-agricultural employment is in wholesale and retail trade, services and manufacturing. This accounts for more than 1,710,100 jobs.

Missouri at a Glance . . .

Missouri ranks 19th in size among the states with a total area of 69,674 square miles. Missouri is larger than any state lying east of the Mississippi River.

Population: 5,468,338 (1999 estimate)
Labor Force: 2,887,590 (1997 annual average)
Unemployment Rate: 3.4 percent (1999)
College Graduates: (age 25 and over) 22.3 percent
Traditional Industries: Agriculture, manufacturing, tourism
Expanding Industries: Business and financial services, chemicals and materials, electrical and electronic equipment, food products, health products and services, information and media, paper products, tourism, transportation equipment.
Ten Largest Cities: Kansas City, St. Louis, Springfield, Independence, Columbia, St. Joseph, St. Charles, Florissant, Lee's Summit and St. Peters.
Capital Punishment State

Topography: Missouri contains four major geographic areas:
- The Glaciated Plains
- The Western Plains
- The Ozarks
- The Southeastern Lowlands

Highest Point: Taum Sauk Mountain in Iron County—1,772 feet above sea level.

Lowest Point: The St. Francois River, near Arbyrd, in the Bootheel—230 feet above sea level.

Miles of Highway: 32,318 miles (1997)

Navigable Waterways: 1,050 miles

Sales and Use Taxes: 4.225 percent state rate. An additional 1.5 percent use tax for local jurisdictions. Communities may adopt a local sales tax, generally ranging from 0.5 to 1 percent. Counties also may adopt a sales tax ranging from 0.25 to 1 percent, with exemptions.

Kansas City's bustling Main Street as it looked in 1871. Looking north from Sixth Street.

Progress often had its price. A train wreck in Vernon County, in 1903.

Commerce & Economic Development

Missouri's central location in the heart of the nation makes it an ideal center for business, industry and tourism. From the manufacture of components for the space program to the brewing of one of America's favorite beers, from beautiful scenery to man-made attractions, Missouri is recognized by businesses and vacationers alike as America's true heartland.

Manufacturing, tourism, agriculture, wholesale and retail trade, and service enterprises are among Missouri's largest industries. Several large employers in the St. Louis area are Anheuser Busch Inc., the world's largest brewery; Monsanto, a leader in genetic technology; and McDonnell-Douglas Corporation, a manufacturer of military aircraft, commercial jets, missiles and electronic equipment used worldwide. Hallmark Inc., is located in Kansas City; Springfield is home to Mid-America Dairymen, Inc., and Procter & Gamble Paper is a major employer in Cape Girardeau. General Motors, Ford and Chrysler are all represented within the state, with assembly plants in both major metro areas.

The state's varying topography produces everything from grapes to wheat. Missouri is among the nation's leading purebred livestock producers, with livestock and related products accounting for 56 percent of the state's agricultural receipts. Hogs and poultry are also quickly expanding. The remaining 44 percent of Missouri's farm income is derived from crops such as corn, cotton, rice, grain, sorghum, hay, soybeans, wheat, fruits and vegetables.

Barite mining by
the Ozark Products
Company in
Bellefountain
in the 1930s.

Below, logging in
southeast Missouri,
around 1900.

Missouri ranks nationally as follows: second leading state in beef cows; second in hay production; sixth in rice production; eleventh in corn production; eleventh in cotton production; twelfth in milk production; and sixteenth in red meat production.

For more information on specific subjects, here are a few of the state agencies you can contact:

Dept. of Agriculture
P.O. Box 630, Jefferson City, MO 65102

Dept. of Conservation
P.O. Box 180, Jefferson City, MO 65102

Dept. of Economic Development
P.O. Box 118, Jefferson City, MO 65102

Dept. of Natural Resources
P.O. Box 176, Jefferson City, MO 65102

Dept. of Revenue
P.O. Box 840, Jefferson City, MO 65105

Division of Tourism
P.O. Box 1055, Jefferson City, MO 65102

William Clark (1770-1838)
Explorer, Missouri Territorial Governor, 1813 - 1820 (Statehood)

Clark, a native Virginian, began his long relationship with what would become Missouri when he and Meriwether Lewis left on their famous expedition together from St. Charles in May 1804. They became national heroes upon their return to St. Louis in 1806. Clark became U.S. Indian agent for tribes west of the Mississippi and was named brigadier general of Louisiana's Territorial Militia. He was based in St. Louis.

Clark's first priority as agent was to assure militia preparedness in the face of British influence among the Native Americans. He respected and reached out to Native Americans. In 1808, he also negotiated an agreement with the Osage Nation to effectively give up their lands in Missouri and Arkansas. Yet he also made some important political gestures towards the Native Americans. His actions in their defense were not popular among citizens of Missouri, and this hurt him in later attempts at public office.

In 1808, he oversaw the building of Fort Clark, now known as Fort Osage. In 1809 he became a partner in the St. Louis Missouri Fur Company.

In 1813, Clark was named territorial governor of Missouri, a position he would hold during the seven years leading up to statehood. His abilities as an Indian diplomat were called into play both during and after the War of 1812. Despite his shortcomings as an administrator, Clark is considered the best of Missouri's territorial governors.

Due to his absentee candidacy, his old political ties, and his support for Native Americans, he was unpopular with the state's newly settled voters and was defeated in his campaign to become Missouri's first state governor. He lived in St. Louis the rest of his life, serving as Indian agent quite effectively until his death in 1838.

Summary & Conclusions

The first Europeans to settle in Missouri were the French, and they were responsible for much of its early culture. The territory was acquired by the United States in the 1803 Louisiana Purchase, and Missouri became a state in 1821. Although the Missouri Compromise of 1820 allowed the state to join the Union and retain slavery, its citizens remained violently divided before and during the Civil War. The state's first constitution established its house of representatives, senate and the election of legislators by county, while later constitutions increased the representation of cities by creating districts according to population.

Missouri's position as the "Gateway to the West" made it an important point for a diverse population in the nation's 19th century westward expansion. In the 20th century, the state's influence on history has become increasingly international in scope.

Charles Drake (1811-1892)

State Representative, 1859-1862
Author of the "Drake Constitution," 1865
U.S. Senator, 1867
Chief Justice of the Court of Claims, 1885

Drake became well respected as a St. Louis attorney during the 1850s and published authoritative and much consulted work. In 1838, he established what would become his most enduring achievement, the Law Library of St. Louis.

In 1859, he was elected to the state legislature as a Democrat. He was vehemently anti-Republican at this time and made many enemies with his defense of slavery. The change which transformed Drake into the most extreme of radical Republicans was dramatic even for a Missouri politician. He soon became one of the most visible and vocal abolitionists, calling for the immediate outlawing of slavery while battling conservative Republicans who wanted a more moderate transition.

Drake's most famous achievement was the Drake Constitution of 1865, drawn up at the peak of the radical Republican's power. Drake's constitution was heavily criticized at the time for its inclusion of radical tenets such as demanding an oath of loyalty to the Union and the abolition of slavery. He attempted to reduce the power of special interests, made great strides towards establishing public schools, and made approbation, or approval, by the general public a requirement for any future amendments to the constitution.

Drake was elected a U.S. Senator in 1867. The Radical Republican party lost its political base two years later, though as a reward for his service as a Republican, Ulysses S. Grant appointed Drake chief justice of the court of claims.

Chapter 1
Overview of Missouri:
   History, Politics & Progress

End of Chapter Questions

Use the text along with outside material to answer the following questions. Be sure to review the key terms and concepts from the beginning of the chapter before you start.

1. What was the Missouri Compromise? Did it solve the problem for which it was designed?

2. Where did Missouri get its name?

3. Why is Missouri called the "Show Me" state?

4. Briefly explain the history of Missouri's ownership.

5. Who were Lewis and Clark, and what did they do?

6. What were some of the differences between Missouri as a territory and Missouri as a state?

7. What were some of Missouri's contributions to the history of the 20th century?

8. How was state representation treated differently from the 1820 Constitution to the 1964 federal court order?

End of Chapter Activities

Use the text along with outside material to complete the following activities.

1. Locate your senatorial and representative districts on the maps in Chapter 5 and on an older map of Missouri's electoral districts. Have the boundaries of your districts ever changed? Why?

2. Look at any map showing the towns and cities of Missouri and list all the French place names you see. Where are most of them located, and why?

3. Research the provisions of the Missouri Compromise. Discuss with your classmates what you think was the original rationale for the plan.

Chapter

The Foundations
of Missouri Government

Key Terms & Concepts

confederal system
constitution
democracy
federalism
federal system
ordinance
political culture
private sector
privatization
public sector
separation of powers
status quo
tax base
unitary system

Introduction to Governance Systems

Governments exercise legitimate authority and direction over the population in a specified territory. Governance systems include all the institutions and processes necessary to maintain peace and security, while developing agreed-upon goals. In a **democracy**, governance systems are supported by free elections of decision-makers, which requires the election process to be fair, honest and lawful.

Law, then, is the foundation of government. An agreed-upon written **constitution** usually sets the legal foundation and parameters for a nation's government. Included in this constitution is the outline for governmental structure.

The constitution may call for a unitary, federal or confederal governing system. In a **unitary system**, virtually all power rests with a central government. A **federal system** divides power between states or provinces and the central government, as in the United States and Canada. In a **confederal system**, the states or other governmental units retain most powers, while delegating some measure of authority to a central government—as was the case of the United States under the Articles of Confederation.

The present U.S. Constitution replaced the Articles of Confederation because the central government did not have the infrastructure to meet its responsibilities effectively. Of course tensions always exist over how much power governments should have over their people. This major theme continues in politics today.

The 10th Amendment to the U.S. Constitution outlines the division of powers between the states and the federal government:

The powers not delegated to the United States by the Constitution, nor prohibited by it to the States are reserved to the States respectively, or to the people.

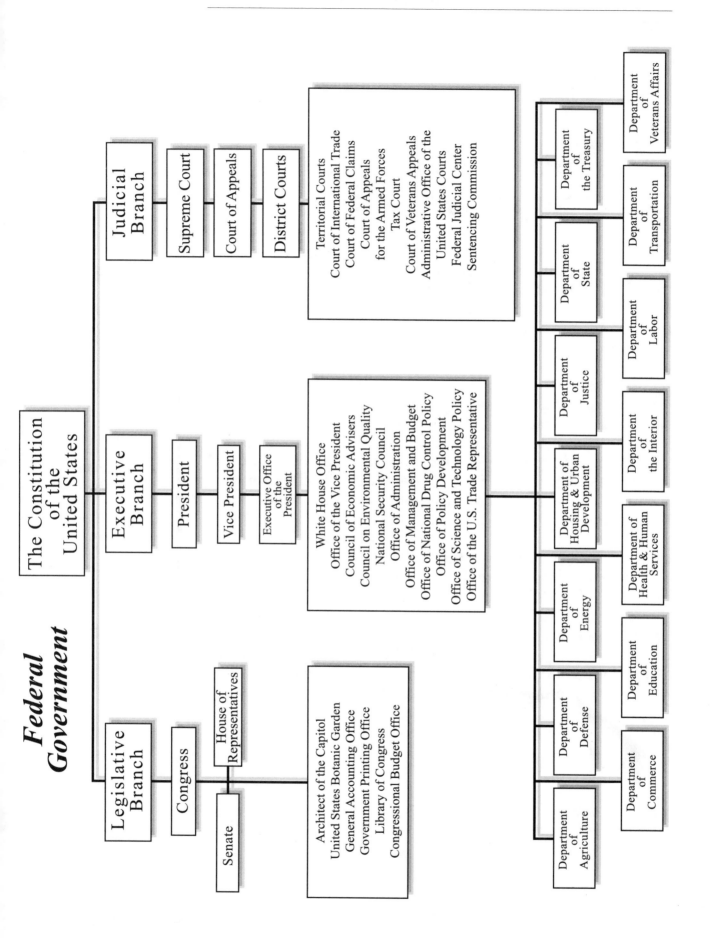

Federal Government

The Constitution of the United States

Legislative Branch
- Congress
  - House of Representatives
  - Senate
    - Architect of the Capitol
    - United States Botanic Garden
    - General Accounting Office
    - Government Printing Office
    - Library of Congress
    - Congressional Budget Office

Executive Branch
- President
- Vice President
- Executive Office of the President
  - White House Office
  - Office of the Vice President
  - Council of Economic Advisers
  - Council on Environmental Quality
  - National Security Council
  - Office of Administration
  - Office of Management and Budget
  - Office of National Drug Control Policy
  - Office of Policy Development
  - Office of Science and Technology Policy
  - Office of the U.S. Trade Representative

- Department of Agriculture
- Department of Commerce
- Department of Defense
- Department of Education
- Department of Energy
- Department of Health & Human Services
- Department of Housing & Urban Development
- Department of the Interior
- Department of Justice
- Department of Labor
- Department of State
- Department of Transportation
- Department of the Treasury
- Department of Veterans Affairs

Judicial Branch
- Supreme Court
- Court of Appeals
- District Courts
  - Territorial Courts
  - Court of International Trade
  - Court of Federal Claims
  - Court of Appeals for the Armed Forces
  - Tax Court
  - Court of Veterans Appeals
  - Administrative Office of the United States Courts
  - Federal Judicial Center
  - Sentencing Commission

Introduction to the Federal Government

In accordance with the plan stipulated by the U.S. Constitution, the federal government in Washington, D.C., divides power between its three branches: executive (the president and his cabinet); legislative (the lawmakers in Congress); and judicial (the Supreme Court, federal appeals and district courts). The resulting **separation of powers** between the three branches is intended to prevent the collection of too much authority in any one place.

The U.S. government operates on a federal model, whereby authority is further distributed between the central government and the states. This qualification is a key of Jeffersonian democracy, so named after Thomas Jefferson, who preferred a weak federal government to prevent abuses of power. It should also be pointed out, however, that Jefferson envisioned the United States remaining a largely agrarian society of self-sufficient farmers, not the highly industrialized and urban nation that was to develop. Likewise, the dynamics of **federalism**, or how much authority the states or the central government should exercise relative to each other, was intended by the founders who drafted the Constitution to remain an open debate that could evolve throughout the nation's history.

The distribution of power at the federal level is reflected in the organization of Missouri state government, which is also divided into three branches. They are the executive branch, the legislative branch, and the judicial branch.

Article IV: Section 4 of the U.S. Constitution protects the right to "majority rule."

The United States shall guarantee to every State in this Union a Republican Form of Government, and shall protect each of them against Invasion; and on Application of the Legislature, or of the Executive (when the Legislature cannot be convened) against domestic violence.

By the 10th Amendment, states have reserved powers, or those not specifically delegated to the federal government.

Concurrent powers are those common to both levels, but a supremacy clause in the U.S. Constitution favors the federal government in case of conflict.

Federal Government
Executive Branch
4 year terms

President

✓ Commands the Armed Forces
✓ Grants reprieves
✓ Executes all laws passed by Congress
✓ Earns $200,000 annually

✓ Controls foreign policy
✓ Makes certain appointments
✓ Presents the administration's budget

Requirements: Must be a citizen of the United States for at least 14 years & must be at least 35 years old.

Vice President

✓ Presides over functions of the Senate
✓ Acts as emissary of the president
✓ Assumes the presidency if the president dies, resigns, is incapacitated or is impeached
✓ Earns $171,500 annually

Judicial Branch
U.S. Supreme Court

✓ Heads the U.S. judicial branch
✓ Appointed for life
✓ Justices earn $164,100

✓ Nine judges
✓ Chief Justice earns $171,500

U.S. Court of Appeals

✓ Judges earn $141,700
✓ Eleven regions plus the District of Columbia

U.S. District Courts

✓ 94 districts (2 in Missouri)
✓ Judges earn $133,000

Legislative Branch (Congress)
House of Representatives

✓ Number determined by population of the state
✓ Minimum age is 25
✓ 2 year terms
✓ Earn $133,600 annually

✓ Missouri currently has 9 representatives
✓ U.S. resident for 7 years
✓ Must reside in the state they represent

Senate

✓ 2 per state
✓ U.S. resident for 9 years
✓ Must reside in the state they represent

✓ Minimum age is 30
✓ 6 year terms
✓ Earn $133,600 annually

Harry S Truman (1884-1972)

Judge, 1922-1924, 1926-1934
U.S. Senator, 1934-1944
Vice President, 1944-1945
President, 1945-1953

Harry S Truman is considered one of the great political figures of Missouri, not only because he rose to the highest office in the nation, but because he remained true to his beliefs and roots through both failure and success.

His first years were spent in and around Independence. He dreamed of becoming a soldier after high school, but his poor vision kept him out of the army. However, he was able to serve in the National Guard and saw action in World War I. Using his reputation as a veteran and upstanding citizen, he ran for the office of Eastern District judge for Jackson County in 1922. His victory owed much to the support of Thomas Pendergast's political ties, or machinery, in Kansas City. Truman's fine reputation helped Pendergast seem more respectable and aided the political boss as much as the favors Truman provided to the machine.

Truman eventually earned an urban following, becoming adept at using the "political machinery" to his benefit. He was an early supporter of civil rights for African Americans in Kansas City. In 1934, he prepared to run for the U.S. House of Representatives, but the Pendergast people preferred that he enter the race for the U.S. Senate. With the statewide influence of the political boss, Truman came out victorious. Although Truman became a consistent supporter of President Roosevelt, members of the administration distanced themselves from the Missouri senator, considering him tainted by the Pendergast machine. Nevertheless, Truman's re-election in 1940 despite Pendergast's imprisonment and the broad-based support for the Missouri senator so impressed Roosevelt's people that they accepted Truman as FDR's running mate in 1944. When Roosevelt passed away on April 12, 1945, Truman became president.

Truman's greatest achievements during his presidency were his early support for civil rights, including desegregation of the military, and his support of Western Europe and the Middle East through the Marshall Plan, Truman Doctrine, and North Atlantic Treaty Organization (NATO). During his administration the first atom bomb was dropped—marking the end of World War II. In 1953, he came home to Independence. Despite his shortcomings and unpopularity nationwide, he was always well respected in Missouri. He remained active for a time in national politics until he was forced to retire in 1963 because of failing health. He died in a Kansas City hospital on December 26, 1972. At his death, he was considered an elder statesman, and he is remembered for many things. He was one of the last politicians who rose to power without the use of mass media.

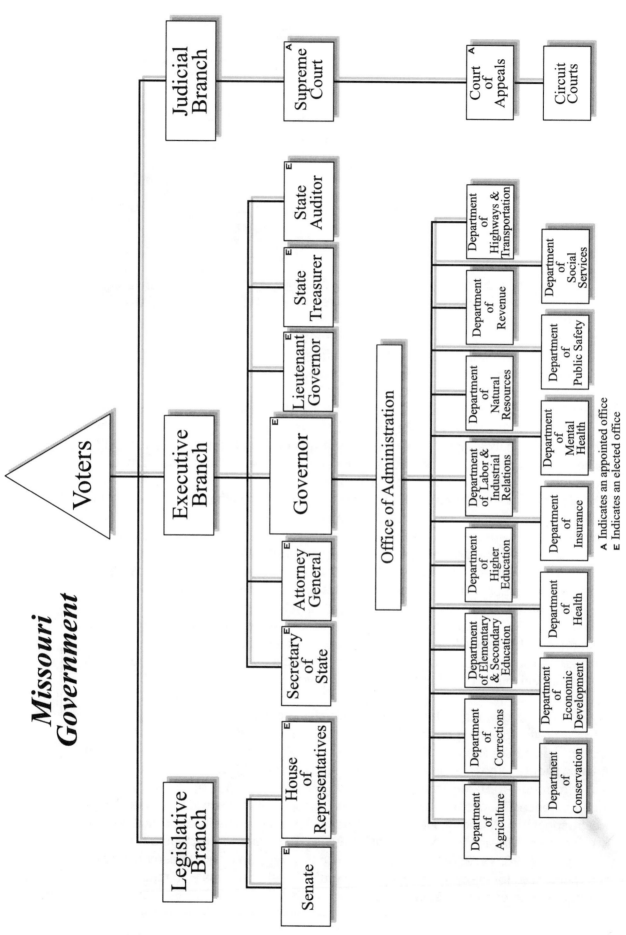

Missouri Government

Introduction to Missouri State Government

Missouri state government is organized much like the federal government. It has three separate branches. The three branches of Missouri government are the executive branch (the governor and his administration); the legislative branch (the lawmakers in the General Assembly); and the judicial branch (the Missouri Supreme Court, court of appeals and circuit courts). This organization is set out in the Missouri constitution (Article II, Section I), much like the federal government's organization is outlined by the U.S. Constitution. Separate chapters of this book will discuss the three branches of Missouri state government, their responsibilities, and their organization at length.

According to the U.S. Constitution, the states may exercise any powers that are not specifically reserved for the federal government. The powers reserved to the federal government are outlined in Article I, Section 8 of the U.S. Constitution. They include regulating commerce with foreign nations, printing money, raising an army and declaring war, and other duties we commonly associate with a nation functioning in the larger world. The individual states may make and enforce laws, as long as they do not conflict with federal law or the U.S. Constitution. The states also administer the policies and programs of the federal government at the state level. But the main purpose of state government is to serve the citizens of the state and their interests.

Preamble of Missouri's constitution:

We the people of Missouri, with profound reverence for the Supreme Ruler of the Universe, and grateful for His goodness, do establish this Constitution for the better government of the state.

Missouri's current constitution is its 4th since it became a state in 1820. The constitution was approved by voters in 1945 and has been amended many times since. Amendments must be approved by voters, but initiation can be by citizen petitions, or by General Assembly joint resolutions.

James Houchin on the campaign trail in Renick, Missouri, in 1902.

President Harry Truman and Winston Churchill in Fulton in 1946.

State Representation in Washington, D.C.

The Road from Missouri...
...to the Federal Government

Missouri has 11 people in Washington, D.C., who represent the state in the U.S. Congress. The U.S. Congress is the legislative, or lawmaking branch, of the federal government. Its purpose is to effectively represent the political voices of the people of the United States. The U.S. Congress is divided into two distinct branches, which are called the Senate (Upper House) and the House of Representatives (Lower House). Its two-year sessions last from each odd-numbered year to the next odd-numbered year.

Missouri's U.S. Senators

Terms of Office

Christopher S. Bond (R)   1986 – 2004

John Ashcroft (R)   1994 – 2000

Missouri's Representatives
in the U.S. House of Representatives*

	District, Office	Terms of Office
William Clay (D)	1, St. Louis	1968 - 2000
James Talent (R)	2, St. Louis	1992 - 2000
Richard Gephardt (D)	3, St. Louis	1976 - 2000
Ike Skelton (D)	4, Jefferson City	1976 - 2000
Karen McCarthy (D)	5, Kansas City	1994 - 2000
Pat Danner (D)	6, Kansas City	1992 - 2000
Roy Blunt (R)	7, Springfield	1996 - 2000
Jo Ann Emerson (R)	8, Cape Girardeau	1996 - 2000
Kenny Hulshof (R)	9, Columbia	1996 - 2000

* elected every two years.

U.S. Senators

"Society in every state is a blessing, but Government, even in its best state, is but a necessary evil. In its worst state, an intolerable one."

—Thomas Paine
Common Sense, 1776

Missouri, like every state, is represented in Washington, D.C., by two senators who are elected to six-year terms. The U.S. Senate provides a smaller body of more experienced lawmakers to counterbalance the operations of the shorter-term (two-year) U.S. House of Representatives. Senators must be at least 30 years old, have been citizens of the United States for at least nine years and must be residents of the state in which they are elected. The terms of one-third of the members of the Senate expire every two years, allowing a regular mixture of experienced and new lawmakers.

The Senate can write new laws and, along with the House, must approve all legislation before it can take effect. It is presided over by the U.S. vice president, and in his absence, the president pro tem, who is elected by his peers in the majority party.

Christopher S. "Kit" Bond
U.S. Senator

Christopher Bond was born March 6, 1939, a sixth generation Missourian. He earned his bachelor's degree at Princeton University and graduated first in his class from the law school at the University of Virginia. His career in Missouri politics began in 1969 with his appointment as assistant attorney general, after which he was elected state auditor in 1970. He was twice elected Governor, in 1972 and 1980. As a U.S. senator, he has distinguished himself by winning elections in difficult years for Republicans: in 1986 he was the only senator to capture a seat previously held by a Democrat; in 1992 he was the only Republican to win in Missouri; and in 1998 he won re-election when many incumbent Republicans lost elections across the nation.

Serving on the Senate Budget Committee and chairing the Appropriations Committee, Bond has worked for a fiscally conservative federal government, passing legislation to balance the nation's budget and provide tax relief to families and small businesses. He has also sought to free small business owners from excess government regulation with his Red Tape Reduction Act. Bond has given especially close attention to the issues facing families and children.

He helped to pass the Family and Medical Leave Act, which allows workers to take time off without fear of losing their jobs when a child is born or a family member is ill. His Parents As Teachers (PAT) program, which seeks to improve learning environments for pre-schoolers, was expanded to include other states beyond Missouri. In 1998 Bond won increased funding to help Missouri law enforcement keep track of juvenile offenders.

His long-term agenda focuses on improving education by returning more decision-making and money to the local level, providing tax relief to small businesses and families, and strengthening social services for the elderly.

During both federal and state level election years, placards supporting a variety of candidates can be found throughout your community.

The U.S. Senate also favors smaller states, since each state is given equal representation, regardless of state size. Of the one hundred senators, one-third are elected every two years for six-year terms. Terms are staggered this way so that only one-third of the U.S. Senate is going out of office at any given time. This ensures continuity of the Senate's objectives.

Each one-third of the U.S. Senate is called a class. U.S. Senators can be re-elected for an unlimited number of terms. This is not uncommon. Many senators have had long careers in the U.S. Senate.

U.S. Representatives

Nine Missourians currently represent Missouri in the U.S. House of Representatives, which has 435 members. Members of the House are elected to two-year terms from districts in the state drawn up according to population. Therefore, heavily populated states have more representatives, and a state's number of representatives will increase or decrease in relation to the state's population. Members of the House of Representatives must be at least 25 years old, U.S. citizens for seven years and residents of the state they represent.

Because members of the House are elected for shorter terms than senators, they are intended to be the most direct "voice of the people" in Congress. Their actions generally reflect the wishes of their constituents more immediately than those of senators.

Like the Senate, the House of Representatives can write new laws, and it must approve all legislation before it can take effect. The House is presided over by the Speaker of the House, a member who is traditionally elected to his position by the majority party.

Richard Gephardt
U.S. Representative

Richard Gephardt is one of Missouri's nine members of Congress serving in the U.S. House of Representatives. He was born in 1941 in south St. Louis, the same district he serves today. He graduated from Northwestern University and the University of Michigan Law School, then entered politics as a precinct captain in St. Louis's 14th ward. He was twice elected to the board of city aldermen before his election to Congress in 1976.

He rose quickly through the House Democratic leadership in the 1980s, distinguishing himself on the Ways and Means and Budget Committees on the issues of health care reform, trade and tax fairness. He helped to found the Democratic Leadership Council, a group that worked to transform the party's too-liberal image, and served as chairman of the House Democratic Caucus. In 1988 he made a bid for the U.S. presidency and won three state primaries before withdrawing. With a Democratic majority in Congress in 1989, Gephardt was chosen house majority leader, the second-ranking post, and after Republicans regained a majority in 1994, he was elevated to the top Democratic slot in the House, democratic leader.

Since then, Gephardt has dedicated himself to regaining a Democratic majority in the House. In the early 1990s he opposed President Bush's tax and economic policies and the House Republicans' "Contract with America," frequently clashing with then-Speaker Newt Gingrich. He also broke with the Clinton administration in opposing the North American Free Trade Agreement (NAFTA). In his legislative record, Gephardt has been a strong advocate of putting families first, and he has become a leading voice on international trade and the protection of American jobs in the global economy.

James Beauchamp "Champ" Clark (1850-1921)

U.S. Congressman, 1888-1889, 1892-1893, 1896-1921
House Minority Leader, 1908-1911, 1919-1921
Speaker of the House, 1911-1919

James Beauchamp "Champ" Clark was born in Kentucky, but settled in Missouri after finishing law school. He worked as an attorney in the small Missouri towns of Louisiana and Bowling Green but coveted political power as much as he did clients. After serving in city and county government, along with a term as state representative in the late 1880s, he ran for the U.S. Congress in 1890 only to lose the nomination of the Democratic party. He won in 1892 but was defeated in his reelection bid of 1894. However, in 1896, he began a 12-term run as U.S. representative for the 9th District of Missouri, eventually becoming the only Missourian to serve as Speaker of the House.

Clark's political views represented the mainstream politics of the Democratic party during the Progressive Era. He regularly supported the direct election of senators, ridding the country of the electoral college, and establishing the primary system to nominate presidential and vice-presidential candidates. He was also a loyal Democrat and worked to unite the urban and rural wings of the party. His own constituents were agrarian, thus Clark was in favor of hard currency and free trade policies to support farmers in the 1890s. He later modified his views to follow his party in its support of the Federal Reserve system and the protection of American industries. It was this partisanship, along with his sometimes excessive rhetoric, that lost him the presidential nomination in 1912 to Woodrow Wilson. His inability to sponsor legislation during his time in Congress was cited by the national press as another of his liabilities.

Clark's greatest glory, however, came when he was elected Speaker of the House in 1911. He was so well respected as Speaker that in a Republican-dominated House, he was reelected Speaker in 1916. Unfortunately, he was defeated in his 1920 bid to win reelection to the House as Republicans gained power after World War I. He is remembered for his staunch Jeffersonian ideals and for his support of progressive issues.

Federal Versus Local Government

What level of government interests students and citizens the most? Most would answer, "the federal government." People feel there is more action at the federal level. Many believe great decisions are only made in Washington, D.C.—not in Missouri's state capital of Jefferson City, or in their local community.

Yet, very often, an individual's life is affected more by local or state government. Recent reform puts more responsibility at the state and local levels, allowing the federal government to downplay its role. Elections are held by local authorities, and land use decisions are made by both city and county governments. If an individual drives drunk, he or she will probably be arrested by local law enforcement officers and face the local judiciary. These are only a few areas in which state and local governments greatly impact the citizenry.

There is an important difference between the relationship of states to the federal government, and the relationship of local units of government to state government. The federal model best describes the state's relationship to Washington, D.C. However, to the surprise of many, the governance system for state and local governments is the unitary model.

Whereas state governments share power with Washington, D.C., state governments totally control the existence of local governments. They breathe life into them, and can put them out of existence as well. We will return to this relationship between state and local government in a later chapter.

The Purposes Governments Serve

Citizens have very different views on the role government should play in their town or community. Whether a community should organize into a government is just the first of many decisions to be made. Once organized, what functions should the government provide? Some people look for government to solve a variety of problems, in addition to providing basic functions such as law enforcement and fire protection. These basic functions are of most concern to business and property owners, who would argue that the purpose of government is to support economic development, which of course requires stability, law and order. Others emphasize improving the quality of life, including assistance for the poor. Government, they would argue, exists to help develop the "good society," that is, to promote harmony and equality.

These two approaches often define conservatives and liberals, but such labels can be misleading. Indeed, many individuals hold varying points of view. They may be conservative on one issue but liberal on another. Of course, there are also those whose views are at one or the other end of the political spectrum. These latter folks add a dynamic factor to politics, but sometimes hinder compromise, which is necessary for democracy to work.

Governance Systems Address Human Needs

Governance systems are crucial for society. Without them there would be chaos. Take a minute to imagine your community—or even the entire state—without a government. Initially, some people might think that no government would be a blessing, but consider the consequences. At the very least, the need for law enforcement, fire protection and roads is critical for a well-ordered community.

With **privatization**, some functions normally reserved for government are turned over to companies that seek to make a profit from offering that particular service. These companies often replace public utilities, offering services as diverse as electricity, trash pick-up, transportation and other needs of the general public. This for-profit environment is called the **private sector.** Government and public services are generally defined as the **public sector**. Privatization can work well because government entities no longer have the expense and burden of performing certain services. Also, delegating the services to a private, competition-based company can often lower costs to the citizens, since the company must offer a competitive price and operate efficiently to stay in business.

But not all functions of government would work as privately run businesses. To whom would a privately owned police force be accountable? Education has a long history of being offered by both public and private institutions, and there is presently much discussion over whether to turn more of it over to the private sector.

Some individuals yearn for a community where everyone contributes in a small way and formal governance is not needed. Undoubtedly, some communities like this exist, but it is not practical for large populations. Also, some citizens argue that the advances of modern civilization could not have been accomplished without governmental institutions, including public education (particularly in science and technology). Regardless, many continue to argue for reduced governance at any cost.

How Geography Affects the Formation & Development of Governments

Geographic factors are often responsible for the creation of governments, especially cities. Towns sprang up on transportation routes, particularly where there was a break in transportation, such as where rivers joined the ocean or other major bodies of water. Goods were off-loaded and loaded again for shipment.

Kansas City, St. Louis, St. Joseph and Cape Girardeau are all examples of Missouri cities that experienced rapid growth in their early days, because of their proximity to the transportation and trade on the Missouri or Mississippi riverways.

Other reasons for town creation included the development of the railway system. Steam engines had to refuel and take on water regularly. Crew change points led almost inevitably to the growth of a whole series of new towns across the nation.

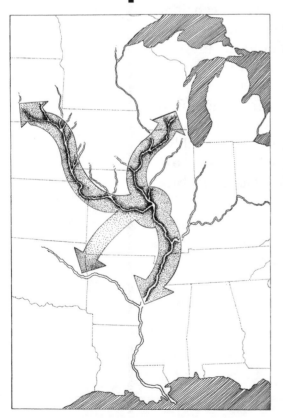

Cities sprang up along water transportation routes. Kansas City, St. Louis, St. Joseph and Cape Girardeau all grew quickly, due in part to their key locations along the Missouri or Mississippi Rivers.

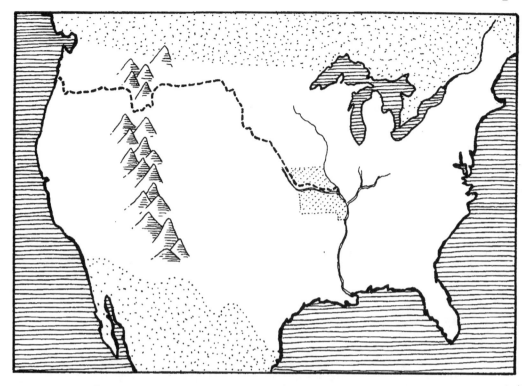

The Oregon Trail was a popular trail for early settlers heading west. Beginning in the 1840s, a steady flow of people migrated west on the trail, which stretched more than 2,000 miles over plains, across rivers and over mountains.

Of course there are other reasons for city creation. Jefferson City was created solely for political reasons. The area where Jefferson City was developed was chosen because of its central location within the state. Even Washington, D.C., was created for political reasons.

Many cities in other countries have been created for political reasons too, such as Brasilia, the capital of Brazil in South America. Brasilia was deliberately located in the interior of the country to draw development inward, away from the congested coasts.

With all of society's improvements in transportation and communication, the location of a capital is not quite as important as it once was. Since World War II, fewer new cities have been built for political reasons. Instead, most government buildings have been placed in pre-existing metropolitan areas and suburbs.

Since the end of World War II, the development of cities has dramatically shifted for another reason, too. Suburban growth has been phenomenal. The origins of suburbs are numerous. Returning soldiers married and found limited housing in the cities. This led them towards the relatively wide-open areas surrounding the cities.

Although urban areas remain the centers of our state's population, there is an increasing trend back to rural areas. This movement has been facilitated by technology such as the Internet and video-conferencing. This new trend where many white collar workers work from home and communicate with their office and peers by phone, fax and e-mail, is called "virtual officing."

An early horse-powered ferry boat near New Haven, Missouri.

Also, these returning soldiers desired the open space, yards and gardens associated with a single family home.

Many veterans were from small towns and rural areas and disliked cities to begin with. Besides their anti-urban attitudes and desire for space, two other important factors contributed to the development of comprehensive suburbs.

The first factor absolutely necessary for suburban living was the automobile. Without such transportation, suburbs would have had to follow mass transit lines and would not have encircled cities as quickly. Americans love their automobiles. An automobile allows a person to live "anywhere" and drive to work, and one-hour commutes are not uncommon nowadays.

The second but equally important factor required for suburbanization was the availability of home loans. Most new families did not have enough cash to buy homes. They needed a loan, preferably an amortized loan (meaning equal monthly payments over time) with an affordable payment and little or no down payment.

These were requests for long-term and low-interest loans, and in this earlier era, banks were generally unwilling or unable to make such loans. Therefore, the federal government stepped in and guaranteed both GI (for government inductees or veterans) and FHA (Federal Housing Authority) loans. The federal government stipulated the length and interest rates of such loans, and many loans for GIs required no down payment. In case of default, the government would pay the lender. With such a guarantor, banks could not lose.

The availability of such loans subsidized the mass building of suburbs and allowed new families to buy free-standing homes with lawns. Federal housing policies definitely helped build suburbs, as did federal highway aid, which literally paved the way for automobiles. All of these factors helped empty the central cities. For example, the city of St. Louis, which had approximately 850,000 habitants in 1950, now has a total population of less than 400,000.

One additional reason for rapid suburbanization relates to race. Besides the anti-urban attitude discussed above, racism was another prevalent cause for suburbanization. As central cities lost population, the citizens who remained were often minorities. African Americans increased their proportion of central city populations, and "white flight" increased in momentum as racial balances tipped.

With the loss of population, central city school systems deteriorated and students filed suit, arguing that earlier state segregation policies adversely affected their schools. They pointed out, among other things, that the state constitution carried a provision for separate schools until 1975. (The U.S. Supreme Court decision of *Brown vs. Board of Education of Topeka* ended school segregation in 1954.) The plaintiffs won and the courts required financial aid (involving both state and local dollars) to help bring about equality with white suburban schools. The state is now suing for an end to this supplemental funding, which has been in effect for more than ten years.

Geography and suburbanization have had yet another impact on government. Suburbs desire additions to their tax bases similar to cities and counties outside metropolitan areas. They fight each other for business and industry and often bend over backwards to accommodate such interests, offering zoning changes, tax incentives and more.

Because of the fragmentation of metropolitan areas into a mosaic of suburban towns and cities, it is not unusual to have residential areas in one suburb adjoin commercial areas in another.

This can be convenient, but it is more often viewed as conflicting land use. Residents of an upscale neighborhood do not usually want to be next door to a commercial area, much less one designated for industry. However, it is difficult to coordinate land use policies when there may be as many as 92 municipalities in one county, as in St. Louis County—most of which are competing for business and industry.

How Missouri's Political Culture Affects Its Governance Systems

Political culture reflects citizens' attitudes towards their laws, institutions and leaders. A state's political institutions are very much affected by the state's earliest settlers, and the views they held of government and society. In the case of Missouri, the fact that St. Louis was the "Gateway to the West" meant that a variety of individuals and groups traveled through it.

Many, of course, chose to settle in Missouri. Yankees from the northeast made their way to northern Missouri. Others from the Middle Atlantic states migrated westward through Kentucky and Tennessee, settling in the Ozark Mountains. Many from the South found Missouri's river bottoms suitable for farming.

These groups held different views regarding government and society, and these differences culminated with the Civil War. Missouri had been a slave state, but its pro-South government was driven into exile by Union troops from St. Louis, and replaced with one supporting the North. Families were torn apart by "the great unpleasantness," as the Civil War was often called, and civil unrest was common even well after the Civil War had ended.

It is not surprising that a large portion of Missourians became disbelieving and suspicious of government—when not even the government could keep the peace. This distrust or dislike of government, then, has a long history in Missouri, and it is further magnified by the state's strongly individualistic character.

Historically, Missouri has been a conservative state. It has been known as a low tax state, ranking 48th among the 50 states in tax collection, and has maintained many legal restrictions upon local governments to make certain that fiscal, or budgetary responsibility, prevails. The Hancock Amendment of 1980 (proposed by ex-congressman Mel Hancock) attempted to restrict state government spending early on, following similar efforts first in California, then in Michigan. It has had mixed results. The Hancock Amendment is an example of the state's conservatism, and such policies are very common. Missouri state government has seen changes, but there has never been a shift away from its basic posture on taxes.

The themes of complexity, conflict and conservatism can be easily traced throughout Missouri's history and are still in place today. Complexity refers to the tortuous legal system with its many controls over local government. Conflict refers to the competition between the many groups and cultures that make up the state's population, and the difficulty of achieving consensus on any issue but low taxation and minimal government. Conservatism is a result of the first two. Distrust of governance systems leads to a conservative outlook regarding public policy and the power of government. This outlook is certainly not confined to Missouri, but the state's motto—"Show Me"—certainly reflects its pugnacious posture and conservatism.

How Governance Systems Serve Economic Functions

Missouri's conservatism creates a supportive atmosphere for business. The General Assembly has been favorable to business by keeping taxes low and not over-regulating business. There is also a Department of Economic Development, which is well supported by the legislature and by recent governors.

Yet, compared to other states, Missouri provides only a moderate business and political climate for economic development. It does not rank high in a study measuring treatment of small businesses, and Missouri rated just above average in two other studies. However, a survey by *Entrepreneur* magazine and Dun and Bradstreet ranked St. Louis fourth and Kansas City tenth in small business activity among major metropolitan areas.

A fairly strong labor movement is confined primarily to the two major metropolitan areas. Southwest Missouri, including the Springfield area, is vehemently against unions, as are many other non-metropolitan areas. Therefore, labor groups have not been able to get legislation allowing collective bargaining for municipal workers. However, labor groups did defeat a well-financed "right-to-work" referendum in the 1970s, relying on its membership for a strong campaign. Lately, however, the business and economic lobby has had greater success than labor lobbyists.

Kansas City's Country Club plaza is an early example of commercial zoning. This photograph was taken in the 1920s.

With evident support of business, economic development and a low tax climate, the question becomes "Why has Missouri not done better in economic development?" Reasons include: (1) low support for certain services such as education, which turns away some potential new businesses, and leaves the labor pool less technologically skilled; (2) not being a "right-to-work" state, which may discourage some industrial leaders from locating new factories here; and (3) decline of the defense industry—McDonnell-Douglas (now Boeing) was and still is a major employer but has down-sized considerably with the end of the Cold War. Other industries that once thrived in Missouri, such as shoe manufacturing, have also gone the way of the dinosaur. However, auto assembly continues to do well, with Missouri ranking third behind Michigan and Ohio.

How Economic Choices Confront Governments

The competition among and within states for economic development is extremely intense. States compete with each other for new large-scale industrial plants, such as General Motor's Saturn automobile plant. After a bitter struggle involving twenty states, Tennessee won out. A goal of state government is often to attract new jobs and supplement the **tax base**, which is money generated by government in the form of sales tax, property tax, automobile licensing and many other taxes that allow government to operate. Property taxes are an important source of funds for schools—and large industrial plants pay mightily. Also, those gaining new jobs contribute to the state and local treasuries through sales and income taxes. Corporate taxes are also important revenues.

Local governments face the same economic pressures as states, but to a higher degree. Local governments, both cities and counties, often desperately seek economic development. Cities will advertise nationwide, describing their business-friendly attributes. They will also, in some instances, subsidize local entrepreneurs with money for expansion or to provide additional services.

Cities will often zone large areas for commercial and industrial development as an added incentive for businesses to locate there. Many times cities designate more land than will ever be needed for such uses. This reflects the wishful thinking of the "build it and they will come" mentality—like the baseball diamond built among cornfields in the Kevin Costner movie *Field of Dreams*.

Counties play an even more important role in Missouri government with respect to zoning decisions. There is much commercial and industrial building outside of cities on land controlled by counties. Many county governments are still rurally dominated, and some are very receptive to zoning changes to accommodate business and industry. Others may resist progress and fight for the **status quo**, preferring the existing conditions or state of affairs to the changes and detriments that progress may bring. If you drive along the highways outside of metropolitan areas, you can see strip malls, which include factory outlet stores, fast food restaurants, all kinds of retail establishments, and other development. In Missouri, many travelers between Kansas City and St. Louis on Interstate 70 wonder when commercial development alongside the highway will be built up to the point of entirely crossing the state.

Most state governments have traditionally delegated zoning powers to local governments, which puts control at the weakest point. Local governments can be most susceptible to economic pressures because of intense business interest in land use decisions and the decision-making of city and county government. Business is vitally interested in local tax and regulation policies, including land use decisions. The business community is always represented on city councils, although not as prevalent in county government, except for agricultural representatives. Business interests often feel they are the most important group in the community—that cities exist for business.

Occasionally, environmental interests prevail on certain issues. For example, a "can ban" ordinance in the city of Columbia was the first in the nation. The **ordinance**, or local law, requires a deposit on all cans and soft drink bottles. This deposit is returned to the consumer after a percentage is retained for administration and handling. Stores selling beverages must collect and store cans and bottles so they can be recycled. Columbia residents voted on the ordinance three times and waited for several favorable court decisions before the ordinance took effect.

Another example of environmental interests prevailing took place in Grand Marais, Minnesota. Grand Marais is located on the shores of Lake Superior, the largest freshwater lake in the world. Sixty acres of public land surrounding the scenic harbor were put into a land trust, which essentially prevents any future development. This conservation easement is to be administered by the Minnesota Land Trust, which was established by the state legislature. Business interests vigorously opposed the signing of the ordinance, arguing that more time was needed for study. The city council, however, under the leadership of the outgoing mayor, voted unanimously for adoption.

Summary & Conclusions

According to the U.S. Constitution, the U.S. federal government separates power between the executive, legislative, and judicial branches of government. It also delegates authority between the central government and the states.

The organization of state governments into three branches mirrors federal government. But state and federal governments have different responsibilities. Many debate which level of government should be responsible for what function.

Missouri is represented in the federal government by two senators in the U.S. Senate and nine members of Congress in the U.S. House of Representatives.

Although the activity of the federal government attracts more media attention, state and local governance systems often affect our lives more directly. Local governments play a huge role in our lives in decisions that affect everything from the geographic boundaries of our cities to the promotion or restriction of economic development in our communities.

Beyond the general agreement to protect citizens' basic security, there is a broad spectrum of opinion about how much government involvement in people's lives is desirable. The history and political culture of Missouri make its citizens generally conservative and skeptical of powerful government.

Geography has been important to the development of government in Missouri, particularly in the major metropolitan areas where suburbs have developed in close proximity to the central cities. Missouri's political culture supports such development, since many prefer the greater choice allowed by many small units of government and the resulting diffusion of power.

Missouri's political climate also favors business, but there is an important and active labor movement. Although there is much support for business, the state has not done as well in economic development as many supporters had hoped. Local governments, however, usually support additions to the tax base. Indeed, regional planning and zoning is sometimes undermined because of the local government's desire for new business.

A Few Words on Flag Etiquette

It is the universal custom to display the flag only from sunrise to sunset on buildings and on stationary flagstaffs in the open. However, the flag may be displayed 24 hours a day if properly illuminated during hours of darkness.

1. When flags of states, cities or localities are flown on the same halyard with the flag of the United States, the latter should always be at the peak.

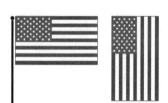

2. When the flags are flown from adjacent staffs, the flag of the United States should be housed first and lowered last.

3. The flag of the United States of America should be at the center and at the highest point of the group when a number of flags of states or localities are grouped and displayed from staffs.

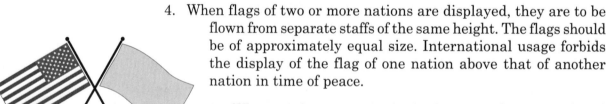

4. When flags of two or more nations are displayed, they are to be flown from separate staffs of the same height. The flags should be of approximately equal size. International usage forbids the display of the flag of one nation above that of another nation in time of peace.

5. When used on a speaker's platform, the flag, if displayed flat, should be displayed above and behind the speaker. When displayed from a staff in a church or public auditorium, the flag of the United States of America should hold the position of superior prominence.

From *The Flag Code of the United States—Public Law 94-344, July 7, 1976*

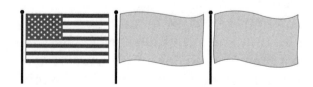

The Pledge of Allegiance

I pledge allegiance to the flag of the United States of America, and to the Republic for which it stands, one nation under God, indivisible, with liberty and justice for all.

Chapter 2
The Foundations of Missouri Government

End of Chapter Questions

Use the text along with outside material to answer the following questions. Be sure to review the key terms and concepts from the beginning of the chapter before you start.

1. Why does the unitary model of government impact you most directly?

2. Why does the federal model best describe the relationship between the U.S. government and the individual states?

3. What is a governance system and why do you think there are so many different types?

4. What are some examples of governance systems that are not democratic?

5. What is the primary function of all types of government?

6. What are frequent motivating factors for the establishment of general purpose governments? What about special purpose governments?

7. Illustrate the basic concepts or beliefs that often differentiate liberals and conservatives.

8. What is the primary function of a constitution? Describe its role in the creation and management of governance systems.

9. What are the most important benefits that citizens gain from governance systems?

10. What does "privatization" mean? Make a list of any of the benefits and/or services that your local government provides that have been privatized.

11. In your own words describe "political culture." Outline some of the different elements of Missouri's history that have shaped its political culture.

12. What were the most significant factors in shaping Missouri's political culture?

13. Briefly discuss why Missouri has a history of skepticism toward central government. What major conflict affected this result and why?

14. What does the term "fiscal responsibility" mean? Why is this concept important in the management of governance systems?

15. Explain the ideas of "complexity," "conflict" and "conservatism" as they apply to Missouri government. Analyze each and provide reasons why each has been used to define Missouri's government structure.

16. In Missouri's conservative culture, why are low taxes and limited regulations important elements that help to support the state's economy?

17. Why are governance systems important for the maintenance and encouragement of economic growth?

18. Describe two ways that local, state, and county government agencies encourage economic activity.

19. Why does the author say that delegation of zoning powers to local governments places control at the weakest point?

20. Why have suburbs become increasingly popular? What were some of the initial reasons for population shifts to the 'burbs? What consequences have resulted from the move from the city to the suburbs?

End of Chapter Activities

Use the text along with outside material to complete the following activities.

1. Compare and contrast the unitary and federal models of government. Look closely at how they differ and what similarities they share. Draw a diagram that shows how each model directly or indirectly affects federal, state, and local governments.

2. List three other forms of governance systems. Compare each to the democratic system. List the potential pros and cons of each.

3. Identify a business or industry in your community that has been dramatically affected (positively or negatively) by a government regulation. Trace both the history of the regulation and its statewide impact. Can you describe why this law was enacted?

4. Look at a map of your community. Contact your local government and identify on the map the various zonings that affect your community's development. How do these laws impact your daily life?

5. Do you feel that race has been an important force in the shift of population to the suburbs? Discuss the impact of this fact on the state of race relations.

Legal Point

Define segregation. Describe why *Brown vs. Board of Education of Topeka* was a critical Supreme Court decision. Specifically, explain how this decision impacts state and local governments.

Out of Class Activity

Describe some of the important geographic features of your community. Also, outline the major geographic features of Missouri and the Midwest. Discuss how these regional and local features have affected state and local government. What specific geographic features play an important role in shaping the local government system of your community?

Chapter

The Basis of Politics: Political Parties

Key Terms & Concepts

adjunct party organizations

committee

election authority

electoral college

merit system

mud-slinging

nomination

non-partisan elections

PACs

party platform

patronage system

planks

political agenda

precinct

primary

pundit

split-ticket voting

statute

straight-ticket voting

ward

Introduction to the Importance of Parties

Some political **pundits**, or political experts, claim that the two major political parties—the Republican party and the Democratic party—are dying due to voter "turn-off," among other reasons. The resulting disenchantment of voters, government observers point out, has led to an increase in support for minor parties, independent candidates who are seen as political "outsiders," and reduced turnout at the polls. However, this diagnosis is premature, at best, and may even be incorrect. Some see the major parties gaining influence because of new funding sources.

The two major parties continue to play a crucial role in our governance system. Candidates for office still largely run as Democrats or Republicans. The major parties play a vital role in the organization of Congress and state legislatures. Having a majority allows the party leadership to make appointments to committees, thus ensuring some party discipline and allowing the party to push its **political agenda**, or set of agreed-upon goals. The Republican "Contract with America"—a much-publicized conservative agenda of goals for Congress to work towards, brought to the U.S. House with the Republican takeover in 1992—certainly demonstrated the vitality of the Republican party and the importance of congressional control.

Our two-party system has been credited with providing stability in the United States, particularly when contrasted with Europe's multi-party governance systems. There are more leadership changes in nations with multi-party systems, leading to greater political instability. In the United States, there is a considerable body of law relating to election systems, which in effect

Political parties are important for many reasons. They provide staffing, organization and leadership to run many campaigns, increase voter interest, finance campaigns and encourage qualified people to seek office.

"To lodge all power in one party and keep it there is to insure bad government and the sure and gradual deterioration of the public morals."

— From Mark Twain's Autobiography

supports the two major parties. Some decry this system's bias, arguing that it should be easier to start and perpetuate new political parties. However, despite difficulties, new parties do appear. And if they generate enough support, their issues are often co-opted by the major parties. In Missouri's 1992 election, the Libertarian party received sufficient votes (2 percent) to qualify for automatic placement on future ballots. It is always impressive when a new party manages to get on the ballot and remains there for future elections.

The parties, then, remain a crucial vehicle for recruiting candidates and voters, raising funds, developing platforms, pushing policies and assisting with campaigning. Although voting percentages for major party candidates are down, major party candidates continue to dominate the governance system. The parties are active in the Missouri General Assembly, county government and some cities, although the extent of their activity varies from area to area.

Adjunct party organizations exist to support the parties. Examples include the College Republicans, the Young Democrats, Jefferson Women's Democratic Clubs, and the Missouri Federated Republican Women. The Pachyderms, another Republican service

Election 1996: Keith Mackie, Republican candidate for the 21st District seat in the Missouri House, addressed a Centralia High School assembly during a candidates' forum.

A campaign photo of Governor Smith with two of his Democratic supporters and a Missouri mule in front of the Missouri State Capitol, circa 1948.

organization, was developed in Missouri to aid the party and now operates in several states. Democrats in Boone County responded by establishing a rival group called the Muleskinners. In conclusion, the major political parties can indeed be called the cornerstones of democracy. It is difficult to imagine our political system without them.

Party Organization

Primaries

Statutes, or state laws, outline election systems on a state-by-state basis, including the organization of parties. In Missouri, statutes outline procedures for, among other things, electing committee members at party primary elections held in August of even-numbered years. Party **primaries** are an election held before a general election to nominate a political party's candidates for office. Since the primary is actually for the parties to select their candidates, voters must declare their party affiliation and poll workers have to accept their declarations. This is the only time party affiliation is an issue. Since proof of party affiliation is not required, crossover voting can occur with Republicans voting a

Democratic ballot and vice versa, since both primaries are held at the same location.

If one party has a strong candidate assured of winning the primary, supporters sometimes vote in the opposition primary. The strategy is to elect the weakest opposition candidate for the November general election. Primary elections, it should be noted, were designed to eliminate candidate selection by party caucuses. Voters, rather than party leaders, make the selections for each of the parties.

New parties in their formative stages have difficulty competing to recruit enough candidates to fill a primary ballot. This tends to hold down the number of voters requesting a minority party ballot.

Presidential primaries operate in the same way. Again, the strategy is to take the candidate selection process away from party leaders and to give it to the voters. A majority of states now hold a presidential primary, and if a candidate wins enough of these, **nomination** at the national convention is virtually assured. Although democracy appears to be enhanced with this process, some question the results. The use of primaries has somewhat diminished the influence of the major parties, but low voter turnout has meant selection by a relatively small number of voters. Missouri used the primary for the first time in 1988 to support Representative Dick Gephardt for president. Bills were then introduced in the General Assembly to make the presidential primary permanent.

Committees

The building blocks of the parties are the **committees**, which leads to a bottom-up rather than a top-down organizational model. Committees are organized in many ways, depending on the issues at hand. Some are organized by townships, legislative districts, or judicial circuits, and some are statewide.

In all 114 counties, a committeewoman and a committeeman are elected from each ward. A **ward** is a subdivision of a city, often used as a legislative district for city council elections. In larger cities, a ward is often further divided into **precincts**. They in turn organize themselves into county party committees (the foundation of the party), and 163 legislative district committees. Chairmen and vice chairs become members of the judicial circuit committees, as well as the state senatorial and congressional committees. Finally, each senatorial committee elects two registered voters from its district to sit on the state party committee.

The state committee develops the party platform, calls for conventions to elect delegates to the national committee and convention, and selects presidential electors. The electors comprise the **electoral college**, which is responsible for actually electing the president of the United States. Technically, a candidate for president is not elected by popular vote alone—he or she must carry a majority of the electors. It is legally possible for a candidate to lose the popular vote but win the election because of carrying the electoral college. The electors from a given state equal the number in the state's congressional delegation (two senators plus representatives). Therefore, the total for the electoral college is the same as the total in Congress, 535.

Among its other responsibilities, the party selects candidates for office in a special election called as a result of a vacancy due to death, resignation, or some other reason. In addition, county committees make recommendations to the governor for filling vacancies in county government. The governor makes the appointment unless a special election is required. Finally, the county committees each submit lists of people to act as election judges for their party to the county election authority. The **election authority**, which is the county clerk's office, then employs the required number to work the polls on election day. Equal numbers of judges from each of the two major parties staff the polls. These judges are usually paired to make certain neither gains unfair advantage. Election judges put in a long day for relatively little pay, but all who have worked usually feel amply rewarded in other ways. Obviously, they are crucial to the election process.

The political parties, then, are semi-public organizations, with their organization defined in a state's election laws. As mentioned, though, there is a system bias towards the two major parties. Third parties have difficulty getting on the ballot, but several have done quite well, as have some independents. In 1992, Ross Perot did well as an independent in his race for president, although he did not fare as well at the head of his Reform party in 1996.

3. Mid-Missouri German counties are traditionally strongly Republican. These immigrants were against slavery and gravitated to the Republican party and its strong anti-slavery stance.

4. Northwest Missouri was settled by immigrants from Iowa, Illinois and Indiana as well as other adjoining states. They and their descendents hold typical midwestern attitudes, emphasizing community, demanding quality government services, and shifting party support in response to the level of agricultural prices.

5. The urban areas in Missouri (which hold over half of the state's population), are strongly diverse and divided between party lines.

Source: David A. Leuthold, *Campaign Missouri 1992*. University of Missouri Press: Columbia, 1994.

Funding

Financing political campaigns has become highly politicized in and of itself. At the national level, both parties have been criticized for their fundraising tactics. Critics have cited donors getting permission to sleep in the Lincoln bedroom in the White House; monies raised from foreign nations; and the use of office phones to solicit campaign funds. Former U.S. Speaker of the House Newt Gingrich was also attacked for using his television college course to raise funds for Republican political purposes. Cries for reform were heard, but neither political party has been overly interested to date.

The cost of campaigning has escalated since the advent of television. Television has proven to be the most effective medium for campaign advertising in geographically large or populous districts. However, the cost of television is much greater than promotions through newspapers, radio, direct mail, lawn signs, bumper stickers or handouts.

The demand for campaign funds has increased, and the political parties have not had enough funds to help many candidates. Consequently, candidates have had to resort to their own devices for money raising. This has led to a greater reliance on interest groups, where "big bucks" can be found. **PACs**, or Political Action Committees, have been established by many special interests with the intention of helping candidates who are sympathetic to them. PACs are criticized for "buying" support, but candidates, too, are criticized for accepting their money. Public financing has been tried in presidential elections, with candidates who meet the required threshold of private donations getting public monies. However, there has been little interest in, and much opposition to, expanding such support. Consequently, fund raising continues to be a major political debate.

Campaign Finance Reform in Missouri

Although campaign finance reform has been debated for a quarter of a century, lately it has been a volatile issue. A law drawn up to restrict campaign contributions in the wake of the Watergate scandal and President Nixon's resignation in 1974 led to a Supreme Court case the following year. In *Buckley vs. Valeo* (1975), the

Supreme Court found that the First Amendment guarantee of free speech protected the amount of money a candidate could spend, but it also supported federal contribution limits of $1,000.

In 1994, the Missouri General Assembly set a $1,000 cap on the amount of money anyone could contribute to a candidate running for governor, lieutenant governor, secretary of state, state treasurer, state auditor, or attorney general. For state senate candidates, the limit was set at $500. A campaign for state representative could receive no more than $250. Limits on races for other local offices depended on the population of the district or county. The limits were placed in order to curb the influence of political action committees and other special interests.

The amounts were later adjusted to $1,075 for statewide campaigns, with $525 and $275 limits on state senate and state representative campaigns, respectively. Nevertheless, the statute soon met with protest from groups around the state.

Shrink Missouri Government PAC, a political action committee run by St. Louis attorney Bevis Schock, was one of the groups opposing the limitations proposed by the Missouri legislature. Schock's group had contributed to Zev David Fredman's campaign for state auditor in 1998. Schock's group filed suit in district court against the state of Missouri, charging that the spending limits violated their right to free speech and association as protected by the First Amendment and the Equal Protection Clause found in the Fourteenth Amendment. The state of Missouri had to prove that they had a compelling interest in reducing corruption by limiting campaign contributions.

The district court upheld Missouri's statute, basing its decision on *Buckley vs. Valeo* (1975). Schock's further opposition to *Buckley vs. Valeo* drew from the fact that the $1,000 limit from 1975 was not marked for inflation, making it worth $400 in 2000. Schock appealed to the 8th Circuit Court which repealed the district court decision, finding in favor of the respondents. The circuit court also reasoned that the limits Missouri had placed on contributions limited candidates' ability to practice "effective advocacy."

On January 24, 2000, the U.S. Supreme Court reversed the 8th Circuit's decision. The high court's reasoning was that large campaign donations by PACs and other special interests might deter the general public from participating in government because of the appearance of influence-buying such contributions could create. Justice David Souter wrote for the court that large gifts made by special interests to politicians gave the impression that these groups "call the tune," which "could jeopardize the willingness of voters to take part in democratic governance."

The ruling does not affect so-called "soft money," which is donated to groups that spend money without regard to specific candidates. Nor does the decision affect the ban on federal spending limits spelled out in *Buckley vs. Valeo*. Missouri thus joins about 60 percent of the states in the union that limit campaign donations.

An example of the legislature's motivation in capping spending can be seen in a recent race for governor. The two candidates, Jim Talent and Bob Holden, together collected around $6 million. Their highest individual contributions have reached $100,000. These donations were made after the 8th Circuit repealed the statute, though the candidates managed to narrow the field of competitors by drumming up some of that money even a year before declaring their candidacies. Some candidates called for their opponents to return some of the excessive contributions, but very little money was expected to be refunded.

Reform Politics: Non-Partisan Elections

The major parties have been impacted by several reforms in the electorate over the years. Some voters have become disenchanted with the major parties, asserting, like Governor Wallace of Alabama and years later Ross Perot, that "there is not a dime's worth of difference between the two." A **party's platform** is a statement of basic principles put forth by a political party, usually at its national convention. The platform, which does not formally bind either the party or its candidates, also contains specific short-term goals and proposals for legislation, known as **planks**.

Still another factor that has impacted major parties is the Reform Movement. In the second half of the 19th century, the Reform Movement took shape to fight the urban political machines (such as Tammany Hall in New York City, and later, up to the 1940s, Boss Tom Pendergast of Kansas City). Some cities had become controlled by a single political party whose desire to stay in power led to corruption of the election process. Control of the election system enabled party supporters to "vote early and often." Although corruption was more widespread than just the election process, reformers considered the political parties to be the "bad guys." Many changes were introduced to "take politics out of city government," since as one politician put it, "there is not a Republican or Democratic way of paving a street."

The adoption of non-partisan elections was one important change. **Non-partisan elections** are elections without candidate party identification. A candidate's name appears on the ballot, but not the name of his or her political party. Reformers thought that this would diminish the influence of **straight-ticket voting**, where a voter marks a box to support all the candidates of one party. Straight-ticket voting has declined drastically over time, even in partisan elections.

Thomas Hart Benton (1782-1858)
U.S. Senator, 1821-1851
U.S. Representative, 1852-1854

Born in North Carolina, Benton became one of the most important national political figures of the first half of the 19th century. Benton entered politics for the first time in 1809, but his political career was interrupted by the War of 1812. He served as a colonel under General Andrew Jackson. After a personal falling-out with Jackson, Benton arrived in St. Louis in 1815 to practice law. He soon began to make a political name for himself through the *St. Louis Enquirer* newspaper.

It was this reputation that led to his election to the U.S. Senate in 1820. He was half of the first team of senators Missouri sent to Washington upon reaching statehood in 1821. It was this experience—learning that he could draw more support from the general populace than from his own wealthy contemporaries—that formed the basis of his populist, Jacksonian ideology. Despite his earlier conflict with Jackson, Benton was greatly advantaged by the rise of the Tennesseean to the presidency in 1828. Although asked to run for president himself several times, Benton preferred the U.S. Senate. Serving in the Upper House for 30 years, he played a major role in the pivotal debates that led up to the Civil War—from the Missouri Compromise to the early threats of secession during the last decade of his life. Although his primary support came from landowners in the West and South, Benton favored a strong union and opposed all efforts at secession.

His pro-Union stance proved his political downfall. His original supporters were in favor of slavery and also supported the South. After being ousted from office in 1851, Benton served one term as U.S. Representative. He then lost a final bid to return to the Senate in 1855 as well as losing Missouri's gubernatorial election of 1856 to the pro-slavery, pro-South candidate Trusten V. Polk. Benton spent his last years in Washington, D.C., writing a history of the American government and a work entitled *Abridgment of the Debates of Congress from 1789 to 1856.* He finished the 16th volume before dying in Washington on April 10, 1858. His body was taken to St. Louis where he had so gallantly served as one of its founding fathers.

At the same time, **split-ticket voting** has increased. In split-ticket voting, voters cast their ballots based on specific issues or candidates instead of voting a straight Democratic or Republican ticket. In today's mass media culture, oftentimes voters are inundated with campaign hype and are unable to clearly define the stances of each party on a particular issue. In some cases, campaigns deviate from the main issues and focus instead on discrediting the opponent's track record. This is called **mud-slinging**. In these cases, oftentimes voters choose a split-ticket vote to focus on a particular agenda or candidate that has risen above the din of the campaign hype.

So politics have not been eliminated but continue in different ways. The parties often circulate sample ballots before elections, identifying their candidates. However, independent candidates seem to stand a better chance of being elected when party identification is not a factor. City elections are often non-partisan, and some judicial elections are as well.

Patronage and Merit Systems

Another reform tactic was to weaken patronage. The **patronage system** refers to officeholders rewarding supporters with jobs, regardless of their qualifications. In previous political eras, upon taking office, newly elected officials would replace the previous staff with their own supporters. Sometimes these appointments required particular qualifications, yet many times incompetent people were hired as a way of rewarding them for their political support. This was an accepted practice and the political parties were important in recommending replacement personnel.

Reformers did not like the system and established civil service at the federal level in the late 19th century. Civil service, later called the **merit system**, required formal recruitment and testing for both entry and promotion in government. Private businesses in many instances adopted the same procedures and established personnel operations. Subsequently, merit systems have been established in all states and many city governments, reducing patronage appointments. U.S. Supreme Court decisions have also restricted terminations for political purposes, holding political affiliation to be a form of protected speech.

Although patronage has been weakened, governors still appoint department heads (with senatorial confirmation in Missouri), staff members and many others. The 164 automobile license offices throughout the state are based upon patronage, though, and the Departments of Revenue and Agriculture are not within the central merit system (although they have adopted some of their provisions). For many years, the Highway Patrol was required to have an equal number of officers from each party. This often meant that non-political graduates of the training academy had to be assigned to a party. Although weakened, the parties are still called upon to make many recommendations and continue to play an important role in the governing process.

Party Strength in Missouri

In Missouri, the two major parties dominate the General Assembly. Democrats have long held majorities in both the house and senate, but Republicans have been gaining seats recently. Party discipline has been more pronounced in the house, where the speaker has had considerable influence due to his ability to make committee assignments. The president pro tem, the top leadership post in the senate, has less authority due to greater "clubbiness," which emphasizes the senate's long-standing tradition of informality and other power-diffusing rules. With this tradition, it has been possible for a few minority party senators with long tenure to wield disproportionate influence due to their knowledge of both formal and informal rules.

At the local level, most counties are highly politicized, generally favoring one of the major parties. There is a mix of one-party counties, those that lean toward one party, and those that are highly competitive. There are about 46 strongly Democratic and approximately 38 Republican counties in Missouri. The other counties either lean toward one party or are highly competitive and divided.

Political parties are important at the local level because they often control the courthouse or county government. They recruit candidates to run for county offices, and their endorsements often lead to election. County-elected officials, in turn, remain highly active in party politics to help in re-election. In cities, the activity

Camden County was originally named Kinderhook, for Kinderhook, N.Y., home of Democrat Martin Van Buren. When Van Buren abandoned the Democratic party in 1848, the horrified county scrambled to change its name. The new name honors Charles Pratt, Earl of Camden, an English politician who supported the colonies in the Revolutionary War.

of the parties varies. In St. Louis, the Democratic party is very active and important, since it is traditionally a Democratic city and there are partisan elections. In Kansas City, parties are less obvious because of reforms such as non-partisan elections, brought about by the reactions and reforms to Boss Pendergast. So party politics continue, but in vastly different and more regulated ways.

Pick a Party

As voting age approaches, you are faced with a decision of whether to lean left, right, or remain in the middle where politics are concerned. In order to make an educated decision in choosing a political party, one must first understand the platforms of the Republican, Democratic and other active parties.

The Republican party has been considered the conservative party in politics. According to Jay Shafritz in *American Government & Politics,* Republicans "have favored increased spending on defense, decreased spending on domestic, educational, and welfare programs, and a general reduction in the size of government by curtailing government regulation and increasing the privatization of selected government programs."

Charles Nickolaus, left, and Bill Rapp hoist Chuck Graham at Big Eight Bar and Grill after he secured the Democratic nomination in the 24th District state house race in 1996.

Former president Ronald Reagan announced at a Republican congressional dinner in May 1982 that the Republican party is "the party that wants to see an America in which people can still get rich." This reflects a generally pro-business stance. Recently, the party has also taken conservative stands on social issues, such as abortion, affirmative action and gay rights, and the phrase "family values" has become a common Republican rallying cry.

Republican John Ashcroft, who served as Missouri governor for two terms, led the fight against abortion. As a U.S. senator, Ashcroft was the author of the landmark Charitable Choice provision of the new welfare reform law, which would allow government funding to support private and religious charities' efforts to find employment for those on welfare. He also sponsored major legislation to enact broad-based middle-class tax relief by making payroll taxes deductible. Ashcroft is widely recognized in Congress for his innovative use of technology and the Internet.

At the other end of the political spectrum, the Democratic party, in recent decades, has developed a reputation for supporting low-income groups, for expanding civil rights protection, and for a greater commitment of government resources to solve social problems like racial and gender inequality, health care access, and gun violence. The party has generally favored more liberal stands on social issues and has historically supported labor over business.

The Democratic party, under the leadership of Governor Mel Carnahan, has worked hard to pass socially and economically progressive legislation for the working families of Missouri. Responsible and targeted tax cuts have also been enforced. Governor Carnahan and Democrats in the state legislature expanded access to quality child care by passing the Family Care Safety Registry. Since Governor Carnahan resumed office in 1993, 350,000 new jobs have been created in Missouri.

Recent issues in local elections that have been hotly debated by Republicans and Democrats are regulation of the tobacco industry, efforts to eliminate the sale of tobacco products to minors, and the ever-popular debates on tax reductions. Legislation to allow the carrying of concealed firearms in Missouri was another heavily debated topic between the two parties. The issues that will affect you as a voting citizen will undoubtedly change in the coming years, though topics such as taxes, education, health care and crime are consistent themes.

Whether or not either of these parties align with your social, moral and political views is not the ultimate issue. What is important is that you contribute at the local and national level of government by voting. Many people choose not to choose a party, which is perfectly acceptable. In this scenario, a citizen votes for a candidate based on his or her individual platform, as opposed to the citizen analyzing their party platform. The choice is yours, but your decision should involve being an active part of the governmental process.

Registration and Mail-In Elections

There is continuing interest in enhancing democracy. One strategy for doing this is to broaden the electorate by increasing registered voters. There are opponents to this way of thinking, though. Opponents assert that increasing registered voters does not assure greater turnouts. They also suggest that if registration becomes too easy, it may increase the likelihood of voting fraud. Regardless of these concerns, the trend has been to make registration and voting easier.

Missouri and the nation now have what is called the "motor-voter" law. This means individuals may now register to vote at drivers license bureaus, welfare offices and wherever they receive state services, as well as at the county clerk's office. Voter registration has increased, but there is no firm evidence of increased election turnouts as of yet.

Ashland voters Roy Sublett and Mary Peterson mark their ballots at the American Legion Hall in a recent election.

Micah Phillips, an 8th grade student, takes voter information from a pager. Junior high students were helping out at polling places by manning beepers used to relay election information.

Mail-in elections have been tried in certain places in Missouri, and the results have been spectacular. In a Kirksville school election involving issues, not candidates, 78 percent returned their mail-in ballots, as opposed to the 19 percent that voted in person in a previous election on the same issue. Some states, including Kansas, are experimenting with voting in advance. During a set period, commonly two weeks prior to election day, voters may cast their ballots at specified places at their convenience. Their ballots are counted with those cast on election day. Several companies are also working on software that would allow voting via the Internet. These programs were used on a trial basis for Arizona's presidential primary in 2000, but it remains to be seen whether Internet voting will become a permanent alternative.

Summary & Conclusions

The dominant two-party political system is sometimes seen as an obstacle to real change, but the parties remain critically important to stabilizing governance, organizing support in elections, and defining political platforms.

Primaries are popular elections to choose a party's candidates for national or local office. Party committees play a vital role in organizing party support throughout a state and in recruiting candidates for office. They send delegates to the party's national convention to nominate the party's presidential candidate. State committees also select presidential electors to vote in the electoral college. And the electoral college ultimately determines the outcome of presidential elections.

The funding of party organizations and of candidates has come under increasing scrutiny as the cost of campaigning has skyrocketed. Despite the enactment of state and national contribution limits, the continuing importance of big donors to political parties has created demands for campaign finance reform. But many question whether setting new limits on contributions is an infringement on free speech.

Reforms to party politics include non-partisan elections, which are an attempt to weaken the grip of political parties on voting, and merit systems for hiring people into civil service regardless of political affiliation or patronage.

Missouri presents a diverse map of political loyalties, with some regions strongly partisan and others more mixed. The Democratic party is generally known as liberal in its support of government solutions for social problems and civil rights issues. The Republican party is known as conservative on the role of government in people's lives and broadly prefers private sector solutions to public problems.

Increased voter participation has become a major objective in American politics recently, since fewer and fewer people are voting at every election level. Recent innovations can make voting more convenient, but there is no substitute for an informed and energetic electorate.

Chapter 3
The Basis of Politics: Political Parties

End of Chapter Questions

Use the text along with outside material to answer the following questions. Be sure to review the key terms and concepts from the beginning of the chapter before you start.

1. In political terms, define liberal and conservative. Based on your initial study, how would you categorize yourself? Why might these broad categories often be misleading?

2. Why are party affiliations such an important part of the political process?

3. What does it mean when a candidate runs for office as an independent? Why do you think there has been a dramatic rise in the number of independent candidates running for office in recent years? Do you think this fact has helped or hurt the political process?

4. According to the author, what has been the two-party system's primary effect on our democracy?

5. What political benefits do candidates typically receive through their association with a political party?

6. What purpose is served by organizations such as the "Pachyderms" and "Muleskinners"? Are these types of organizations active in your community? If so, list them and describe how they function locally.

7. What function do primaries serve? When are these special elections typically held and who typically participates?

8. Compare and contrast local, state and national primaries.

9. Why does the author call committees "the building blocks of parties"?

10. Explain in detail the process for electing the president of the United States (from the bottom up). How is it possible for a presidential candidate to lose the popular vote (the vote of the people) yet still win the presidential race or vice versa? How do you feel about the role of the electoral college in presidential elections?

11. What does the term "special election" mean? How are special elections typically used in the political process?

12. What roles do election authorities and election judges play in the election process?

13. Why does the author say that political parties are "semi-public organizations"? In your own words, describe what this means.

14. What is one of the principal reasons for the dramatic rise in the cost of running political election campaigns?

15. What are PACs and how do they function in the political process?

16. Describe what is meant by "reform politics." How has this reform movement affected the political process? Do you think that the political process needs to be "reformed"?

17. What effects have so-called non-partisan elections had in the election of candidates in recent years?

18. What does it mean to vote a "split ticket"?

19. What are the likely advantages and disadvantages of patronage versus merit systems?

20. Historically, why have the Democrats held the majority in Missouri politics?

21. How would you describe the political climate of the county in which you live? Explain your answer based on historical data and trace how this tendency has affected the outcomes of political races in recent years.

22. What benefits could possibly come from "broadening the electorate"?

23. Explain Missouri's "motor-voter" law. What has its impact been on the election process?

24. How do you feel about "mail-in" and Internet elections? Do you think individuals would be more likely to participate in the election process if this option were made available throughout the state? Explain your answer.

End of Chapter Activities

Use the text along with outside material to complete the following activities.

1. In your own words, outline the major differences and similarities between Democrats and Republicans.

2. Outline some of the other political parties (besides Democrats and Republicans) that are active today. Describe how these parties were initially formed and highlight the important points in each party's political platform.

3. List some of the major PACs operating today in Washington, D.C. Outline their respective platforms and, if possible, identify their direct effects on government in recent years.

4. In recent years, much attention has been paid to limiting or restricting election spending. What do you think the advantages and/or disadvantages of limiting campaign spending would be?

5. Examine voter turnout statistics for elections held in the last ten years at the local, state and national levels. What is striking about these numbers? What do you think these numbers say about the public's interest in the political process?

Chapter

The Executive Branch: Membership, Powers, Authority & Influence

Key Terms & Concepts

appointment

autonomy

collegial model

commute

confirmation

extradition

industrial model

line item veto

pardon

reprieve

veto

Introduction to the Executive Branch

Elective Offices

The executive branch consists of all state elective and appointive employees, except those of the legislative and judicial branches. The governor is Missouri's official leader and is responsible for carrying out the laws of the state. He or she does this by directing the executive branch of government. In addition to the many duties that are specifically assigned to the governor in the Missouri Constitution, they have many other duties that are assigned to them by statute and by custom.

The executive branch of Missouri state government is quite different from the legislative and judicial branches. The executive branch approximates an **industrial model** of organization. The governor presides over a large bureaucracy, similar to a CEO (chief

Each year, the governor delivers the "State of the State" address to the General Assembly and submits a state budget for the legislature to act on. Following action on a bill by the legislature, the governor has the option of signing the bill into law or exercising "veto power" to prevent the bill from becoming a law. The legislature can override a governor's veto with a two-thirds majority vote.

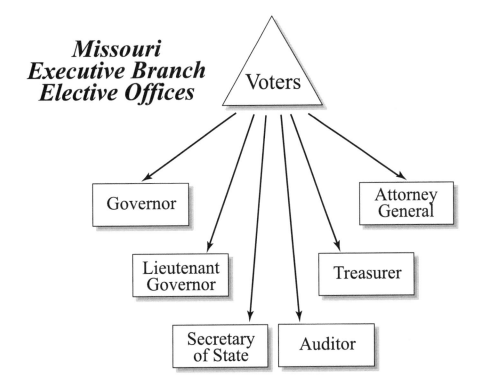

Missouri Executive Branch Elective Offices

Missouri's Executive Branch
Elected Officials

	Elected:	Term Expires:
Governor Mel Carnahan	Nov. 5, 1996	January 2001
Lieutenant Governor Roger Wilson	Nov. 5, 1996	January 2001
Secretary of State Rebecca McDowell Cook	Nov. 5, 1996	January 2001
State Auditor Claire McCaskill	Nov. 3, 1998	January 2003
State Treasurer Bob Holden	Nov. 5, 1996	January 2001
Attorney General Jeremiah (Jay) Nixon	Nov. 5, 1996	January 2001

executive officer) of a private corporation, and makes many appointments. This model is like a pyramid with the governor at the apex.

This model contrasts with the legislative and judicial branches, which are multi-membered bodies without chief executives. They more closely resemble what is called a **collegial model**. In a collegial model, members are equals, except for the leaders selected by members themselves. Such leaders are sometimes called "first among equals." The image might be one of a flattened out pyramid with no top.

It is through the executive branch that the greatest portion of state services are delivered. The Constitution (Article IV, Section 12) and the Reorganization Act of 1974 have established a number of executive departments to deal with specific areas of interest. These departments are outlined later in this chapter.

The governor's office will be addressed in the following pages. Then other elective offices will be explained, followed by descriptions of the executive branch departments.

Governor's Office

Qualifications for Governor

The requirements for the office of governor include candidates being (1) at least 30 years of age, (2) citizens of the United States for at least 15 years, and (3) residents of Missouri for at least 10 years. Although the office is open to anyone, governors to date have all been white males. As of 2000, the last eight have been attorneys.

The highest state office that a woman has held to date has been lieutenant governor, with Harriet Woods serving from 1985 to 1989. However, women have become more active in politics and have served as state auditor and secretary of state—positions that have often been stepping stones to higher office. For example, former State Auditor Margaret Kelly challenged Governor Mel Carnahan in his quest for a second term, but lost.

The office of governor has been the last stop in the political careers for some politicians. Recently, however, two younger Republican governors have gone on to the U.S. Senate (Christopher Bond and John Ashcroft). Of the last four governors, only Joseph Teasdale has not made a run for the U.S. Senate.

Missouri
Governor – Lt. Governor

Governor

Term: 4 years

Qualifications:
- ✓ At least 30 years old
- ✓ U.S. citizen for 15 years
- ✓ Live in Missouri for 10 years

Basic Powers:
- ✓ Administers Laws
- ✓ Appoints and Removes Officials
- ✓ Liaison with Federal Government
- ✓ Recommends Laws and Budget
- ✓ Signs or Vetoes Bills
- ✓ Calls Special Sessions
- ✓ Commands National Guard
- ✓ Grants pardons, reprieves
    or commutations
- ✓ Ceremonial Head of State

Lieutenant Governor

Term: 4 years

Qualifications:
- ✓ At least 30 years old
- ✓ U.S. citizen for 15 years
- ✓ Live in Missouri for 10 years

Basic Powers:
- ✓ Ceremonial Head of State
- ✓ President of the Senate
- ✓ Succeeds to Governorship
- ✓ Acting Governor When
    Needed
- ✓ Volunteer Coordinator
- ✓ Ombudsman

The Governor's Terms of Office

The governor is elected for a term of four years and, since the 1960s, may serve a second consecutive term. Governor Warren Hearnes was successful in getting the constitution amended in 1965 and was the first to succeed himself. Governor Phil Donnelly served two non-consecutive terms, 1945–1949 and 1953–1957. Since then, all governors except Joseph Teasdale have served two terms, although Christopher Bond's terms were also non-consecutive. (Bond was defeated in his re-election campaign by Teasdale, but won in a rematch four years later.)

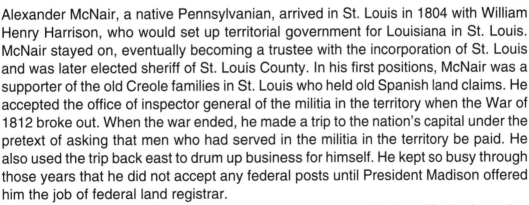

Alexander McNair
(1775-1826)
**Trustee of the City of St. Louis,
Missouri's First Governor, 1820**

Alexander McNair, a native Pennsylvanian, arrived in St. Louis in 1804 with William Henry Harrison, who would set up territorial government for Louisiana in St. Louis. McNair stayed on, eventually becoming a trustee with the incorporation of St. Louis and was later elected sheriff of St. Louis County. In his first positions, McNair was a supporter of the old Creole families in St. Louis who held old Spanish land claims. He accepted the office of inspector general of the militia in the territory when the War of 1812 broke out. When the war ended, he made a trip to the nation's capital under the pretext of asking that men who had served in the militia in the territory be paid. He also used the trip back east to drum up business for himself. He kept so busy through those years that he did not accept any federal posts until President Madison offered him the job of federal land registrar.

As land registrar, McNair began to support squatters' rights, effectively cutting off his relationship with his early support among the old families of Missouri. This proved a politically astute move as the new generation of Missouri voters elected him into office as governor against William Clark. McNair's administration was not known for great political activity. He proposed few items and because the Missouri constitution did not allow him to run for a second term, he retired from politics. He lost nearly all of his estate following the economic panic of 1819 and by the time he died in 1826, his family was left destitute.

The Governor's Executive Powers

The Missouri state constitution vests the governor with "supreme executive authority." The governor sees to it that the laws are enforced and that peace is maintained. In the past, many students of government felt the powers of the governor were limited—that the office did not provide enough formal authority to allow much leadership. Since the 1960s, though, with two consecutive terms available and reorganization of the executive branch, the office is comparable in authority to those in most other state governments.

Reorganization was most important in creating an Office of Administration, headed by a professionally trained administrator, which brought improved budgetary control and oversight to the executive branch. A governor's goals became more important (including the choice to be conservative or an activist) and reorganization allowed political and leadership skills to become more effective. In addition, it became more helpful if the legislature were controlled by the governor's party, but not absolutely necessary for program achievement. Governor Ashcroft was quite successful in accomplishing some parts of his program, despite having the General Assembly controlled by the opposition.

The governor has many other powers as well. He or she can call special elections and serve on a variety of boards and commissions. In the area of intergovernmental relations, the governor represents the state of Missouri when it deals with other states and federal government entities.

The Governor's Appointment Authority

Governors have considerable authority to appoint officials. They get to choose their department heads (with senate confirmation) and make a variety of other political and administrative appointments. **Appointments** are the act of designating someone for an office or position. According to analyst David Leuthold,

> One chief executive's assistant estimated that a governor made approximately two hundred "political plum" appointments. Another governor's assistant ... suspected there might be as many as two thousand appointments to process, counting members of numerous state boards and commissions, replacements for vacancies for county offices, and members of advisory commissions.

Obviously, there is a great deal of work involved in checking out people for various positions. Leuthold reported that Governor Ashcroft's transition team received about 4,500 resumes from applicants in 1984, and interviewed 2,000–3,000 people.

The governor's actions also influence local government. Governors appoint members of the boards of police commissioners in St. Louis and Kansas City and their election officials, as well as those in Platte and Clay Counties. Governors also fill vacancies in county governments. Their duty of appointing police and election commissioners in the two major cities dates back to an earlier era of corruption. Although there have been some recent efforts to get this changed, they have been unsuccessful to date.

Governors make political appointments by filling short-term vacancies in statewide elective offices and congressional openings. They also appoint members of most commissions in state government, as well as curators and regents for the University of Missouri and state regional universities. The University of Missouri has constitutional status, though, which gives it a certain amount of **autonomy**, or independence, from state government control.

It should be noted that most major appointments require **confirmation** by the Missouri Senate. This limits the governor's authority because the senator from the appointee's home district has veto power over the appointment. If the home senator is opposed, senatorial courtesy obliges other senators not to support the candidate, and the appointment is dead.

The Governor's Role in Peace Keeping

The governor is also charged by the constitution with preserving the peace. The governor is commander in chief of the state militia, except when it has been called into service by the federal government. The governor has general authority over civil defense and disaster relief. Previously, the governor had direct control over the Missouri State Highway Patrol, but this was changed in the reorganization of the executive branch in 1974. With reorganization, the patrol was assigned to the newly created Department of Public Safety. (Of course, the governor, with senate confirmation, appoints the director of Public Safety.)

Missouri State Constitution Article IV. Section 51

The appointment of all members of administrative boards and commissions and of all the department and division heads, as provided by law, shall be made by the governor. All members of administrative boards and commissions, all department and division heads and all other officials appointed by the governor shall be made only by and with the advice and consent of the senate.

The Governor's Legislative Powers and Veto

The governor's legislative role involves recommending measures to the General Assembly. This is done through the "State of the State" address, which is given at the start of each legislative session. Governors usually restrict their recommendations, for it is much easier to kill than pass legislation. Therefore, it behooves governors to concentrate their efforts on just a few of the measures they consider most important. The governor's staff lobbies actively for the desired bills and closely follows their progress through committee hearings. Also, the governor may become personally involved and lobby for favored measures. Some "log rolling" (exchange of favors to gain support) may be involved in this process, but it is hard to document. Finally, as a last resort, a governor may make a direct appeal to voters through radio and other media, urging them to bring pressure on legislators to pass or defeat certain measures.

Again, how much governors decide to press for in their legislative program is important. Usually, governors will not push for extensive tax measures, since they are unpopular. Governor Hearnes lost much popularity in his second term (1969-1973), after being re-elected by a large margin, by supporting a substantial tax increase. However, Governor Carnahan in his first term (1993-

Mel Carnahan (1934-)
Governor, 1992-2000

A native of Birch Tree, Missouri, and son of a U.S. Congressman for Missouri, Mel Carnahan first took public office as a municipal judge in 1961 in Rolla. In 1963, he won election to the Missouri General Assembly as a representative. After losing a race for the state senate in 1966, Carnahan stayed out of politics until 1981 when he was elected state treasurer. The state treasurer's office was in great need of modernization and Carnahan's achievements saved the state great amounts of money, although his success proved insufficient to win the Democratic nomination for governor in 1984.

After another brief retirement in Rolla, Carnahan served as lieutenant governor in 1989—the only Democrat in a statewide office. Fortunately for Carnahan during his 1992 campaign for governor, he was not the lone Democrat to win. In his position as chief executive of the state, Carnahan continued the mission he adopted as treasurer: redirecting unused funds towards education, job development and law enforcement. His most outstanding achievement was the passage of the Outstanding Schools Act in 1993, which increased the teaching staff in elementary education, shifted funding towards career centers for those high school graduates who do not go on to college, and provided full backing of the Parents As Teachers program. As of this printing, Carnahan was running for a seat on the U.S. Senate.

1997) surprised pundits by managing to push through an extensive tax package for schools, albeit with the help of the state court system. (A circuit court was threatening to act if nothing was done, and this was very intimidating to legislators.) For a high success rate, then, a governor's goals must be realistic and attainable.

The governor's **veto** authority, or ability to reject bills, is formidable, indeed. He or she can veto bills passed by the General Assembly or, in the case of appropriations bills, only parts of the proposal. This is called a **line item veto**. Because of the crucial nature of fiscal measures, it is deemed advisable to let the governor veto certain items, rather than the whole bill. This allows continued state operation while the legislature considers an override. Missouri legislatures almost never override vetoes although they may do so by a two-thirds majority in each house. (A constitutional amendment approved in 1970 allows a September special session for consideration of veto overrides.) Nationally, governors veto about 5 percent of legislatively approved bills, and about one in 25 are overridden. In Missouri, there has been a history of even fewer overrides.

Lloyd Stark (1886-1972)
Governor, 1936-1940

Born into a world-famous horticulturist family, Lloyd Stark expanded his family's Stark Brothers Nursery into an international force in its field during the 1920s. He first entered politics through the Missouri-Illinois Bridge Company where he came into contact with Tom Pendergast's Kansas City political organization, or "machine" as it is often called. Stark launched a campaign for governor in 1928, but failed without Pendergast support. By 1932, the political boss was left with no choice but to support Stark, who was considered an outsider to Kansas City politics.

Unfortunately for Pendergast, Stark turned on his former patron and began to appoint reformers to important posts around the state. Maurice Milligan, a federal district attorney supported by Stark, uncovered election fraud by Pendergast and the great Kansas City machine began its downfall. Stark was able to court quite a bit of political power himself, particularly through the money provided for social programs by Franklin D. Roosevelt's administration. The governor became recognized as a progressive in his support for health, education and labor. He increased public school funding and was the driving force behind what would become Ellis Fischel Cancer Center in Columbia. With such success under his belt, Stark set out to unseat Harry S Truman in the 1940 Senate race. But further political prosperity was not to be for Lloyd Stark. Truman had consolidated a large base of support throughout the state, which brought him victory. Milligan had also entered the race, succeeding only in splitting the reformer vote with Stark. In defeat, the former governor retired to a life of horticulture and agriculture until his death in 1972.

A referendum is an alternative strategy that may be implemented to overcome a governor's veto. Referendums can be called by the General Assembly or through the initiative (citizen petition) route. In both cases, they allow a vote of the people on the desired measure. If approved by voters, referendums become law without needing the governor's signature. Initiative and referendum will be explained in more detail in the next chapter.

Warren Hearnes (1923-)
State Representative, 1950-1961
Secretary of State, 1961
Governor, 1965-1973

A World War II veteran, Hearnes first ran for office after receiving his discharge in 1950. He was elected to the Missouri House of Representatives. He also studied for his law degree at the University of Missouri-Columbia. He served in the house until 1961 when he ran successfully for secretary of state for Missouri, a position he used as a springboard to the governor's office.

When Hearnes ran for governor in 1964, he took on an established political machine that had kept his party in power for decades. Hearnes was not in line to run for governor as the Democratic candidate, so he first had to overcome seemingly insurmountable odds just to win the nomination. He ran as a populist, painting his opponent as the tool of special interests. When Hearnes won both the nomination and the general election, he took charge of both his party and the state.

One of Hearnes' first moves as governor was allowing a person to hold the office for two consecutive terms. He used this change to his advantage four years later when he won re-election. His wife Betty, who would later run for various offices, also lobbied the legislature to fund the Missouri Council of the Arts, and Missouri became only the second state to fund such a body. The governor pushed bills through to fund education and mental health. After leaving office, he made two unsuccessful bids for office, once for U.S. senator in 1976 and then for state auditor in 1978.

Governor Hearnes signing civil rights legislation in 1965.

The Governor's Political Influence

Before governmental restructuring in the 1960s and 1970s, the powers of the governor were considered somewhat weak. Now most citizens feel there is sufficient authority for a governor to be effective. Still, some governors have greater success at accomplishing goals than others. Obviously, something else is necessary for effectiveness, and this relates to an individual's political skills as well as their popularity and charisma. As noted, a governor must have sufficient acumen to know which goals to pursue and sufficient skills to accomplish them. If a governor also has charisma and enjoys popularity, there is a greater possibility of success.

Legislators will be less likely to oppose governors if they feel there may be a backlash from voters should they do so. It is difficult to measure how great a role popular backing plays in the success of a governor's legislative package, but it is obviously important. Of additional importance is whether the governor's party controls the General Assembly.

The governor can further maximize influence by selecting the state party chairman. Governor Hearnes did so and "purged" many old party regulars who had opposed him in the bitterly fought Democratic primary in 1964. Hearnes challenged the "designated" Democratic candidate in the primary and won in an upset. He was almost assured victory in the general election because of the weakness of the Republican party during this period.

Governor Ashcroft (1985–1993) appointed a Kansas City attorney—Woody Cozad—as Republican state party chairman. Cozad was a prominent and strong activist who gained additional influence as a member of the University of Missouri's Board of Curators. (He held both positions for over a year, but some felt his role as a curator was compromised by his appointment as Republican party chairman.) Although the political parties have been weakened, they and the party chairmen can still be important for governors in both elections and legislative programs.

Joseph Folk (1869-1923)
Governor, 1904, Champion of the "Missouri Idea"

Born in Tennessee, Joseph Folk earned his law degree from Vanderbilt University in 1890. Folk arrived in St. Louis in 1893 to practice law with an uncle. He became a well-known figure when he negotiated an end to a public transit strike in 1900. After his election to circuit attorney for St. Louis later that same year, Folk immediately went after the same political machinery that had put him in office.

Despite the efforts of those whose trust Folk had betrayed, his work was recognized on a national level as shining a spotlight on urban corruption. In 1904, the year Republicans across the country rode Teddy Roosevelt's coattails into office, Folk won the governor's seat in Missouri as a Democrat. He brought a much-needed sense of morality to the governor's office and fought graft and trusts equally. The "Missouri Idea" was born at this time, meaning that the state could empower its people in such a way that they could make the law work in their favor.

His last two years were his most successful. He passed many of his initiatives with the support of the Democrats in both houses of the state legislature. His greatest actions as governor included passing Missouri's initiative and referendum amendment, enacting a statewide direct primary law, putting into effect various child welfare laws, approving further railroad regulation, establishing state examiners in many industries, and creating a commission for public libraries throughout the state. His attempts to run for U.S. Senator were thwarted by the enemies he had made in the state's political machinery. Folk spent his last years based in Washington, D.C., working in private law practice and in international negotiations following World War I. Shortly thereafter, Folk died of a heart attack in New York City in 1923.

Missouri Governors
Through 2000

Democrats 39
Republicans 11
Unionist 2

John Ashcroft (1942-)
State Attorney General, 1976
Governor, 1984-1992
U.S. Senator, 1994

John Ashcroft returned to his hometown of Springfield after receiving an undergraduate degree from Yale and a law degree from the University of Chicago. He taught business law at Southwest Missouri State until he entered politics in a race for the Republican nomination for U.S. Congress in 1972. He was unable to obtain the nomination, though he was appointed state auditor under Governor Christopher "Kit" Bond later that year. He was defeated when he ran for governor in the election of 1974.

Ashcroft found success in 1976, winning the race for state attorney general. His efforts as a tough opponent of crime made him the frontrunner in the gubernatorial race in 1984. One of Ashcroft's greatest political skills is to present his ideas in a concise, coherent manner that communicates effectively to the voter. By winning the governor's race, Ashcroft became the first Republican to follow another Republican into that office in Missouri since 1928. As governor, Ashcroft supported education through his Excellence in Education Act, which increased school funding in return for improved performance. He also set up an international trade office in Seoul, South Korea. Ashcroft remained proud of keeping Missouri's taxes very low, even with the accompanying reduction in funding for many social services.

After leaving office, Ashcroft worked in a St. Louis law firm until 1994. He unsuccessfully sought the chairmanship of the Republican National Committee. In 1994, he joined Kit Bond as the junior U.S. Senator from Missouri. In the Senate, Ashcroft distinguished himself by both remaining in close contact with his home state and having excellent attendance in Senate sessions. A natural conservative, Ashcroft has pushed for tax cuts and reform, direct funding of public schools as well as local control of school districts, and strengthening of law enforcement agencies in the fight against illegal drugs. He is a visible presence on Capitol Hill, but most importantly with his own constituents, stopping in each of the state's 114 counties several times since his election to the Senate.

The Governor's Pardon

The governor, in addition to the responsibilities of carrying out the laws and powers of appointment, has the power to pardon criminals. To grant a **pardon** is to excuse or free someone from punishment. The granting of a pardon is a serious action and is never undertaken in haste. In most cases, a pardon is granted only after a lengthy investigative process has been completed. A governor may also grant **reprieves**, which delay punishment, or he may **commute** a sentence, which changes a punishment to a less severe one. Additionally, the governor maintains the duty to extradite fugitives from justice that escape from other states into Missouri. **Extradition**, also called rendition, is a power authorized to the governor by the federal constitution.

David Francis (1850-1927)

Mayor of St. Louis, 1885-1888
Governor, 1888-1892
Secretary of the Interior, 1896-1897
President of the Louisiana Purchase Exposition, 1897-1904

David Francis, a native of Kentucky, came to Missouri to study at Washington University in St. Louis. Upon graduation, he did not have the money to pursue a law degree, so he went to work at his uncle's grain commission house. Francis was so successful that within six years he had started his own business. He became so well known for his success at a young age that he was elected mayor in 1885. As mayor, he aimed to streamline city administration and fight corruption.

After being elected governor in 1888, Francis enacted many early progressive measures, such as railroad regulation, state grain inspectors, and Missouri's first antitrust law. He also fought efforts to relocate the state university after fire destroyed the first administration building on the Columbia campus. Upon leaving office, he campaigned for President Grover Cleveland who named him Secretary of the Interior in return for his efforts. Towards the end of the 1890s, Francis directed all of his strength towards lobbying successfully for St. Louis to host the centennial celebration of the Louisiana Purchase and the World's Fair in 1904. Perhaps Francis' greatest mission was undertaken in the last years of his life when he was named ambassador to Russia in 1916. But the political turmoil in Russia and Europe in the following years proved too strenuous for him. He eventually came back to St. Louis where he died in 1927.

Governors of Missouri

Name	Political Party	Year Elected
Alexander McNair	Democrat	1820
Frederick Bates	Democrat	1824
Abraham Williams	Democrat	President of the Senate*
John Miller	Democrat	1825 (special election)
John Miller	Democrat	1828
Daniel Dunklin	Democrat	1832
Lilburn Boggs	Democrat	Lt. Governor*
Thomas Reynolds	Democrat	1840
Meredith Marmaduke	Democrat	Lt. Governor*
John Edwards	Democrat	1844
Austin King	Democrat	1848
Sterling Price	Democrat	1852
Trusten Polk	Democrat	1856
Hancock Jackson	Democrat	Lt. Governor*
Robert Stewart	Democrat	1857
Claiborne Jackson	Democrat	1860
Hamilton Gamble	Unionist	1861 (by state convention)
Willard Hall	Unionist	Lt. Governor*
Thomas Fletcher	Republican	1864
Joseph McClurg	Republican	1868
Benjamin Brown	Republican	1870
Silas Woodson	Democrat	1872
Charles Hardin	Democrat	1874
John Phelps	Democrat	1876
Thomas Crittenden	Democrat	1880
John Marmaduke	Democrat	1884
Albert Morehouse	Democrat	Lt. Governor*
David Francis	Democrat	1888
William Stone	Democrat	1892
Lon Stephens	Democrat	1896
Alexander Dockery	Democrat	1900
Joseph Folk	Democrat	1904
Herbert Hadley	Republican	1908
Elliot Major	Democrat	1912
Frederick Gardner	Democrat	1916
Arthur Hyde	Republican	1920
Sam Baker	Republican	1924
Henry Caulfield	Republican	1928
Guy Park	Democrat	1932
Lloyd Stark	Democrat	1936
Forrest Donnell	Republican	1940
Phil Donnelly	Democrat	1944
Forrest Smith	Democrat	1948
Phil Donnelly	Democrat	1952
James Blair Jr.	Democrat	1956
John Dalton	Democrat	1960
Warren Hearnes	Democrat	1964, 1968
Christopher Bond	Republican	1972
Joseph Teasdale	Democrat	1976
Christopher Bond	Republican	1980
John Ashcroft	Republican	1984, 1988
Mel Carnahan	Democrat	1992, 1996

* Inherited governorship rather than elected.

Other Elective Offices of the Executive Branch

Lieutenant Governor's Office

Missouri's lieutenant governor must be at least 30 years old, a U.S. citizen for at least 15 years and a resident of Missouri for at least 10 years before being elected to the office. The lieutenant governor is elected for a four-year term and may be re-elected.

Under the constitution, the lieutenant governor is *ex officio* (because of office) president of the Missouri Senate. This means upon the governor's death, conviction, impeachment, resignation, absence from the state or other disabilities, the lieutenant governor acts as governor. By law, the lieutenant governor is a member of many boards, including the Board of Fund Commissioners; the Missouri Housing Development Commission; the Missouri Rural Economic Development Council; and the Tourism Commission, among others. The lieutenant governor is the state's official advocate for Missouri's elderly.

Thomas Eagleton (1929-)
Attorney General, 1956
Lt. Governor, 1960
U.S. Senator, 1968-1986

Thomas Eagleton was born September 4, 1929, in St. Louis. After graduating with honors from Amherst and Harvard Law School, he began practicing as an attorney in St. Louis. Eagleton rose steadily through the politics of the state. He first served as circuit attorney for St. Louis in 1956. He became Missouri's attorney general in 1956. After a term as lieutenant governor, Eagleton began a three-term tenure in the U.S. Senate in 1968. He received notoriety in 1972 when presidential candidate George McGovern picked Eagleton as his running mate, only to drop him later.

As senator, Eagleton spoke widely on affairs ranging from foreign relations and intelligence to education and health care. Eagleton retired in 1986. His place was filled by former Republican governor Christopher Bond, giving the Republicans a monopoly on Missouri's U.S. Senate seats. After retiring from the U.S. Senate, Eagleton accepted a position as University Professor of Public Affairs at Washington University in St. Louis. His courses focus on business, government and public policy. Eagleton also writes a national newspaper column and is a public speaker.

Secretary of State's Office

The secretary of state is elected to a four-year term. He or she must be a Missouri resident for at least one year. The secretary of state's office is the "information place" of Missouri government. This office's many diverse responsibilities are all linked by the common theme of information. The office is responsible for compiling, storing and publishing a variety of state documents. As keeper of the Great Seal of Missouri, the secretary of state authenticates official acts of the governor. In addition, the secretary of state is Missouri's chief elections official.

Functions of the office are divided into six areas: elections, securities, business services, records services, state library, and administrative services. The executive deputy secretary of state is charged by law with implementing the policies and procedures of the secretary, and supervising day-to-day operations of some phases of the office. The office has approximately 270 employees.

State Auditor's Office

The state auditor is elected to a four-year term and must meet the same qualifications as the governor. He or she must be at least 30 years old, a U.S. resident for at least 15 years and a Missouri resident for at least 10 years. The auditor's office determines if tax dollars are being spent efficiently, economically and legally, and to determine how well governmental units and agencies protect against fraud and abuse of the public funds under their control.

The office audits all state agencies, boards and commissions, the state court system, and the counties that do not have a county auditor. The state auditor may also be called on to audit local units of government by citizen petition. Approximately 200 state agencies and programs, the state's 45 judicial circuits (including approximately 400 municipal divisions) and 93 counties must be regularly audited by the state auditor. Approximately 20 audits of local government entities, petitioned by local voters, are performed each year. Other legal duties are detailed in Chapter 29 of the Revised Statutes of Missouri.

State Treasurer's Office

The treasurer is also elected. The qualifications are the same as for the secretary of state. The state treasurer is Missouri's chief financial officer. The duties of the treasurer as defined by the Missouri constitution and statutes are to be the custodian of all state funds and to invest those funds not needed for daily state operations.

The treasurer serves a term of four years, and a person may only serve as a treasurer for two terms. The treasurer's office manages Missouri's $17 billion in annual state revenues. It directs the state's banking and investment services. The office also safeguards and tries to locate the rightful owners of unclaimed property that has been turned over to the state by banks, businesses, insurance companies and government agencies.

The treasurer also serves as a member of many boards, including the Missouri Housing Development Commission, the Missouri State Employees Retirement System, the Missouri Cultural Trust, the Missouri Investment Trust and others.

Attorney General's Office

The attorney general is elected to a four-year term. He or she must be an attorney and must live in Jefferson City while holding office. The attorney general is the attorney for the state. He or she represents the legal interests of Missouri and its state agencies but does not represent individual citizens in private legal actions.

As the state's chief legal officer, the attorney general must prosecute or defend all appeals to which the state is a party, including every felony criminal case appealed to the Missouri Supreme Court and courts of appeal. The attorney general also is required to institute, in the name and on behalf of the state, all civil suits and other proceedings that are necessary to protect the state's rights, interests or claims. The attorney general may appear, answer or defend any proceedings when the constitutionality of a statute is challenged.

The attorney general also renders official opinions to the executive and legislative branches and the county prosecuting attorneys on questions of law relating to their duties.

The attorney general may institute proceedings to oust any corporation doing business in Missouri if it has violated state laws; or anyone unlawfully holding office; or, more specifically, any public official, for malfeasance in office. Malfeasance means wrongdoing, particularly by a public official.

By law, the attorney general is a member of numerous boards, including the Board of Fund Commissioners, the Governor's Committee on Interstate Cooperation, the Missouri Highway Reciprocity Commission and others.

The Non-Elective Executive Branch

Executive Branch Departments

1. Office of Administration
2. Department of Agriculture
3. Department of Conservation
4. Department of Corrections
5. Department of Economic Development
6. Department of Elementary & Secondary Education
7. Department of Health
8. Department of Higher Education
9. Department of Insurance
10. Department of Labor & Industrial Relations
11. Department of Mental Health
12. Department of Natural Resources
13. Department of Public Safety
14. Department of Revenue
15. Department of Social Services
16. Department of Transportation
    ... and more than 350 boards and commissions

1. Office of Administration

The Office of Administration serves as the state's service and administrative control agency. The emphasis of this department is to combine and coordinate the central management functions of the state government. This is accomplished through the Division of Accounting, Division of Budget and Planning, Division of Data Processing and Telecommunications, Division of Design and Construction, Division of Facilities Management, Division of General Services, Division of Personnel, and Division of Purchasing and Materials Management.

2. Department of Agriculture

The Department of Agriculture enforces the state laws that assist in regulating the agricultural industry of Missouri. The agency also protects the interests of Missouri agriculture and fiber producers while promoting the products in Missouri, throughout the United States, and abroad.

3. Department of Conservation

The Department of Conservation's objectives are to protect and manage Missouri's fish, forest and wildlife resources. The department also serves the public, facilitates their participation in resource management activities, and provides opportunities for enjoyment and education of fish, forest and wildlife resources.

4. Department of Corrections

The Department of Corrections is a law enforcement agency dedicated to public safety. It maintains control of criminals sentenced to prison or parole. It also administers programs to help rehabilitate offenders.

5. *Department of Economic Development*

The Department of Economic Development executes laws and department policies in economic development, the regulation of business and financial institutions, and professional registration.

6. *Dept. of Elementary & Secondary Education*

The Department of Elementary and Secondary Education is primarily a service agency that works with local school officials and other groups to identify needs within the educational system and to improve educational opportunities and programs.

7. *Department of Health*

The Department of Health is comprised of many offices, all with the goal of protecting the health and welfare of the state of Missouri's residents. The offices included in the Department of Health are: Office of the Director, Division of Administration, Division of Environmental Health and Communicable Disease Prevention, Department of Health Standards and Licensure, Division of Maternal, Child and Family Health, and the Division of Chronic Disease Prevention and Health Promotion. Each of these divisions initiates, implements, manages and supervises programs designed to further their particular interest areas and promote general health issues.

8. *Department of Higher Education*

The Department of Higher Education identifies statewide needs for higher education, plans for post-secondary education, evaluates student and institutional performance, and reviews and enhances institutional missions. The department's duties also include the development of effective and economical specialization among institutions, the administration of a performance funding program encouraging the achievement of statewide priorities, the submission of a unified budget request for public higher education to the governor and the Missouri General Assembly, and the approval of new degree programs offered at public schools and universities. The department's planning activities include the state's independent institutions as well as its public institutions.

9. Department of Insurance

This department regulates the Missouri insurance industry. It provides consumer protection for the insurance-buying public. The department includes four divisions: Financial Regulation, Market Regulation, Consumer Affairs, and Resource Administration.

10. Department of Labor & Industrial Relations

This department administers programs that promote job placement, provides an income for those without employment, mediates between management and labor groups, regulates wages,

---

George Caleb Bingham (1811-1879)
Artist, State Representative, 1848
State Treasurer, 1862
Adjutant General, 1875-1876

Bingham is one of the most famous Missourians from the 19th century because of the masterful paintings that bear his signature. Born in Virginia in 1811, Bingham settled in Franklin, Missouri, in 1818. A chance encounter with the portrait painter Chester Harding inspired the nine-year-old Bingham to follow the same calling. He began portrait painting in 1828. On a trip to Philadelphia in 1838, he discovered genre art, the style he would master with such works as *Fur Traders Descending the Missouri.*

It was earlier, in 1834, back in central Missouri that Bingham began a friendship with attorney James Sidney Rollins, which brought him into contact with politics for the first time. His political aspirations were not realized until 1848 when he won a seat in the Missouri legislature as a Whig. Although Bingham had been a slave owner like his friend Rollins, he became a strong unionist in the 1850s. He was so respected as an enemy of secession that he was chosen captain of a home guard unit in Kansas City when the Civil War started. Governor Hamilton Rowan Gamble subsequently appointed Bingham state treasurer in Missouri's pro-Union government.

Bingham witnessed many of the worst abuses by Union officials against Missouri's citizens. His paintings from the period reflect these injustices and he became a committed Democrat. In 1875, Charles Henry Hardin was elected governor of Missouri and named Bingham adjutant general. In this role he was able to represent Missouri in claims the state had with the federal government dating from the war. Unfortunately, Bingham died in 1879—in relative artistic obscurity. His paintings were largely forgotten until the 1930s when museums in New York and St. Louis began a revival of his art. It was the famed muralist from Neosho, Missouri, Thomas Hart Benton, whose acknowledgment of Bingham's mastery that gave Missouri's first artist the recognition he deserved.

promotes safety in the workplace, enforces anti-discrimination statutes, promotes equal access for those with disabilities, and investigates claims of workers' compensation fraud and noncompliance with the state's labor laws.

11. Department of Mental Health

The Department of Mental Health works to prevent mental disorders, developmental disabilities, and substance abuse by treating and rehabilitating persons, by offering family support, and by educating the public. Its major goal is to provide a higher quality of life and increased independence for Missourians. One important step toward this goal is to combat public prejudice about mental illness.

12. Department of Natural Resources

This department serves citizens through many environmental and natural resource related issues. The department deals with energy and mineral resources and preserves the state's historic and cultural heritage. The department's five divisions are Energy, Environmental Quality, Geology and Land Survey, Administrative Support and State Parks.

13. Department of Public Safety

This department coordinates statewide law enforcement, criminal justice and public safety efforts for the purpose of ensuring a safe environment for Missouri citizens. The department is divided into: Office of the Director, Missouri Capitol Police, Missouri State Highway Patrol, Division of Liquor Control, Division of Fire Safety, Division of Highway Safety, Missouri National Guard, State Emergency Management Agency, Missouri Veterans Commission, and the Missouri Gaming Commission.

More than 80 state parks and historic sites are managed by the Department of Natural Resources, offering diverse recreational opportunities from fishing to mountain biking.

14. Department of Revenue

The Department of Revenue collects all revenue for the state. Its primary duties are to collect taxes, to title and register motor vehicles, and to license drivers. They also enforce and administer laws that apply to taxation, motor vehicles and driver's licenses.

15. Department of Social Services

The Department of Social Services provides public assistance to children and parents, access to health care, services to the elderly, child support enforcement, and specialized assistance to troubled youth. While many programs give needed financial assistance and services, other programs work towards reducing financial dependency of citizens on government.

16. Department of Transportation

MoDOT is responsible for Missouri highways, aviation, waterways, public transit and railroads. This includes the design, construction and maintenance of Missouri's 32,000-mile highway system.

Case Study

Conserving Nature

Missouri has been inhabited for thousands of years. Humans have always depended on wildlife for survival: food, clothing, shelter, tools, and trade. With the state's large beaver and buffalo population, the fur trade became the earliest industry in this territory. St. Louis soon developed into the fur capital of the world. In 1803, President Thomas Jefferson purchased the entire Louisiana Territory. This led to a tremendous growth in the trapping industry and the settling of new territory.

Beginning in 1813, many people migrated west. As more settlers arrived in Missouri, many species were hunted or became endangered due to habitat destruction. No laws existed to monitor the number of animals that were killed. Most landowners saw nature as part of their property. Animals were killed in excessive numbers since their abundance seemed to indicate an endless supply. Finally in 1883, the U.S. Supreme Court ruled that wildlife belonged to all people—not individual landowners.

Despite the few laws that existed, without enforcement, by 1936, much of our wildlife was gone. Cutting forests, plowing prairies and draining swamps and marshes led to great soil erosion. There were fewer than 200 beaver, 2,000 deer and 2,500 wild turkeys left in Missouri. The passenger pigeon and timber wolf became extinct in Missouri.

In 1937, the Missouri Department of Conservation was formed. The Conservation Department assists in the wise use, enjoyment and protection of our natural resources. This department does research, makes and enforces laws and teaches people to be safe and responsible outdoors.

After the formation of the Conservation Department, our fish, forests and wildlife resources began to be restored, but still more assistance was needed. In 1976, citizens of Missouri voted to pay a conservation tax anytime they bought an item. One penny of every eight dollars spent in Missouri would go to conservation (costing each Missourian six to seven dollars a year). The tax allowed for the study of our natural environment. Rules were written and enforced to preserve our surroundings.

Due to the work of citizens and the Department of Conservation, wildlife is once again plentiful. Missouri has one of the best fish, forest, and wildlife programs of any state. White-tailed deer again roam in abundance. Wild turkeys and bobcats can again be found in many parts of the state. Fish populations are on the rise. The beaver, after being hunted almost to extinction, is now common. Wooded areas continue to furnish habitat. New strides are also being made along our major waterways to increase habitat for migratory birds and aquatic species.

Summary & Conclusions

The executive branch of Missouri state government includes the governor's office and all of the elected and appointed officials of the governor's administration, including the lieutenant governor, secretary of state, state auditor, state treasurer, and attorney general. The executive branch also includes departments that direct the state's oversight of education, tax collection, law enforcement, agriculture, economic development, conservation, health, and more. Because of its broad responsibilities, the executive branch is the largest of the three branches of Missouri state government.

The executive branch of government is organized on the industrial model, with the governor presiding like a corporate CEO over a large bureaucracy. The governor appoints officials to serve in the state government, proposes legislation to the General Assembly, vetoes legislation he deems objectionable, and selects the state chairman for his political party. The governor's leadership skills and popularity can play a considerable role in gaining support for a legislative agenda.

Chapter 4
The Executive Branch: Membership, Powers, Authority & Influence

End of Chapter Questions

Use the text along with outside material to answer the following questions. Be sure to review the key terms and concepts from the beginning of the chapter before you start.

1.   Compare and contrast the primary differences between the industrial model of the executive branch and the collegial model of the legislative branch.

2.   What does "supreme executive authority" mean? What effect does this authority have on the state's governance system?

3.   What function does the governor's appointive authority serve?

4.   In what ways can a governor have direct impact upon local government?

5.   Why do you think that most major appointments made by governors require confirmation by the legislature? Discuss in detail how this "check" benefits the governance system.

6.   What purpose does the governor's veto power serve?

7.   Why is it often favorable for the governor to utilize the "line item veto"?

8.   What is the purpose of a referendum and what is the basis for its existence?

End of Chapter Activities

*Use the text along with outside material to complete
the following activities.*

1. Draw a pyramid that describes the executive branch of the Missouri legislature.

2. Identify and analyze important pardons that have been granted by Missouri governors in recent years. Why is this process another important "check" on governmental authority?

3. Outline the primary powers of the governor. How do each of these powers influence government at the state and local levels?

4. Research and review the major points of the current governor's legislative agenda.

5. Outline the process by which a governor's veto can be overridden by the legislature.

Out of Class Activities

1. What is the "merit system" and how does this system affect the appointments made by the governor? Do you think this is a good system? Why or why not? Analyze some of the current governor's appointments and describe how the merit system may have influenced his selections.

2. Visit the website www.mdn.org/newsbook. This site is maintained by the Missouri School of Journalism. It contains up-to-date news from the capitol and useful information for covering the legislature. Research and report on a recent event involving the executive branch.

Chapter

The Legislature: Organization & Function

Key Terms & Concepts

bicameral

census

General Assembly

house of representatives

independence

initiative

law

lobbyist

lower chamber

quid pro quo

reapportionment

referendum

representativeness

senate

special interest group

unicameral

upper house

Introduction to the Legislative Branch

"The rule of law." This phrase is often applied to our democracy, and means that all citizens—even the president—are subject to the rule of the law, not the whims of any given leader.

Laws form the necessary underpinning for any modern society, and laws are made by legislatures. Although one political cartoon noted that watching the making of law is similar to watching sausage being made (both seem messy and unpleasant), the time-consuming and complicated process is crucial. The legislative process is conducted in Congress at the federal level, and at the state level, in the state legislature and in city councils.

In Missouri, the state legislature is also known as the **General Assembly**. The General Assembly is **bicameral**, meaning it consists of both an upper house and a lower house. The **upper house** is the senate. The **lower house,** or chamber, is the house of representatives. It holds annual sessions, which are held from January through mid-May. There are also provisions for special additional sessions.

An extraordinary or special session of the General Assembly can be called by the governor at any time.

The special session is limited to 60 days.

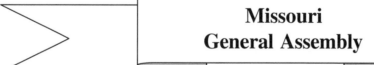

Missouri General Assembly

Senate (Upper House)

Presiding Officer: Lt. Governor
34 members • 4-year terms

Requirements:
At least 30 years of age
Missouri voter for 3 years
District resident for one year

Salary: $29,080 annually
plus expenses (1998)

House of Representatives (Lower House)

Presiding Member: Speaker
163 members • 2-year terms

Requirements:
At least 24 years of age
Missouri voter for 2 years
District resident for one year

Salary: $29,080 annually
plus expenses (1998)

Interestingly, all states except Nebraska have adopted similar models with bicameral, or two-chambered, legislatures. Nebraska, during a reform era, changed to a **unicameral**, or one-chambered, legislature.

State laws are known as statutes and can be enforced. There are also rules and regulations for implementing and enforcing state laws developed by state agencies and commissions, but these are made and changed without General Assembly action.

The Missouri General Assembly has been rated 36th among the 50 states on several measures, including representativeness and independence from the governor. **Representativeness** refers to how well the legislature reflects the social complexity of the state. **Independence** refers to policy-making and how independent, or autonomous, the legislature is from lobbyists, state agencies, and the governor in developing policy.

The Missouri Senate

The **senate** consists of 34 members elected from districts with approximately equal populations. This means that senatorial districts outside of metropolitan areas are geographically larger. For example, the 12th District in northwest Missouri contains 16 counties and approximately 150,000 people. The size of the Missouri senate is small compared with others in the nation, which is quite strange because the House of Representatives ranks among the nation's largest.

Senators must be at least 30 years of age, and they serve four-year terms. They must be qualified voters of their districts for one year and must have lived in the state for three years. Elections are staggered, meaning that half of the senators are elected every two years. Under recent term limit restrictions, they are limited to two terms for a total of eight years.

Both senators and representatives are paid $29,080 annually (1998), although cost of living increases are now in effect, as well as an increase in the daily expense allowance (per diem, or per day). A citizen salary commission recommended substantial increases as of January 1997, but they were turned down by the General Assembly. Identical resolutions had to be passed by both houses to defeat the salary increases. The house of representatives was the first to defeat the measure, but many assumed the senate would take no action, or different action, from the house of representatives by the deadline of February 1997. This would have validated the increases. Evidently, pressures against the large increases were extreme, and the measure was rejected by substantial margins. Many of those opposed to salary increases consider the legislators to be part-time, since they are in session only from January through May.

Leadership in the senate includes the lieutenant governor, who presides over the chamber and votes in case of ties. This relationship becomes interesting when the lieutenant governor is of a different party from the majority. This happened when William Phelps (Republican) held the office from 1973-1981. Disputes between the lieutenant governor and the Democratic majority led to a change in the rules. The authority to assign committee bills and rule on points of order was taken from the lieutenant governor and reassigned to the president pro tem, who is elected by senators of the majority party, in this case the Democrats. A court decision in 1974 upheld this change.

Theodore McNeal (1905-1982)

First African American State Senator, 1960-1970; Civil Rights Advocate

A chance visit to St. Louis after graduating from high school changed the life of Arkansas-born Theodore McNeal. After some factory work, he eventually found employment as a porter on a Pullman car. McNeal became one of the founding members of the International Brotherhood of Sleeping Car Porters in St. Louis. He experienced such success as a union negotiator that he rose to be the union's national vice-president. He also began fighting for civil rights as early as 1942, organizing a demonstration to call for equal employment in high-paying jobs in the war industries.

It was not until 1960, at age 54, that McNeal entered politics for the first time, becoming the first African American to serve as Missouri state senator. Among his accomplishments were the support he gave to the first civil rights bill in Missouri history and the call for a St. Louis campus of the University of Missouri. He was recognized as one of the most powerful African Americans in a state legislature in the country. Upon his retirement in 1970, he was tapped to serve on the Board of Curators of the University of Missouri, the first African American to do so. He later served on the St. Louis Board of Police Commissioners. He retired in 1973.

Missouri Senatorial Districts

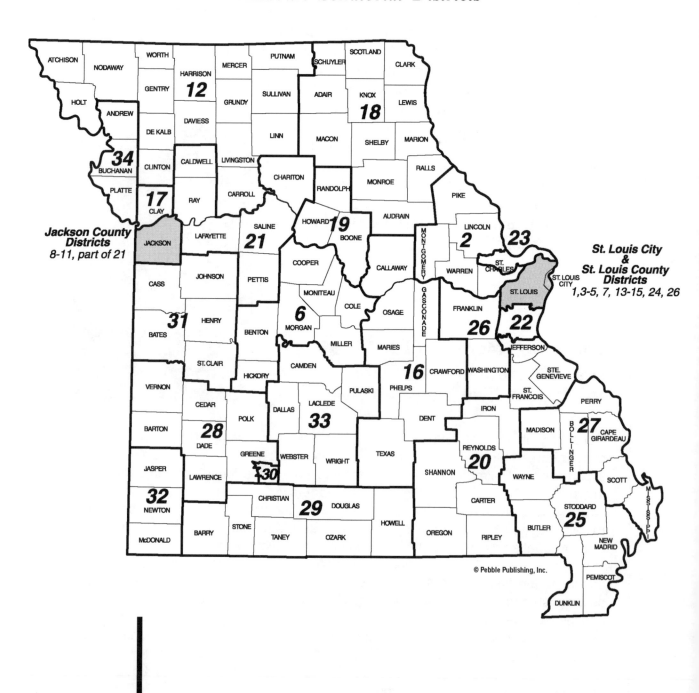

Jackson County
Districts
8-11, part of 21

St. Louis City
&
St. Louis County
Districts
1,3-5, 7, 13-15, 24, 26

© Pebble Publishing, Inc.

Naturally, this increased the power and influence of the president pro tem. Other senate leaders include the majority and minority floor leaders, the caucus chairs, and the caucus secretaries, as well as some administrative posts.

Committee chairs are also part of the leadership. The senate presently has 22 committees. Obviously, being chair is not possible for all senators, but with another 22 vice chairs, committee leadership is available to all, together with multiple committee assignments. For example, former senator Joe Moseley from mid-Missouri chaired the education committee (with the University of Missouri in his district) and sat on three other committees as well. Interestingly, the minority party makes its own committee assignments. In the house of representatives the majority party, via the speaker, handles assignments. This makes for more decentralization in the senate and dilutes the power of the majority party. The senate, with its many traditions and greater informality, has been described as being more of a "club" than the house of representatives. When Harriet Woods was lieutenant governor, she frequently pointed out how the senate was an "old boys' club," which had some difficulty in adjusting to a female presiding officer.

"Although the Senate is much given to admiring its members—a superiority less obvious or quite invisible to outsiders—one senator seldom proclaims his inferiority to another, and still more seldom likes to be told of it."

— Henry Adams, 1907

Missouri Senate Standing Committees

1. Administration
2. Aging, Families & Mental Health
3. Agriculture, Conservation, Parks & Tourism
4. Appropriations
5. Civil & Criminal Jurisprudence
6. Commerce & Environment
7. Education
8. Elections, Veterans' Affairs & Corrections
9. Ethics
10. Financial & Governmental Organization
11. Gubernatorial Appointments
12. Insurance & Housing
13. Judiciary
14. Labor & Industrial Relations
15. Local Government & Economic Development
16. Pensions & General Laws
17. Public Health & Welfare
18. Rules, Joint Rules & Resolutions
19. State Budget Control
20. Transportation
21. Ways & Means

A photograph from inside the capitol during a session of the 80th General Assembly.

Missouri State Senate Facts

1. Senator Michael Kinney was the oldest senator who ever served and he also served the longest—56 years. He was elected in 1912 and retired in 1968 at the age of 92.

2. Missouri's first woman senator, Mary Gant, served from 1972 until 1980.

3. At least 40 Missouri senators have attained higher statewide office or have become a U.S. senator or member of Congress for Missouri.

4. Senator J.O. Morrison and Senator James L. Mathewson were the longest serving presidents pro tem in Missouri history. They each served 8 years.

5. More than half of all senators reside in one of Missouri's three largest metropolitan areas (Kansas City, St. Louis and Springfield).

6. Senator Gwen Giles, elected in 1977, was the first African American woman to serve as a Missouri senator.

7. The Democratic party has held the majority of senate seats since 1949. Senator M.C. Mathes was the last Republican president pro tem.

8. All senate meetings are open to the public and the media.

9. The shortest bill introduced in the senate was one line long. One of the longest bills introduced was SB 52 (897 pages) in 1993.

10. The most debated subjects in the senate are taxes, education and crime.

The Missouri House of Representatives

The Missouri **house of representatives**—or house, as it is often called—has 163 members elected from districts that average 31,000 people. The house is also referred to as the lower house, or chamber. Missouri's house ranks among the largest in the nation.

Some argue that the large number of representatives means better representation. Their thinking is that citizen access to legislators is easier because there is a better ratio of constituents to representatives, and that a larger body can better represent the great diversity of Missouri.

Others dispute this theory, arguing that larger legislative bodies are dysfunctional. They contend that the legislative process becomes more complicated with such large numbers of representatives and so many committees. Indeed, complexity can be a problem. However, it works to the advantage of those who have served the longest and have learned the intricacies of politics. Yet, with term limits, there are fewer years for an individual to gain expertise. Many argue that longevity is the greater problem. Long tenure, they argue, leads to "careerism" and a lack of accountability.

Deverne Lee Calloway (1916-1993)
First African American Woman to Serve as Missouri State Representative, 1962-1982

Calloway played an important role in shaping state government attitudes about race and the under-privileged. She was one of the few African Americans with a college degree before World War II. It was her Red Cross experience during the war that exemplified her leadership qualities. Stationed in the Far East, she headed a demonstration against the policy of segregating black patients within Red Cross facilities.

After the war, she was involved in local Chicago politics until her marriage to Ernest Calloway brought her to St. Louis in 1946. She began her string of ten terms in the Missouri state legislature in 1962, becoming the first black woman elected to that post in the state. As representative, she fought for public education, aid to Missouri's less fortunate, and prison reform. Calloway was involved in the St. Louis area through many community boards in the 1970s. After serving her tenth term in office, she retired in 1982. She died at the age of 76 in her hometown of Memphis, Tennessee.

Missouri House of Representatives Districts

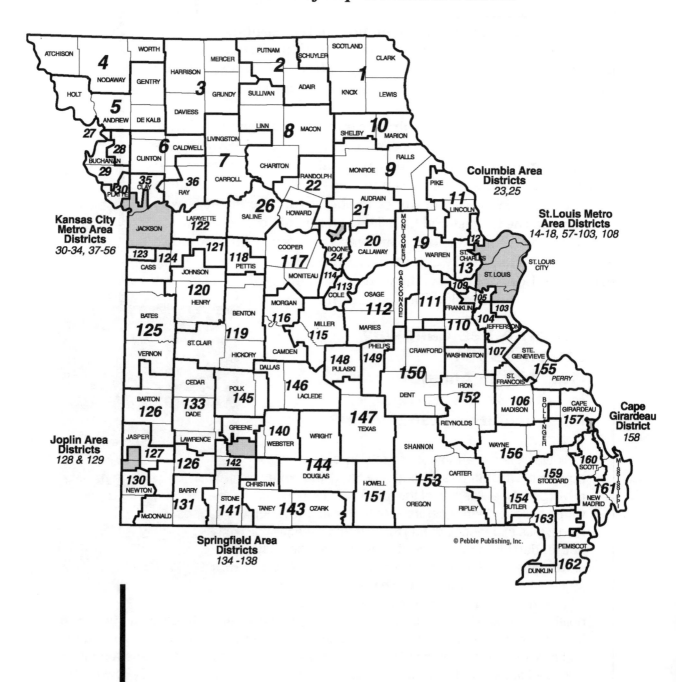

Representatives must be at least 24 years of age, and they serve two-year terms—up to a maximum of four. They must be qualified voters of their district for at leat one year, and of the state for at least two years.

The top leadership post in the house of representatives is the speaker of the house. The speaker is elected by the majority party. The speaker appoints all committee members and chairmen, assigns all new bills to house committees, and signs all official actions of the house. The speaker pro tem presides in the speaker's absence. Both the speaker and the speaker pro tem are nominated by the majority caucus and elected at the opening of the first regular session of each General Assembly. The majority and minority floor leaders manage floor action on behalf of their parties; they are ex officio members of all committees. The majority whip directs support of members of his or her party to various party objectives.

Robert Griffin, Democrat from Cameron (District 6), was speaker of the house from 1981 to1995, and accrued considerable power and influence during his long tenure. This was the longest any speaker had served. Power was concentrated in his office during his leadership. Those opposing him were often banished to unfavorable committee assignments, or as some call it, the "political wilderness."

Bob Griffin (1935-)
Speaker of the House, 1981-1995

Bob Griffin has become one of the most infamous figures in Missouri politics, joining a tradition of conspicuous Missourians, running from the corrupt territorial governors through the machinery of influence and graft of Thomas Pendergast. Born in Braymer, Griffin's first public office was as Clinton county prosecutor in 1963 after his law degree from the University of Missouri and a stint in the U.S. Air Force. He left the office of county prosecutor in 1970 to run for the General Assembly. He also served on state and national Democratic committees.

Griffin became the speaker pro tem during the 79th and 80th sessions of the Missouri General Assembly. In 1981, he was named Speaker of the House and served in that position until political scandal forced him to resign in 1995. A federal jury in 1997 found Mike Fisher, former head of the AFL-CIO in Kansas City, guilty of paying bribes to Griffin while the latter served as speaker of the house. Griffin was acquitted on three counts and the jury could not reach a verdict on six others. Griffin later entered a plea of guilty to bribery and mail fraud and was sentenced to four years in prison.

Reapportionment & Redistricting

Changes in population could easily bring about a different majority in the General Assembly, particularly if they occur in the right places. **Reapportionment**, or the changing of election district lines to assure substantially equal populations, is required with every 10-year census. A **census** is an official count of the inhabitants of the United States. It is performed every ten years.

Missouri House of Representatives Standing Committees

1. Accounts, Operations & Finance
2. Agribusiness
3. Agriculture
4. Appropriations
    Education & Public Safety
5. Appropriations
    General Administration
6. Appropriations
    Health & Mental Health
7. Appropriations
    Natural & Economic Resources
8. Appropriations
    Social Services & Corrections
9. Banks & Financial Institutions
10. Budget
11. Children, Youth & Families
12. Civil & Administrative Law
13. Commerce
14. Consumer Protection & Housing
15. Correctional & State Institutions
16. Criminal Law
17. Critical Issues
18. Education
    Elementary & Secondary
19. Education–Higher
20. Elections
21. Environment & Energy
22. Ethics
23. Federal /
    State Relations & Veterans' Affairs
24. Fiscal Review
25. Governmental Organization & Review
26. Insurance
27. Judiciary
28. Labor
29. Local Government & Related Matters
30. Miscellaneous Bills & Resolutions
31. Motor Vehicle & Traffic Regulations
32. Municipal Corporations
33. Professional Registration & Licensing
34. Public Health
35. Public Safety & Law Enforcement
36. Retirement
37. Rules, Joint Rules, Bills Perfected
    & Printed
38. Social Services, Medicaid
    & the Elderly
39. State Parks, Natural Resources
    & Mining
40. Tourism, Recreation
    & Cultural Affairs
41. Transportation
42. Urban Affairs
43. Utilities Regulation
44. Ways & Means
45. Workers' Compensation
    & Employment Security

One occurred in 2000, and the next will occur in 2010. The political parties become very outspoken during the redistricting process. Districts that have grown in population have to give up population to those that have lost population or have stayed the same. This is done in order to keep the populations of the various districts substantially equal. This is usually no more than a 10-percent variance above or below the average.

The General Assembly has not been good at reapportionment or redistricting because so much is at stake. The political parties get into life and death struggles over redistricting. A legislator can effectively lose his or her seat if too many opposition votes are added to the district, or if too many supporters are subtracted. If a redistricting bill manages to get through the legislature, it is often challenged in court. The courts have been heavily involved in this process of late.

Richard Webster (1922-1990)
State Representative, 1948-1962
Speaker of the House, 1954
State Senator, 1962-1990

Richard Webster became the longest-serving Republican in the Missouri legislature. Born in Carthage, he entered politics after receiving his law degree at the University of Missouri-Columbia. He was first elected as state representative for Jasper County in 1948. He ran unsuccessfully for attorney general in 1952 and returned to the house in 1953. He became speaker of the house in 1954—the youngest in the state's history at that point. In 1962, he was elected to the state senate and held that office until his death in 1990.

Although a member of the Republican party, Webster championed many liberal issues, including education, civil rights, workers' benefits, and the disadvantaged. His most important legacy is Missouri Southern State College, which he sponsored as a two-year college in 1965. It was accredited as a four-year institution in 1977. The first residence hall on the campus was named Webster Hall in his honor.

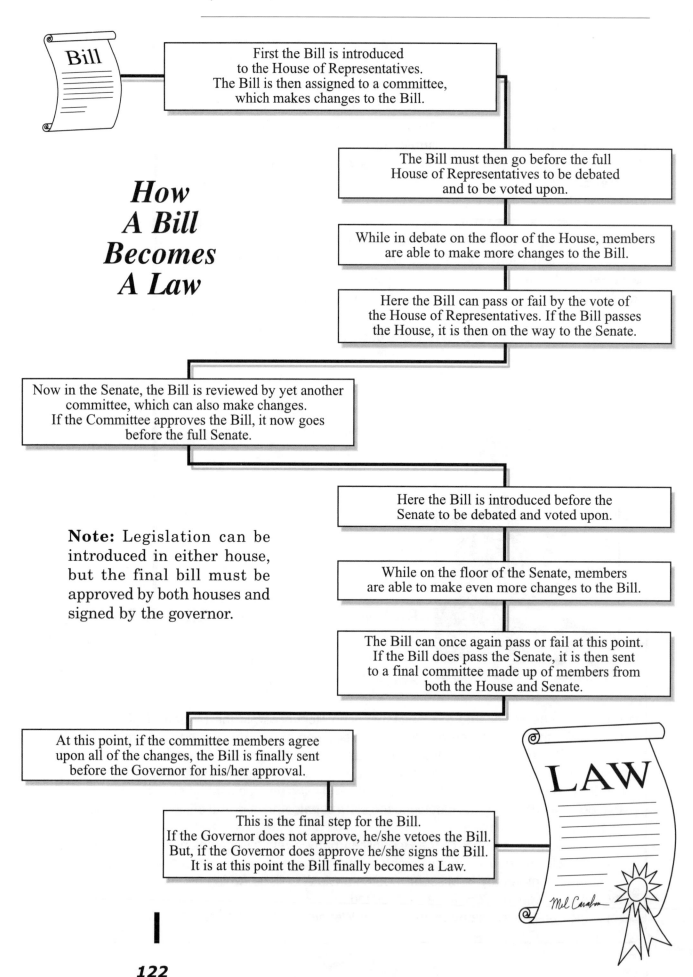

Bill

First the Bill is introduced
to the House of Representatives.
The Bill is then assigned to a committee,
which makes changes to the Bill.

*How
A Bill
Becomes
A Law*

The Bill must then go before the full
House of Representatives to be debated
and to be voted upon.

While in debate on the floor of the House, members
are able to make more changes to the Bill.

Here the Bill can pass or fail by the vote of
the House of Representatives. If the Bill passes
the House, it is then on the way to the Senate.

Now in the Senate, the Bill is reviewed by yet another
committee, which can also make changes.
If the Committee approves the Bill, it now goes
before the full Senate.

Here the Bill is introduced before the
Senate to be debated and voted upon.

Note: Legislation can be
introduced in either house,
but the final bill must be
approved by both houses and
signed by the governor.

While on the floor of the Senate, members
are able to make even more changes to the Bill.

The Bill can once again pass or fail at this point.
If the Bill does pass the Senate, it is then sent
to a final committee made up of members from
both the House and Senate.

At this point, if the committee members agree
upon all of the changes, the Bill is finally sent
before the Governor for his/her approval.

This is the final step for the Bill.
If the Governor does not approve, he/she vetoes the Bill.
But, if the Governor does approve he/she signs the Bill.
It is at this point the Bill finally becomes a Law.

LAW

Mel Casalon

The Legislative Process

Legislatures are most often associated with the passage of bills to raise and spend money. In earlier times, English kings had to give away some authority to a legislature to gain monies necessary for wars and governance. The English parliament became important in this way, for it had the power of the purse. Since then, all modern legislatures have approved money bills, even though the bills may originate with the chief executive. (The governor develops a budget for the General Assembly to approve or reject, as does the president with Congress.)

Approximately 1,500 bills are introduced annually on a wide range of matters, and about 10 to 15 percent become law. Most bills, while introduced by legislators, are developed by state agencies or **special interest groups**, such as bankers, teachers, utilities, insurance companies, labor, and so on. Individual legislators sometimes draft their own bills, but this is not too common anymore. There is a committee of legislative research for the house of representatives and a senate research staff to help draft bills and provide background information. In addition, all bills now require a fiscal note—in order to inform legislators what costs can be expected if a bill becomes law.

The legislative process in Missouri and most states involves a number of steps. Legislation can be introduced in either house, but the final bill must be approved by both houses and signed by the governor to become law. A bill can stall in committee or either house, or be vetoed by the governor. Given the length of the process, it is not difficult to understand why it is much easier to kill than pass legislation. The legislative process is extremely complicated—and is designed to be that way.

It would be virtually impossible for every member of the legislature to take the time to study every aspect of all new laws proposed at each session of the General Assembly. As a result, the house and senate members work in specialized legislative committees that consider the validity and need for a particular bill. Committee membership includes representation of both political parties. However, the members of the majority party always outnumber those of the minority party. Committee chairmen are always appointed from the majority party by the speaker of the house and the president pro tem of the senate. The committees are set up according to the rules of each house, and they are established based on the proposed bill's subject matter.

According to David Valentine, Director of Senate Research, "Most observers agree that there are too many [committees]. . ."

Valentine makes another important observation. In the 1970s, he points out, the minority Republicans followed a strategy of cooperating with the Democrats, and were fairly successful in gaining legislation they wanted. In contrast, Republicans in the 1980s and 1990s changed strategy and decided to emphasize campaign positions. The result was fewer Republican-favored bills, but a gain in Republican seats in both the house and the senate. Democratic majorities are much narrower than earlier, and the chambers could easily switch majorities in the near future.

If the Missouri General Assembly passes a law that conflicts with the U.S. Constitution, the state or federal judicial system can strike the law down, deeming it unconstitutional.

Case Study

How The Safe Schools Act Is Improving Public Schools Safety

Between classes, a student entered the restroom at a high school in St. Louis and discovered the battered body of a freshman. As stated in the *Journal of The Missouri Bar*, "Evidence indicated that she had been beaten... and her assailant had attempted to drown her... in the toilet." A St. Louis county circuit court convicted a 15-year-old fellow student. This was the convicted student's second day at the victim's high school after having been suspended from another school for behavioral problems.

In response to this and other violent incidents that have recently taken place, the Safe Schools Act was passed in 1998 to protect students from further harm. This law involves stricter operation of a school district concerning student admission and enrollment, residency issues, policy development and suspensions, reporting requirements, and record keeping.

The Safe Schools Act also increases the punishments for crimes that occur on school property. The crime of making a false bomb report was changed from a class A misdemeanor to a class D felony. Section 160.261 allows zero tolerance for weapons at school. "The discipline policy must dictate that a student who has brought a weapon to school be suspended for at least one year or be expelled," reads the statute.

Schools should be a safe zone for students. The Safe Schools Act is a legislative step in the right direction, by helping to keep weapons out of schools and keeping violent students from remaining in the classroom.

Initiative & Referendum

Missouri citizens have two direct processes that they can use to either enact or reject laws: the initiative and the referendum.

The **initiative** process can be used to pass or reject laws or amendments to the state constitution independent of the General Assembly. In order to propose an initiative, a petition with a designated number of signatures must be presented to the secretary of state no less than four months prior to the election in which the initiative will be voted upon (currently there is debate on extending this to six months). The number of signatures shall be no less than 8 percent of the legal voters in no less than two-thirds of the congressional districts in the state if a constitutional amendment is being proposed, and no less than 5 percent of such voters if a law is being proposed.

Missouri citizens may also reject any act of the General Assembly by referendum. A **referendum** may be proposed by either a petition signed by not less than 5 percent of the legal voters in each of two-thirds of the state congressional districts or by the General Assembly as other bills are enacted. Referendums must be filed with the secretary of state not more than 90 days after the final adjournment of the session of General Assembly that passed the bill on which the referendum is demanded.

The number of legal voters is determined by the total number of votes cast for governor of Missouri in the election immediately preceding the filing of any initiative or referendum.

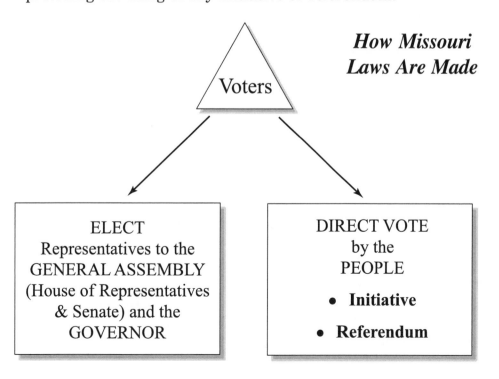

How Missouri Laws Are Made

Voters

ELECT
Representatives to the
GENERAL ASSEMBLY
(House of Representatives
& Senate) and the
GOVERNOR

DIRECT VOTE
by the
PEOPLE

- **Initiative**

- **Referendum**

Common Legislative Terms

Caucus: A voluntary organization of members of the house or senate. Each chamber has partisan caucuses as well as caucuses organized around geographical and interest groups.

Companion Bills: Bills introduced in the both the house and the senate in identical form.

Concurrent Resolution: A resolution that is passed by both the house and the senate. It may originate in either body. If it has the effect of law, it must be handled like a bill.

Confirmation: Approval of an appointment to office by the governor. The constitution gives this power to the state senate.

Consent Bill: A noncontroversial bill that does not cost anything to implement and does not reduce revenues.

Constitutional Majority: The constitution requires approval by a majority of members elected to the senate and to the house for a bill to be considered passed. This are 18 members in the senate and 82 members in the house.

Filibuster: A delaying of action by extending debate.

General Revenue: State revenues which are not designated for a specific use but which may be appropriated for any legal use.

Impeachment: An indictment of a statewide elected official or a state judge for crime or misconduct in office. The constitution gives the power of impeachment to the house of representatives.

Joint Resolution: An enactment of the General Assembly that places a proposed amendment to the state constitution before the voters, or that approves an amendment to the U.S. Constitution. Either called a House Joint Resolution, or a Senate Joint Resolution.

Joint Session: A session of both the house and senate. Joint sessions are held in the house chamber and are normally called to hear the governor or the chief justice of the Supreme Court.

Quorum: The number of members required for a body to do business. The rules of each chamber set this number for committees. The state constitution requires a majority of members to be present for the house and the senate to conduct business.

Reading: A step in the legislative process. First reading occurs when a bill is introduced, second reading when it is referred to a committee, and third reading when it is approved by a constitutional majority of a chamber.

Resolution: An act of the house or senate or of both together that ordinarily has no effect of law. It either commends some achievement, expresses an opinion, urges another entity such as Congress to take some action, or takes some internal action such as establishing a committee.

RSMo: Abbreviation for Revised Statutes of Missouri.

Session: When the General Assembly meets. The regular session is January through May. The session in odd-numbered years is called the first regular session; that in even-numbered years is called the second regular session.

The Role of Lobbyists

A **lobbyist** is a person representing a special interest group that attempts to influence legislators. Lobbyists represent a wide array of public and private interest groups. A lobbyist acts as the voice of these larger groups and impacts the political process directly via his or her involvement. Lobbyists are crucial to the legislative process, although many citizens find interest group activity unsettling. Lobbyists are sometimes referred to as "influence peddlers," but they are of great importance to the process. They provide valuable information to legislators and must play it "straight" if they want to succeed over the long run. In other words, they should not misrepresent their stands on issues or give false or distorted information.

Lobbyists round up sponsors and supporters for the bills they favor, and follow the bills closely throughout the legislative process. A lot of their efforts focus on the committees, where crucial votes are held. (State agencies do not have lobbyists per se, but some of their staff act in this capacity.) While lobbyists furnish important information to legislators, particularly with respect to the stands of their groups, some critics of the legislative process find lobbying obtrusive and annoying and claim that corporate special interests are disproportionately represented.

The suspicion is that lobbyists are corrupting the process by exchanging campaign contributions for the legislation they want. **Quid pro quo**, or one thing in return for another, is the phrase used to describe this exchange. This practice adds fuel to the perceived "crisis in ethics" that has plagued the U.S. Congress and often the presidency. In recent years, lobbying—and the entire election process—has been in an unfavorable public light. Both political parties scream about the cost of elections and call for spending limitations and greater control over special interests and their lobbyists. Thus far, some limitations exist on financial contributions to election campaigns, but not on expenditures. Contribution limitations are easily circumvented by the creation of PACs, which can give unlimited amounts to any candidate. Limiting expenditures, or what may be spent on any given campaign, is considered an infringement on First Amendment freedom of speech, say the courts, at least up to now. A clear solution to this problem has been difficult to find, since one voter's "lobbyist" is another voter's activist. One voter's "special interest" is another's sacred cause.

Rep. Jim Barnes, (D-Raytown), confers with Rep. Sue Shear, (D-Clayton), in January 1996, after he resigned as speaker pro tem.

Legislative Intern Program

The Legislative Intern Program is sponsored by the Missouri General Assembly. It selects the best students in relevant fields from Missouri colleges and universities and provides them with an opportunity to gain valuable practical experience in the processes of state government. The program offers interns the opportunity to use skills gained through their academic studies and other experiences to provide vital staff support to members of the General Assembly. As well as gaining knowledge and experience for themselves, interns provide a real service to the people of Missouri. Some interns spend one day each week at the Capitol, while full-time interns work five days a week. Individual schedules are arranged by each student with his or her legislator and school. For more information, write to the Legislative Intern Program Coordinator, c/o The House Post Office, State Capitol, Jefferson City, MO 65101.

Summary & Conclusions

Missouri's bicameral, or two-chambered, General Assembly is similar to other state legislatures, except for unicameral Nebraska. The General Assembly is comprised of the senate, or upper house, and the house of representatives, or lower house (or chamber).

The Missouri senate is one of the smaller upper houses in the nation, while in contrast, the house of representatives is one of the largest lower houses.

Approximately 1,500 bills are introduced each year, but relatively few survive the gauntlet to become laws.

The legislative process is designed to allow legislators to carefully consider each and every bill. Consequently, procedures are complex and numerous. Experienced legislators are often influential because they are extremely familiar with the rules and procedures.

Lobbying is also an important part of the lawmaking process, even though many citizens find interest group activity unsettling. Lobbyists do, however, provide valuable information to legislators. But some critics say corporate and other special interests are unfairly over-represented.

A legislative tradition: Stacks of paper are flung into the air at the stroke of noon on the last day of regular session.

The Missouri General Assembly has been rated 36th in the nation in "representativeness" and "independence" from the governor. Representativeness refers to how well the legislature reflects the social complexity of the state. Independence from the governor refers to its independence in policy-making.

Recent developments at primarily the national level have put the legislative process and lobbying in a bad light. Furthermore, campaign spending has gotten out of hand. It will be interesting to see what reforms might be forthcoming to counter these trends. Still, legislatures are central to democracies and provide an extremely important check on chief executives.

Chapter 5
The Legislature: Organization & Function

End of Chapter Questions

Use the text along with outside material to answer the following questions. Be sure to review the key terms and concepts from the beginning of the chapter before you start.

1. Why is it important that all citizens, including elected officials, are subject to the rule of law?

2. Why do you think term limits were enacted in the Missouri legislature? Do you think they are beneficial to our governance system? Support your view with three reasons why term limits are or are not beneficial to our governance system.

3. According to the author, why do larger numbers of representatives translate into increased representation? Why do some argue that having so many representatives is actually a disadvantage?

4. Explain the concepts of "majority" and "minority" parties. What important political powers do individual members typically get from being a member of the "majority"?

5. What is one of the primary functions of the legislature?

6. What is a lobbyist? What part do lobbyists typically play in the state legislature? Why does the author say lobbyists are crucial in the legislative process?

7. Why do shifts in population tend to have powerful effects on the political process?

8. Why are reapportionment and redistricting such important issues to elected officials?

9. Why is the law making process intentionally complicated?

End of Chapter Activities

Use the text along with outside material to complete the following activities.

1. Make a list of the current elected leaders of the General Assembly. Include in your list their party affiliations and the date that they will be eligible for re-election. Be sure to list each leader's major role and principal responsibilities.

2. List the qualifications for office for both senators and representatives. Discuss each and try to explain why each qualification is important in terms of both representation and the electoral process.

3. Identify one special interest group that is currently active in the legislature. Briefly outline their agenda and the impact, if any, they have had on state government, such as helping with the passage or defeat of a bill.

4. Briefly outline the major steps in the process of how a bill becomes a law. Do you think all of these steps are needed to create good laws?

Out of Class Activities

1. Visit the website www.mdn.org/newsbook. This site is maintained by the Missouri School of Journalism. It contains up-to-date news from the capitol and useful information for covering the legislature. Research and report on a recent event involving the legislative branch.

2. Visit the website http://stateline.org, a free online news service written by journalists for journalists, policy-makers and citizens. Each day it provides information and news on all 50 states. Research Missouri's legislative branch for the current year. Report on a recent event you find interesting.

Chapter

The Judicial System: Law & Order

Key Terms & Concepts

appellate court
associate division
capital punishment
circuit court
civil trial
criminal trial
felony
grand jury trial
impeachment
juvenile division
misdemeanor
municipal court
original jurisdiction
peremptory challenge
petit jury trial
probate division

Introduction to the Judicial Branch

The third branch of government, although certainly not third in importance, is the judicial branch. It is composed of the many courts in the state. It has equal standing with the executive and legislative branches. The Missouri Constitution devotes an entire article to it, as it does for each of the other two branches of Missouri government.

Article Five of the Missouri Constitution outlines the structure and powers of the courts in Missouri and generally how they should operate. As stated in the introduction of this book, organized societies rely upon the rule of law, without which there can be no effective governance, peace or order.

The judicial branch, then, is crucial for effective government. It is the branch that continues to define the rule of law, and to mediate when conflict arises. The courts are needed to resolve conflicts between governments and branches of government, as well as cases regarding individual civil rights. Furthermore, they hear criminal cases, determine guilt or innocence, and make determinations between contesting parties in civil disputes.

Organization of the Courts

Prior to 1979, the Missouri court system was highly decentralized. Municipal and magistrate judges lacked adequate legal training, there was little coordination, and financing was inadequate with some judges paid on a per-case basis. These problems led to a push by the Missouri Bar for a unified court system with adequate financing. The General Assembly drafted a proposed constitutional amendment to replace the judicial article and submitted it to voters in a referendum in August 1976. It was narrowly approved, and the General Assembly then drafted a more detailed, 230-page bill to implement court reform. Known as the Court Reform and Revision Act, it became law on January 2, 1979.

The Court Reform and Revision Act provided for three areas of major change. First, it upgraded standards for judges, mandating

Article V, Sections 1-3 of the Missouri Constitution:

Section 1. The judicial power of the state shall be vested in a supreme court, a court of appeals consisting of districts as prescribed by law, and circuit courts.

Section 2. The supreme court shall be the highest court in the state. Its jurisdiction shall be coextensive with the state. Its decisions shall be controlling in all other courts. It shall be composed of seven judges, who shall hold their sessions in Jefferson City at times fixed by the court.

Section 3. The supreme court shall have exclusive appellate jurisdiction in all cases involving the validity of a treaty or statute of the United States, or of a statute or provisions of the constitution of this state, the construction of the revenue laws of this state, the title to any state office and in all cases where the punishment imposed is death.

The Missouri Constitution provides five major areas of law, over which the Missouri supreme court has exclusive jurisdiction:

1) Cases involving the validity of a statute or treaty of the United States;

2) Cases involving the validity of a statute or provision of the constitution of this state;

3) Cases involving the construction of the revenue laws of this state;

4) Challenges to the title to any state office;

5) All cases where the punishment imposed is death.

Unless a case involves one of these questions, the party appealing the lower court's decision must take its appeal to the proper district of the court of appeals. If the case falls into one of these categories, however, the supreme court must hear it because it has exclusive jurisdiction in such cases. (Exclusive jurisdiction in a particular court means that that court, and no other, may hear a case.)

that municipal judges must be lawyers in cities with a population of more than 7,500. In less populated cities, non-lawyer municipal judges are now required to attend state-provided training programs. Second, it changed the system of finance for the courts system, with the state picking up the salaries of circuit clerks, circuit judges, and associate circuit judges. This meant the state could provide comparable pay for comparable work, uniform personnel policies, uniform fringe benefits, and similar staffing for similar courts. In addition, the state prohibited judges from being paid on a per-case fee basis.

The opposition to per-case fee basis resulted primarily from speed traps set up by some municipal police forces. Speed traps were designed not only to reduce speeding but to provide revenue to the city through court fines. Critics charged that speed limits were sometimes set unrealistically low in order to enhance revenues. One municipality near the Lake of the Ozarks had become notorious for writing tickets to generate income.

Third, the judicial reform brought unification to the previously decentralized court system. It created a three-tiered system with the lowest level being the circuit courts, then the courts of appeal, and at the top the Missouri Supreme Court. The **circuit courts** now include all courts of limited jurisdiction: probate, juvenile, common pleas, etc. (In pilot test counties a family court division has been established, which combines domestic relations, juvenile cases, adult and child abuse, and related criminal cases.) These courts are headed by presiding judges who are responsible for managing the system and can reassign judges or cases to eliminate bottlenecks or backlogs. Consequently, their role has been enhanced under the new system.

Traditional Writs

Writs are formal written documents ordering or prohibiting some action. Below are several commonly used writs.

Writ of habeas corpus: An order to bring a person held in prison or similarly detained by authorities before a court, for inquiry into the lawfulness of that detention.
Writ of mandamus: An order to a public official to enforce the performance of a specific public duty.
Writ of certiorari: An order from a superior court to call up for review the records of an inferior court.
Writ of quo warranto: An order requiring a person to show by what right he or she exercises an office, franchise or liberty.

Judicial Branch

Missouri Supreme Court

- ✓ Chief Justice presides over court
- ✓ 7 judges
- ✓ 12-year terms
- ✓ Highest court in the state
- ✓ Hears cases on appeal from lower courts or transferred from appeals court

Requirements:
- ✓ Must be at least 30 years old
- ✓ Must be a citizen of the United States of America for at least 15 years
- ✓ Must be a qualified Missouri voter for at least 9 years

Court of Appeals

Eastern District – 14 judges
Western District – 11 judges
Southern District – 7 judges

- ✓ 12-year terms
- ✓ Hears cases on appeal from lower courts
- ✓ Must be at least 30 years old
- ✓ Must be a citizen of the United States of America for at least 15 years
- ✓ Must be qualified Missouri voter for at least 9 years
- ✓ Annual salary $98,728

Circuit Courts

- ✓ 6-year terms for circuit court judges
- ✓ 4-year terms for associate circuit court judges
- ✓ 45 circuit court districts
- ✓ Circuit court judge's salary: $98,947
- ✓ Associate circuit court judge's salary: $87,235

Note: Each circuit court has at least one circuit judge. In circuit courts with more than one county, each county must have at least one resident associate circuit judge. All cases under the law first come to trial in one of the state's judicial circuit courts.

Missouri Supreme Court

At the top of the judicial system is the Missouri Supreme Court. It consists of seven members, with one member serving as chief justice on a rotating basis for two years. The Missouri Supreme Court has **original jurisdiction**, or cases that only it can try, in all cases involving:

(1) the validity of a treaty or statute of the United States,
(2) a statute or provision of the Missouri Constitution,
(3) construction of the state's revenue laws,
(4) the title to any state office, and
(5) cases involving the death penalty.

It also has exclusive appellate jurisdiction, where certain cases may only be appealed to it.

In addition to its decision-making powers, the Missouri Supreme Court supervises the entire court system in the state. The Office of State Courts Administrator, created in 1970, aids it in this responsibility. This office provides management services, technical assistance, education and training programs, and other court improvement projects. The court also licenses all practicing attorneys and disciplines those found guilty of violating the legal rules of professional conduct. The court hears oral arguments three times a year in January, May and September.

The Dred Scott case was decided by the Missouri Supreme Court on March 22, 1852. The decision, upheld by the Supreme Court of the United States, was one court decision that helped precipitate the Civil War.

The Supreme Court Library contains more than 108,500 volumes, from old case reports dating from revolutionary times to the most up-to-date legal reports and periodicals.

State of the Judiciary Address, 1998, By Duane Benton, Chief Justice, Missouri Supreme Court

"The judiciary is working smarter today than ever before. Facing increasing caseloads, the courts are efficiently serving Missourians. The judiciary is doing more and more with proportionately less and less. The judicial branch is the smallest of the three branches of state government. We spend less than three-fourths of 1 percent of the total state budget.

Though a separate, equal branch of government, the judiciary is smaller than 13 of the 15 departments in the executive branch. While our cost is small, our impact is great; we deliver services to all citizens of the state. Court employees work in all 114 counties and the City of St. Louis, in all 34 senate districts, and in almost all, if not all, of the 163 House districts.

(1) We decide cases that affect citizens throughout this state, from traffic offenses and consumer-merchant disputes, to death penalty cases and multi-million dollar lawsuits. (2) We provide ways for people to resolve their disputes informally in small claims court, and for abused persons to get immediate protection from their abusers. (3) We do all this in a way that benefits both the people of this state as well as those who make the system work: quickly and for as little expense to the state as possible."

Missouri's Supreme Court Justices:

	Appointed:	Term Expires:
Chief Justice		
William Ray Price, Jr.	April 1992	December 2006
Justices		
Duane Benton	August 1991	December 2004
Ann Covington	December 1998	December 2002
John Holstein	October 1989	December 2002
Stephen Limbaugh, Jr.	August 1992	December 2006
Ronnie White	October 1995	December 2008
Michael Wolff	August 1998	January 2002

The Missouri Supreme Court holds three sessions each year—beginning in January, May and September—to hear oral arguments in cases on appeal. On these occasions, attorneys for the parties involved appear personally before the court and orally argue the merits of their cases and answer the questions of the judges. Before these arguments take place, the lawyers in the cases present detailed briefs fully stating all of their arguments and the basis for them (past court decisions, laws, scholarly articles and the like). The briefs and oral arguments are considered by the court in researching, deciding and writing its opinion in a case. When not hearing oral arguments, the judges are busy researching the cases that have been heard and writing opinions. Researching and writing a single opinion often requires several weeks.

Court of Appeals

The wheels of justice move slowly, it has been said, and the appeal process is partly responsible. The Missouri Court of Appeals, or **appellate court** as it is often called, relieves the Missouri Supreme Court of extra work by handling all appeals, except for those where the supreme court has exclusive jurisdiction.

The court of appeals, which is not a trial court, reviews both the facts and the application of law in cases referred to it. Decisions are final unless they are further appealed or transferred to the Missouri Supreme Court.

A single court of appeals was established in 1970 by a constitutional amendment. It consists of three districts—western (11 judges), eastern (14 judges) and southern (7 judges). Court is held in a variety of locations, but primarily in Kansas City, St. Louis and Springfield.

Circuit Courts

Within the circuit court, there are three levels of jurisdiction. These are the circuit division, the associate division and the municipal division. If you, the reader, become involved in the legal process, it could very well be through the circuit court. Circuit courts have absorbed the other lesser courts in the new unified judicial system, and are the courts of original jurisdiction. This means that most every civil or criminal action starts in circuit court. These courts occasionally even handle cases involving the federal constitution, unless one of the parties elects to use the federal courts. There are 45 circuit courts in the state of Missouri.

Circuit Division

The circuit division is where most jury trials are held. The division handles everything not specifically assigned to other divisions, including:

(1) all felony cases,
(2) civil cases exceeding $25,000,
(3) equity cases, such as injunctions and domestic relations,
(4) probate matters in counties with populations of more than 65,000,

(5) misdemeanor cases that are initiated in this division,

(6) extraordinary remedy cases, and

(7) cases reassigned from other divisions.

Felonies are major crimes such as murder or arson. Felonies can involve sentences from a year in prison to life. In some cases, the sentence for a felony is **capital punishment**, also called the death penalty.

The circuit division has two types of juries—grand and petit. **Grand jury trials** involve a special panel of 12 citizens, who may be selected by a judge, and who examine evidence to see if there are sufficient grounds for criminal prosecution. (Their only role is to discover evidence, not to convict.) The proceedings are secret, and hearsay or secondhand testimony is permitted. Only nine of the 12 grand jurors must vote for indictment.

Grand juries are required for federal prosecution, but states have the option of using them or utilizing some other method. In Missouri, they are used continuously in metropolitan circuits, but only occasionally in rural areas. They are particularly useful in investigating public officials and violations of state election laws. Previously, they were often called to reduce backlogs of cases, but reorganization has lessened this use. If the grand jury believes there is sufficient cause to prosecute, indictments are issued for a regular **petit jury trial**.

For most people charged with crimes, though, a preliminary hearing is held before a judge where information is gathered. If sufficient evidence is found for prosecution, the judge orders a petit jury trial. In a petit jury trial, in criminal cases, verdicts must be unanimous—12 of 12—for conviction.

In a democracy there is the expectation that all citizens are equally able to serve on a jury. However, Missouri has several automatic disqualifications, including judges of courts of record, lawyers, those with very serious mental or physical handicaps, military persons on active duty, illiterates, convicted felons who have not had their civil rights restored, those convicted for misdemeanors involving moral turpitude, and those who have served on grand juries within the previous ten years.

In addition, there are many people who may ask to be excused. These include those over 65; professors or teachers; clergy; those engaged in the practice of medicine, osteopathy, chiropractic, or dentistry; government employees and those whose employment would be jeopardized by jury duty. Also, a person must be at least

21 years of age to serve. Although there have been attempts to reduce this to 18, the requirement still stands.

Potential jurors are selected from "master jury lists," which are compiled by county boards of jury commissions. Lists used to be drawn exclusively from voter registration records, but there has been a move to use driver's license records, which expands the pool. Names are drawn at random and those selected are usually asked when they can serve.

Whether or not a person will serve is still problematic. They may be excused by the defense or prosecution in criminal cases for prejudice or bias, or by a **peremptory challenge**, meaning at the discretion of the attorneys. There is no limit to the number of persons who can be disqualified, but peremptory challenges are usually limited to six for each side. Jury selection becomes very important, even crucial in deciding the outcome of a case. Different ethnic and racial groups view the prosecution and defense differently, with some generally favoring one over the other. The location of a trial also becomes important because of the general orientation of the community or pretrial publicity.

The circuit division also includes courts of special jurisdiction. This include the probate division, the juvenile division, drug courts and family courts, among others.

The **probate division** oversees the settlement of wills, making certain the terms are carried out, as well as processing the estates of those who die without wills. In addition, the probate division conducts the affairs of those who have been declared incompetent. Prior to reorganization, probate judges were elected in every county except Jackson and St. Louis, where the non-partisan selection basis is used (see section on the non-partisan court plan).

In the **juvenile division**, 17 is the defining age for being considered a young adult. Those who come into contact with the legal system and are under the age of 17 are assigned to the juvenile division. The division, it should be noted, is not responsible for punishing violators, but for providing treatment and rehabilitation for children needing care, education, protection and guidance. Cases heard range from adoptions to those involving abuse, as well as truants and those with criminal tendencies.

Associate Division

The **associate division** of the circuit court handles a variety of cases, including those that have been reassigned from circuit court, if their dockets, or schedules, are full. Disputes between citizens that involve less than $25,000 are handled by the associate division.

The associate division also provides a small claims court for sums of less than $3,000. Small claims court is an inexpensive way to settle disputes and can handle matters not usually heard in regular courts. No juries are used. Hiring a lawyer is optional. Judges make the decision unless one or both parties request a jury trial (an option seldom used). Most small claims court cases involve tenant-landlord relations (very prevalent in college towns), unpaid accounts or vehicle damage suits. Several television programs air the proceedings of small claims courts. These are cases being heard in an associate division court.

The associate division also handles criminal cases involving misdemeanors, traffic cases involving state laws, or cases where a jury trial is desired. **Misdemeanors** are minor violations generally resulting in fines or a jail sentence of less than one year.

Since the associate division handles small claims court proceedings, the following pages are devoted to the small claims court process. But before branching out into a detailed study of the small claims process, the third division of the circuit court— the municipal division—will be briefly discussed.

Municipal Division

The third division of the circuit court is the municipal division. This division handles traffic and code violations (zoning, housing, electrical, plumbing, etc.) for municipalities that have no courts. Municipalities have the option of either retaining their **municipal courts**, or turning the process over to circuit court. Again, this was part of the reorganization and unification of the courts system in 1979. The argument for reassigning such operations to circuit court is cost savings; cities would no longer have to pay court costs including judges' salaries. However, most municipalities have kept their court operations to maintain some local control and, more important, to retain revenues from fines and charges. Municipal courts do not have jury trials, so if a participant wants one, it must go to the associate division or the circuit court.

Introduction to Small Claims Court

The small claims court is a division of the circuit court presided over by an associate circuit judge. The small claims court is a people's court and was established to help people handle their small cases without an attorney. Small claims proceedings are informal in nature. You must fill out all required forms and present your own evidence in court. There are no jury trials. While the small claims court system was designed to settle uncomplicated disputes, filing and winning a claim as well as collecting your money can be far from uncomplicated. There are specific rules that must be followed if you are to succeed on your claim.

You can file a claim in small claims court only against someone who owes you money. The court cannot force anyone to return property to you, nor can the small claims court be used by landlords to evict tenants. The court is also not responsible for collecting the money that the judge may determine is owed to you.

Depending on the type of claim you are making, you have a certain amount of time in which to file the claim. This is called the statute of limitations. The time period begins to run when the injury or damage occurs or when the injury or damage should have been discovered. The statute of limitations varies for different types of claims. Claims for personal injury, property damage, and claims for money damages for breach of contract must be filed within five years. To be safe, you should file your claim as soon as possible.

Pursuing a claim in court is a serious matter with unpredictable results. If you sue you may lose. Be sure you feel you can adequately explain and prove your claim to a judge. Even if you win, you are responsible for collecting the money from the defendant. For more information, contact the small claims court clerk at your county courthouse.

Sample Petition
Small Claims Court

IN THE CIRCUIT COURT, DIVISION XXX, _____ COUNTY, MISSOURI

_____
Plaintiff

_____
Street Address

_____
City   State   Zip Code

_____
Telephone

vs.

_____
Defendant

_____
Street Address

_____
City   State   Zip Code

_____
Telephone

_____
Case Number

_____
Amount Claimed

_____
Date & Time of Hearing

The Plaintiff states he has a claim against the Defendant in the amount of $_____. The claim arose on or about the _____ day of _____, 20___, as a result of the following events:

The Plaintiff states that the information contained in this Petition is true and correct to the best of his or her knowledge, that he or she is not an assignee of this claim and that he or she has not filed more than six other claims in any Missouri small claims court during this calendar year.

Plaintiff understands that should he or she be successful in this action and obtain judgment, and if Defendant does not appeal within ten days, this judgment becomes final. The Plaintiff cannot commence another action involving the same parties and issues.

Signature of Plaintiff:

How to Use Small Claims Court

This information, reprinted from a pamphlet prepared by the Cole County Circuit Court, explains how to use small claims court. Here are some facts and advice:

❏ You should try to settle the problem before bringing it to court.

❏ Before you sue, ask yourself if it's possible to win the case. Can you explain it well enough and provide enough evidence to be convincing?

❏ Make sure you have the correct name and address of the person you're suing so he can be summoned to court. If suing a company, name a corporate officer or registered agent.

❏ No more than $3,000 can be recovered from any action. That is the state's limit on small claims.

❏ To file a case in a particular county, at least one defendant must live in that county, or one plaintiff must be a resident and one defendant must be found in the county. Or, the case may be filed in that county if the cause of action took place there.

❏ You must pay a filing fee of $30 if you're suing for less than $100, and $35 if you're suing for $100 or more. You also must pay the sheriff's cost of delivering the summons. If you win, the defendant may be ordered to reimburse you.

❏ A defendant is entitled to file a counterclaim within 10 days after being summoned.

❏ To prepare for court—as either plaintiff or defendant—gather all documents pertinent to your case. Ask any witnesses to appear in court with you. If a witness refuses, you can subpoena him.

❏ On court day, show up on time and present your case in an orderly fashion, showing the evidence to the judge.

❏ If you do not like the court's decision, you have 10 days to file for a new trial. The form may be obtained from the small claims court clerk.

❏ If the judge has awarded you money, and the other party has not appealed the decision within 10 days, you can start collecting. If the judgment is not paid voluntarily, you can start collection proceedings with the clerk of the small claims court with a $20 fee added as court costs.

Common Small Claims Court Terms

Appeal: The process of asking a higher court to review the lower court's decision. An appeal of a small claims case is called a "trial de novo."

Assignee: A person or business that purchases or otherwise acquires the right to a claim.

Associate Circuit Court: The lowest level state court in Missouri, which can hear claims up to $25,000 in amount. The small claims court is a part of the associate circuit court.

Bond: In small claims court, a deposit of money for the court to hold to prevent the winning party from collecting its money while the losing party appeals the case.

Continuance: The postponement of a court hearing until a later date or time.

Counterclaim: A claim presented by the defendant against the plaintiff.

Default Judgment: A judgment in favor of the plaintiff because the defendant failed to show up for the trail, which the defendant had a duty to do.

Defendant: The person against whom an action is brought.

Docket: The court's list of all cases to be heard on a particular day.

Execution: The legal process of enforcing a judgment.

Garnishee: A third party, such as an employer or bank, who has money belonging to the losing party. The third party is ordered to give the money to the court rather than to the losing party.

Garnishment: Process whereby the winning party is paid by a third party who owed money to the losing party. Wages owed by an employer or deposits held by a bank are most commonly used.

Judgment: The decision of the court.

Judgment Debtor: A person who owes money to someone else according to the decision of a court.

Next Friend: A person, appointed to act formally for a minor in small claims court, who is not the minor's regular guardian.

Petition: A written request to the court.

Plaintiff: A person who brings an action against another person.

Statute of Limitations: The time period in which one must file a claim.

Subpeona: A legal method used to require someone, such as a witness, to appear in court if that person does not want to appear voluntarily.

Summons: A document used to notify a party that a claim has been filed and that the party is required to answer the claim in court.

Trial de Novo: An appeal of a small claims case decision. A trial de novo is a new trial before a judge other than the one who originally decided the case.

Typical Courtroom Setting

| Witness Stand | | Judge |

| | Court Reporter | Bailiff |

| Jury |

| Prosecutor or Plaintiff and Plaintiff's Attorney | Defendant and Defense Attorney |

 Public

Missouri Judges

Qualifications & Terms

Municipal judges can be selected in a variety of ways, with methods decided by the city council or charter. Terms, however, may not be less than two years. In municipalities of 7,500 people or less, judges need not be attorneys.

Associate circuit judges and circuit judges are popularly elected, and serve four- and six-year terms, respectively.

Appellate and supreme court justices are selected under the non-partisan court plan (see later section), for 12-year terms.

Qualifications vary, but the most stringent apply to appellate and supreme court justices. They must be at least 30 years old, U.S. citizens for at least 15 years, registered Missouri voters for at least nine years, and licensed attorneys in Missouri.

Election & Appointment

Most of the judges in Missouri are popularly elected on partisan ballots. This means that candidates must win their party's nomination (Republican, Democrat or Independent) in the August primary, and then run again in the November general election. Elections can be intense if candidates are really determined—and high salaries can add to their determination. (Appointment to office is now limited to some municipalities, where the governing body or mayor makes the selection.)

Some critics of partisan elections for judges question whether or not issues can be adequately developed to differentiate candidates. Also, they argue that the most qualified candidates will not subject themselves to the election process, which can be intense. Critics of partisan elections argue that using the appointment process will assure better judges. To them, the individual seeks the office in the election process, whereas the office seeks the individual through appointment.

Supporters of the election process, though, argue that voter accountability not only is more democratic, but is vital to the integrity of the system. Another Missouri compromise resulted in a combination of the two.

Election & Appointment of Judges

Supreme court and appellate court judges . . .

. . . are selected under a non-partisan plan by an appellate judicial commission, which includes:

7 members:

> ➤ *1 chief justice,*
> ➤ *3 lawyers,*
> ➤ *3 non-lawyers*

This commission nominates 3 candidates and then the governor makes the appointment. After serving a year, the judge must be voted in.

Circuit court judges are . . .

**. . . elected on party ballot
 by voters of the respective district.**

Except that . . . circuit judges and associate circuit judges within the city of St. Louis and Jackson County are elected similarly to appellate court judges.

Non-Partisan Court Plan

A non-partisan court plan was developed in Missouri. It has become known throughout the nation as The Missouri Plan. It combines both appointment and election processes in an attempt to gain the strengths of both methods. A panel of seven members selects three candidates. One of these is chosen to be judge by the governor. The panel consists of three attorneys selected by the bar and three lay persons selected by the governor. It is chaired by the chief justice of the Missouri Supreme Court. Voters must ratify the governor's appointment in the first general election following 12 months of service. The judge's name appears on a separate ballot without party designation, and voters are asked to vote "yes" or "no" on retention of the judge. Retention votes are further required at the end of the judge's regular term. The non-partisan plan is required for appellate and supreme court justices, as well as circuit and associate circuit judges in the City of St. Louis and Jackson County. It also applies to circuit and associate judges in St. Louis, Platte and Clay Counties, and municipal judges in Kansas City.

The non-partisan plan is intended to "get politics out of the judicial selection." But this is easier said than done. One study found there was little difference between the qualifications of those selected by election, by appointment, or by the non-partisan plan. Also, the politics were merely shifted from the wider election process to a narrower process involving the lawyers on the nominating commission and the governor. However, the plan eliminated, until lately, the need for judges to run expensive election campaigns. Recently, there has been a decrease in the percentage of voters favoring retention, and some judges have campaigned to explain the non-partisan plan to voters.

Discipline & Removal

Judges may be either disciplined or removed from office through the impeachment process. For **impeachment**, or removal, the house of representatives initiates proceedings, and the supreme court conducts the trial. Only six circuit judges have ever been removed from office. The Commission on Retirement, Removal and Discipline reports and makes recommendations to the supreme court, which makes a final decision on the case.

Automation

Since the passage of Senate Bill 420 in 1994, the Missouri Court Automation Committee has been working on a project with enormous potential for the people of Missouri. This 10-year project to automate all the courts in the state will provide Missouri citizens with the most timely and responsive judicial system possible. The office is organized into Administration, Information Technology, Adult and Juvenile Court Programs, and Court Services.

Missouri's court system is expected to be fully computerized by the year 2004. A $7 filing fee per case has been levied since 1994 to pay for the changeover. Although the fee ended in 1999, the court administration has hopes to get the General Assembly to extend it through 2004. If extended, the fee will raise approximately $55 million dollars.

When the system is completed, all state courts will be interconnected, and everyone will have access to documents and information around the clock, as long as they have a computer link. Eventually, lawyers will file pleadings by computer, and court records, which are generally open to the public, will be accessible by computer. Video arraignments will also be possible, which would reduce the security problems of moving prisoners. Pilot projects for the new system began in 1997.

The new system will add considerably to a unified state court. Court reform provided much integration in 1979, but the process will be enhanced with computerization. As Chief Justice John Holstein stated in April of 1997, "All courts now have a chance to move together into an integrated network of courts that could bring us closer to the public we serve."

Acting under the direction of the Missouri Supreme Court, the Office of State Courts Administrator (OSCA) is responsible for vigorously pursuing a judicial system for Missouri that is accessible, equitable and swift. The duties and responsibilities assigned to the state courts administrator are broad in scope and relate to all levels of the state court system.

Since the appointment of the first courts administrator in 1970, the office has been assigned responsibility to provide technical assistance, management services, education and training programs, data processing and systems analysis, administrative procedure evaluation, compilation of statistics, and case processing assistance to the courts.

In the wake of nationwide protests against ever-increasing taxes in the early 1980s, the Hancock Amendment to Missouri's constitution placed a limit on the amount of tax that the state could collect from its citizens. By fixing the tax rate on personal income at the 1981 level, the amendment attempts to ensure that even if Missourians' income goes up, their state taxes will not. As of 1996, only four states had lower tax rates than Missouri.

The office also assists courts in developing and implementing court improvement projects in areas such as child support collection, child abuse and neglect, juvenile services, family preservation, criminal history reporting, crime victims' rights, mediation services, alcohol and drug abuse treatment and prevention, and the implementation of time standards for case disposition. In recent years, these latter areas have assumed increasing importance as ways to deal with both the cause and effect of growing criminal and civil caseloads.

Judicial Vocabulary

Use this chapter and outside resources to define these important terms relating to the judicial system.

1. case
2. adversary system
3. plaintiff
4. defendant
5. judicial review
6. civil case
7. damages
8. negligent
9. tort
10. liable
11. criminal case
12. misdemeanor
13. felony
14. majority opinion
15. concurring opinion
16. dissenting opinion
17. unanimous
18. "hung jury"
19. indictment
20. "plea bargain"
21. verdict
22. constitutional law
23. statutory law
24. criminal law
25. common law
26. administrative law
27. equity law
28. injunction
29. original jurisdiction
30. appellate jurisdiction
31. concurrent jurisdiction
32. exclusive jurisdiction
33. writ
34. writ of habeas corpus
35. probable cause
36. bond
37. warrant
38. arraignment
39. grand jury
40. preliminary hearing
41. probation
42. appeal

Significant Missouri Court Cases

1798 ..... Petition to Zenon Trudeau, Lieutenant Governor
1800 ..... Petition to Louis Lorimier, Commandant, Cape Girardeau
1801 ..... Petition to Charles Tayon, Commandant, St. Charles
1806 ..... Chevalier vs. Chouteau
1806 ..... United States vs. Ouipinicaka
1807 ..... Tayon vs. Celeste
1807 ..... Moses Austin vs. John Smith T
1810 ..... In re estate of Meriwether Lewis
1811 ..... Decelle vs. John Smith T
1811 ..... Petition to William Clark, Superintendent
           of Indian Affairs
1815 ..... Thomas vs. Austin
1817 ..... Becknell vs. Robidoux
1838 ..... State vs. Joseph Smith
1838 ..... In re estate of William Clark
1848 ..... Irene Emerson vs. Dred Scott
1855 ..... State vs. James L. Minor
1855 ..... Wells vs. Sanger
1858 ..... Birch vs. Benton
1867 ..... Blair vs. Ridgely
1870 ..... Burden vs. Hornsby
1873 ..... Minor vs. Happersett
1874 ..... Chilton vs. St. Louis & Iron Mountain Railway Company
1882 ..... State vs. Jesse James
1883 ..... State vs. Frank James
1887 ..... State vs. Boyt
1888 ..... State vs. Matthews
1902 ..... State vs. Butler
1905 ..... State vs. Standard Oil Company
1910 ..... State vs. Hyde
1914 ..... In re estate of William Rockhill Nelson
1937 ..... State ex rel. Lloyd Gaines vs. S.W. Canada
1941 ..... Donnell vs. Osburn
1945 ..... Kraemer vs. Shelley
1946 ..... State ex rel. McKittrick vs. American Insurance Company
1947 ..... State ex rel. Wood vs. Board of Education
1972 ..... In re estate of Harry S. Truman
1988 ..... Cruzan vs. Harmon

Brief Overview of Select Missouri Lawsuits

Chevalier vs. Chouteau
1806

Indian slavery was common in territorial Missouri until Spanish officials ordered an end to the practice in 1769. Unhappy slaveholders resisted the order, but some slaves saw in it a chance for freedom. For over three decades, descendants of Afro-Indian slave Marie Jean Scypion petitioned Missouri courts for freedom from slavery based on the fact that Scypion's mother was an Indian. The long court battle included ownership suits between the heirs of Scypion's owner as well, as factions vied for the power to grant or refuse freedom voluntarily. These cases set precedent for other slave freedom suits in Missouri, although later cases primarily involved Afro-American slaves.

United States vs. Ouipinicaka
1806

Frequent confrontations occurred between white settlers and Native Americans in the Missouri territory. Maintaining amicable relations with Indian tribes was important, so when depredations occurred, U.S. officials attempted to obtain justice for both sides. This garnered the criticism of both white settlers and Native Americans as their concepts of justice differed greatly. When members of the Mascoutan tribe were charged with killing two Frenchmen, a chief testified on their behalf, saying the tribe was "desirous of peace and tranquillity with the white people." Expressing remorse for the actions of his braves, he begged for the court to have pity upon his people.

Thomas vs. Austin
1815

Bitter rivalry marked the relationship between Moses Austin and John Smith T, both territorial entrepreneurs in the southwest Missouri lead-mining business. Various court battles over titles to productive mines were just one sign of their long-standing feud that often forced residents of the Ste. Genevieve district to choose sides as the arguments threatened to explode into all-out war. Their hostile relations also periodically affected the political stability of the district, as the two struggled for influence and power in the government of the Louisiana Territory.

State vs. Joseph Smith
1838

The 1830s were a time of religious conflict between the Mormons and their neighbors in western counties. Driven out of Jackson and Clay Counties, the Mormons settled in newly created Caldwell County in 1837 and 1838. County population swelled with Mormon migration. The overflow into surrounding counties concerned non-Mormons. When violence and raids escalated between the two groups, Governor Lilburn Boggs ordered the militia to "exterminate or drive the Mormons from the state" to keep the public peace. In the wake of the hostilities, the Missouri legislature appointed a committee to investigate and report on the situation.

Irene Emerson vs. Dred Scott
1848

"Once free, always free" was a doctrine traditionally upheld in Missouri courts when the ruling regarded slave freedom lawsuits. Dred Scott sued for his freedom on the basis of this doctrine—he had been a resident of the free state of Illinois and the Wisconsin Territory. However, his decision to pursue freedom in Missouri courts came at an inopportune time. The controversy over slavery during the 1850s divided Missouri's politics no less than it did the nation's. Although the St. Louis courts granted the family freedom, the state supreme court remanded the Scotts to slavery due to the aggressive stance of its pro-slavery judges. In upholding the state's decision, the U.S. Supreme Court made perhaps the most controversial decision in its history, sharply intensifying the sectional controversy that would lead to civil war.

Minor vs. Happersett
1873

The Civil War's end brought voting rights to black males. In 1867, Missouri women petitioned the General Assembly for suffrage as well, which was denied. In 1872, Virginia Minor attempted to register to vote with St. Louis election authorities. When they refused, Minor sued in the St. Louis County Circuit Court, protesting that the 14th Amendment forbade any state from impairing the privileges and immunities of citizens. Upon her lawsuit's dismissal, Minor appealed to the Missouri Supreme Court, which unanimously sustained the refusal to register Minor. In 1874, the U.S. Supreme Court upheld the decision, affirming that voting rights were under state jurisdiction, necessitating a constitutional amendment to give women the right to vote.

Burden vs. Hornsby
1870

In September 1870, a Johnson County courtroom was the setting for the "most celebrated dog case. . . in the world." When Leonidas Hornsby shot his brother-in-law Charles Burden's best hunting dog, Old Drum, Burden threatened to kill Hornsby, but sued instead for $100. After two trials, Burden was awarded $25, but that judgment was later reversed. At the third trial Burden's lawyer, George Graham Vest, who later became a U.S. senator, delivered his emotional "Eulogy for a Dog" as the closing argument. When he finished, the jury was in tears. They awarded Burden $50. Hornsby appealed to the Missouri Supreme Court, but the decision stood. Vest's closing argument is reprinted below.

A Tribute to a Dog
by George Graham Vest

Gentlemen of the Jury: The best friend a man has in this world may turn against him and become his enemy. His son or daughter that he has reared with loving care may prove ungrateful. Those who are nearest and dearest to us, those whom we trust with our happiness and our good name, may become traitors to their faith. The money that a man has, he may lose. It flies away from him, perhaps when he needs it the most. A man's reputation may be sacrificed in a moment of ill-considered action. The people who are prone to fall on their knees to do us honor when success is with us may be the first to throw the stones of malice when failure settles its cloud upon our heads. The one absolutely unselfish friend that a man can have in this selfish world, the one that never deserts him and the one that never proves ungrateful or treacherous is his dog.

Gentlemen of the Jury, a man's dog stands by him in prosperity and in poverty, in health and in sickness. He will sleep on the cold ground, where the wintry winds blow and the snow drives fiercely, if only he may be near his master's side. He will kiss the hand that has no food to offer, he will lick the wounds and sores that come in encounters with the roughness of the world. He guards the sleep of his pauper master as if he were a prince. When all other friends desert, he remains. When riches take wings and reputation falls to pieces, he is as constant in his love as the sun in its journey through the heavens. If fortune drives the master forth an outcast in the world, friendless and homeless, the faithful dog asks no higher privilege than that of accompanying him to guard against danger, to fight against his enemies, and when the last scene of all comes, and death takes the master in its embrace and his body is laid away in the cold ground, no matter if all other friends pursue their way, there by his graveside will the noble dog be found, his head between his paws, his eyes sad but open in alert watchfulness, faithful and true even to death.

Donnell vs. Osburn
1941

Despite Missouri's strong Democratic tradition, Republican Forrest Donnell won the govenorship in 1940 by over 4,000 votes. Unwilling to give up the chief executive's office and its powers of patronage, Democratic officials devised a strategy whereby Democratic Speaker of the House Morris Osburn, who was constitutionally authorized to examine and publically announce election returns, pointedly omitted Forrest Donnell from those legally elected. When he did so, Donnell filed suit in the Missouri Supreme Court to force announcement of his victory. The court unanimously supported Donnell, who was inaugurated February 26, 1941.

Kraemer vs. Shelley
1945

The practice of racial housing covenants, which prevented selling or leasing property to African Americans, was challenged in 1945. J.D. and Ethel Shelley, a black couple from Mississippi, bought a home in a racially restricted area of St. Louis. A lawsuit filed on behalf of Louis and Fern Kraemer, residents in the restricted area, fought the purchase. When the St. Louis Circuit Court, citing Missouri real estate law, dismissed the lawsuit, the Kraemers successfully appealed to the Missouri Supreme Court. The Shelleys, in turn, appealed this decision to the U.S. Supreme Court. While the U.S. high court did not outlaw the practice of such covenants, it held them unenforceable, striking the first significant blow against legal discrimination in housing.

Cruzan vs. Harmon
1988

In 1983, Nancy Cruzan was severely injured in a car wreck. Four years later, her comatose body was still being kept alive by artificial nutrition. With no chance of Nancy's recovery, her parents sued to have the feeding tube removed. When their wish was granted, medical authorities appealed to the Missouri Supreme Court. In a four to three vote, the judges struck down the order, choosing to "err on the side of life." Their decision, which put Missouri in the center of the national "right to die" controversy, was overturned by the U.S. Supreme Court in June 1990. Nancy Cruzan was allowed to died shortly thereafter.

Summary & Conclusions

Although the judiciary is the smallest branch of government, it plays an important role. With the 1979 court reform, Missouri's judicial branch went from a decentralized to an integrated system with better financing. The judicial system is currently a three-tiered system with the Missouri Supreme Court at the top, then the court of appeals, and at the bottom, the circuit court, which includes all courts of limited jurisdiction.

The supreme court has original jurisdiction in certain areas and is also the court of final appeal. In addition, it has the responsibility of supervising all other courts and has an Office of State Courts Administrator to help with this task.

Judges are either elected or appointed, with a combination used in the Missouri, or non-partisan, court plan. In the Missouri Plan, judges are selected by the governor from a pool of three candidates identified by a panel of lawyers and citizens. Then, the newly appointed judge faces periodic retention elections.

The idea of the Missouri Plan was to take politics out of the process, but studies indicate that although politics have changed,

The Sunshine Law in Missouri

The Sunshine Law is important to citizens because it allows the monitoring of public meetings. In this manner, it discourages illegal proceedings from occurring at these gatherings. The Missouri Sunshine Law indicates a commitment to openness by Missouri government. It states in Section 610.011, "It is the public policy of this state that meetings, records, votes, actions, and deliberations of public governmental bodies be open to the public unless otherwise provided by law."

All independent regulatory commissions are required by the law to give advance notice of the date, time, place, and agenda of their meetings. Closed meetings are allowed if circumstances warrant, but citizens have the right to file suit in the circuit courts if they feel there was no justification for the closed meeting.

In 1998, the *St. Louis Post-Dispatch* newspaper sued the St. Louis Police Board over "its refusal to allow access to board minutes, financial records and crime reports," as declared in a *Post-Dispatch* article. The police board was found guilty of violating the Sunshine Law. The judge, Robert H. Dierker, Jr., ordered the board to let the public view minutes of all its meetings in the last half of 1998. Much controversy arose over the validity of the judge's ruling.

they have not been eliminated. There continues to be a division of opinion on the selection of judges. Popular election is favored by many to make judges sensitive to all citizens. However, many others favor appointment because appointment allows greater independence in decision-making. It could be said that in a popular election, the candidate seeks the office, whereas with appointment, the office seeks the candidate.

Automation is a recent development at the Missouri Supreme Court level. When the automation system is completed, all state courts will be interconnected, and everyone will have access to documents and information through computers. This promises to make the courts operate more smoothly even with their continually growing case load, as well as to allow the judicial system to run cost effectively. Eventually, other aspects of the process will be handled by computers and the goal of a fully integrated or unified court system will be achieved.

Ann Covington (1942-)

First Woman on the Missouri Supreme Court, 1988-2002
Chief Justice of Missouri Supreme Court, 1993-1995

A native of Fairmont, West Virginia, Judge Ann Covington arrived in Missouri to study for her juris doctorate, which she earned from the University of Missouri-Columbia in 1977. She holds degrees from Duke and Rutgers and did postgraduate work at New York University. Covington also spent two years teaching in England. Her first position in public service was that of Missouri assistant attorney general in 1977. After a two-year stint, Covington started her private practice in 1979 in Columbia.

Covington has served on various boards, including the Juvenile Justice Advisory Board, City of Columbia Industrial Revenue Bond Authority, and the Mid-Missouri Legal Services Corporation. Covington was appointed to the western district of the Missouri Court of Appeals in September 1987. She was the first woman to hold that post. In December 1988, she became the first woman to serve on the Missouri Supreme Court. Among other important posts, Covington acted as a member of the Advisory Committee on Evidence Rules and was named vice president of the Conference of Chief Justices of the United States, the latter during her two-year term as chief justice of the state supreme court.

Chapter 6
The Judicial System: Law & Order

End of Chapter Questions

Use the text along with outside material to answer the following questions. Be sure to review the key terms and concepts from the beginning of the chapter before you start.

1. What powers does Article V of the Missouri Constitution define? Make a brief outline of the most important points of Article V.

2. What was the central purpose of the Court Reform and Revenue Act? How has it affected the state's judicial system?

3. At what level in the state court system do most civil and criminal cases begin?

4. Although municipalities can turn over their local courts to the state circuit court system, why do many continue to maintain their own courts?

5. What is the primary role of the juvenile division? How is it different from other divisions that deal with adults?

6. What advantage does the availability of small claims court offer?

7. What types of cases typically do not require juries? In what division of the court system are these cases usually held?

8. What are the two major types of jury trials? How are they different from each other?

9. What is the primary function of a grand jury?

10. Describe the differences between the number of jury members needed to achieve a conviction in a civil case versus a criminal case. Why do you think this difference exists?

11. Describe the eligibility and selection process for jury members. Who may or may not be excused from selection?

12. What function does a court of appeals serve? Do you think the right to appeal is an important part of the legal process? Explain your answer.

13. List the five types of cases that the Missouri Supreme Court is charged to handle. Give examples of types of cases that would be representative of each type.

14. What function does the Office of State Courts Administrator serve?

15. Explain the non-partisan court plan. How does this plan form a compromise between the election and the appointment of judges?

16. By what process can Missouri judges be disciplined or removed?

17. How will automation of the Missouri court system affect the state's judicial system? What is its primary advantage over the current system? Explain what a "unified state court" means.

18. What was the Dred Scott case, and why was it a critical precursor to the Civil War?

End of Chapter Activities

Use the text along with outside material to complete the following activities.

1.   Outline Missouri's three-tiered court system. Define each level's principal functions.

2.   Outline the procedure for filing a claim in small claims court. Identify the common types of cases that are handled by this court as well as the types of damages that are generally awarded.

3.   Make a diagram of the Missouri Supreme Court like the one in this book. List the names of each justice and identify the chief justice. In your diagram, be sure to include each justice's party affiliation and when his or her term will expire.

Out of Class Activity

What's the Verdict?

Visit a court in your community while it is in session. Evaluate the case, determining the type of proceedings. Is the case civil or criminal? What is the argument of the plaintiff? What is the defense of the defendant? Note the final verdict that was reached. Why do you believe the judge came to this decision? Do you agree or disagree with his or her ruling? Support this statement with proper evidence.

Chapter

Juvenile Justice in Missouri:
A Series of Lessons

Prepared by
Millie Aulbur
The Missouri Bar

Key Terms & Concepts

certification
juvenile
Miranda rights
status crime

Juvenile Justice in Missouri

This chapter focuses on a series of activities that explore juvenile justice in Missouri, especially the revised 1995 juvenile code. Your teacher may ask you to complete all of the following activities, or only selected ones. In this chapter, you will learn:

- juvenile law in Missouri
- your rights and responsibilities as juveniles
- the certification, disposition and sentencing processes
- the many factors involved in certification proceedings
- the many factors involved in sentencing proceedings.

Lesson 1:
Survey of Missouri's Juvenile Laws

Explore some of the basic concepts of Missouri's juvenile laws by filling out the following questionnaire, and discuss your answers using the following pages.

Study the next page and mark your answers on a separate piece of paper. Complete the opinion poll carefully.

Lesson 1:
Opinion Poll on Juvenile Law in Missouri

Directions: Read the statements below and decide whether you agree (A), disagree (D), or are undecided (U). Be prepared to discuss your opinions with the class. Remember, this is not a test that will affect your grade.

_____A. A juvenile is anyone under the age of 17.

_____B. Hitchhiking, although dangerous, is not a crime.

_____C. It is not a crime to set an abandoned house on fire.

_____D. If a juvenile is convicted of possessing either alcohol or illegal drugs, it is up to the judge whether the juvenile loses a driver's license for one year.

_____E. When a juvenile is stopped by a police officer, the juvenile has the right to remain silent and ask for an attorney.

_____F. It is not a crime to hide a stolen item for a friend if you have not participated in stealing that item.

_____G. Throwing rolls of toilet paper in someone's yard for fun or smashing Halloween pumpkins is against the law.

_____H. A juvenile must be at least 14 years old before the court may try him or her as an adult.

_____I. The judge must treat all juvenile offenders equally.

_____J. At age 17, all juvenile records are destroyed and a juvenile offender begins adulthood with a clean record.

_____K. Anyone who is 15½ years old is treated as an adult under Missouri's traffic laws.

_____L. Having a switchblade handy under your car seat is a crime.

_____M. Skipping school may make parents angry, but it is not unlawful.

___N. The judge may not place a juvenile offender in a foster home when the juvenile has committed only one crime.

After completing the poll, have one student serve as a secretary and one student as a clerk. As the class goes through each item on the poll, indicate whether you agree, disagree or are undecided about each statement. The clerk then counts the number of each response and has the secretary record them on the board. Then read the following answers and discuss each statement.

A. Statement: A juvenile or minor is anyone under the age of 17.

It depends. Under Missouri law, it depends upon the circumstance as to when someone is a juvenile. Usually anyone under 18 years of age is considered a **juvenile**. However, anyone 17 or older who is charged with a crime will be considered an adult and tried as one. Consider the following:

- You must be 21 to possess, use or buy alcoholic beverages.

- You must be 21 to serve on a jury. Missouri is one of only two states that do not allow jury service at age 18.

- You must be 18 to get married without your parents' permission. If you are under 15, you must receive permission from a judge to get married.

- You may vote at 18.

- At age 18, you may sue in court and someone may sue you.

- You may make a will, sign a contract and sign a lease at 18.

- At age 18, if you are a male, you must register for military service.

- You must be at least 18 to consent to your own medical treatment. If you are under 18, you must have your parents' permission for any kind of medical treatment, including abortion. There are a few exceptions to this law. Some hospitals or clinics allow you to consent to your own testing and treatment for pregnancy, sexually transmitted diseases, drug and alcohol abuse, or AIDS at any age. Others allow you to consent to your own treatment only if you have reached age 13. If you are younger than 18 but are married or in the military, you are considered emancipated, or on your own, and you may seek medical treatment without your parents' permission.

- At age 16, you may get a driver's license; at 15½ years old, you may get a special license to drive with your parents or guardian.

- At age 15½ years old, you are treated as an adult under Missouri's traffic laws and will go to a regular traffic court if you violate a traffic law.

- At any age, if you are the victim of a crime, you have the right to be paid for damages done to you and to attend any hearings and trials about a case arising from the crime. If the person who committed the crime against you is a juvenile, you may attend the hearings in juvenile court. If the person is an adult or will be tried as an adult, you may go to the hearings and the trial in circuit court.

B. Statement: Hitchhiking, although dangerous, is not a crime.

True statement. Hitchhiking, itself, is not a crime. However, the Missouri Highway Patrol routinely checks on all hitchhikers and, if they are juveniles, returns them to their homes. Furthermore, the juvenile authorities could charge a juvenile with a "status" crime. A **status crime** is an act that is not a criminal act for an adult but is for a juvenile. For example, running away from home is a status crime. Thus, if a hitchhiker were a runaway, he or she would be breaking the law. Another status crime is acting in a way that is injurious to one's health. In some instances, hitchhiking might be considered injurious to one's health.

Although not illegal, hitchhiking can be dangerous. You may be wondering why there are signs posted at every access to interstate highways that expressly forbid hitchhiking—that is because interstates are federally funded and, therefore, federal laws govern them.

C. Statement: *It is not a crime to set an abandoned house on fire.*

False. Burning a building, even an abandoned one, is second-degree arson, a Class C felony, Section 569.050 RSMo 1994. An adult convicted of a Class C felony can be imprisoned for up to seven years and fined up to $5,000. Any act that is a crime for a person 17 and over is also a crime for a juvenile. There are also other crimes involving burning. Under 569.055, a person is guilty of a Class D felony if he or she knowingly burns or causes an explosion that damages another's property. A Class D felony is punishable by a prison sentence of up to five years and a fine of up to $5,000. Under 569.060, 569.065 and 569.067, other acts of burning are prohibited. Pranks with fires or fireworks can certainly constitute criminal behavior.

D. Statement: *If a juvenile is convicted of possessing either alcohol or illegal drugs, it is up to the judge whether the juvenile loses his or her driver's license for one year.*

False. Missouri's Abuse and Lose It Law (Section 577.500 RSMo 1994) clearly states that anyone who is found guilty of—or pleads guilty to—any alcohol or drug related offense shall have his or her license revoked for one year. In other words, the judge must revoke the license of anyone who is found guilty of any drug or alcohol related offense and who is under 21 years of age. Alcohol and drug related offenses include consumption of, sale of, or possession of alcoholic beverages and illegal drugs.

E. Statement: *When a juvenile is stopped by a police officer, the juvenile has the right to remain silent and ask for an attorney.*

True. When a juvenile officer or a law enforcement officer takes a juvenile into custody, the officer must read the juvenile their **Miranda rights**, which include the right to remain silent and the right to an attorney. Authorities may keep a juvenile in custody only 24 hours before filing a petition. A petition alleges that the juvenile has committed an offense.

F. Statement: It is not a crime to hide a stolen item for a friend if you have not participated in stealing that item.

False. Under Section 570.080, RSMo 1994, it is a Class C felony to receive stolen property. Hiding such property would come under this crime. Merely riding in a stolen car or just being with others who have stolen items can lead to trouble with the law even if the juvenile is not involved with the actual crime.

G. Statement: Throwing rolls of toilet paper in someone's yard for fun or smashing Halloween pumpkins is against the law.

True. These are common pranks among teenagers and appear harmless. However, several communities are cracking down on these kinds of actions. There are several offenses these actions could come under. First, littering is against the law, Section 577.070, RSMo 1994. Second, trespassing is against the law, Section 569.160.

H. Statement: A juvenile must be at least 14 years old before the court can try him or her as an adult for committing a crime.

False. This was the law until the 1995 session of the Missouri Assembly. Now at any age, if you are alleged to have committed a serious offense such as murder, sale of drugs, robbery, rape, or assault, or if you are a repeat offender, the juvenile court may certify you as an adult and transfer you to the adult criminal system. At age 12, the juvenile court may also certify you as an adult for other serious crimes, such as stealing a car, drug possession and carrying a weapon. "Certification as an adult" is explained later in this chapter.

I. Statement: The judge must treat all juvenile offenders equally.

False. Suppose two 15-year-old boys are brought before the judge. Both have been accused of stealing a car. The judge has several options available for dealing with each juvenile. For example, the judge can return the juvenile to his home in the custody of his parents with visits to the home made regularly by a juvenile officer. Or the judge can return the juvenile to the custody of his parents with the agreement that the parents and the juvenile visit a juvenile center periodically for counseling. Or the judge can place the juvenile in foster care, a juvenile detention center or other institution. In deciding what to do with the juvenile car thieves, the judge will consider each boy's attitude, the number of times he has been in trouble, his school record, his family life and the kinds of friends he has. Unless both boys have the same background, it is unlikely the judge will dispose of the cases in the same way.

J. Statement: At age 17, all juvenile records are destroyed and a juvenile offender begins adulthood with a clean record.

False. At age 17, a juvenile offender may ask the court to destroy juvenile records, but the court does not have to destroy the records. The records may be used by the military to refuse admittance into military service. The records may be used by probation officers in the event that the juvenile offender commits crimes as an adult. The records may surface in a background check for someone wanting to become a lawyer or FBI agent. The records could also be used for impeachment purposes at a trial. Indeed legislators every year consider making the juvenile record less confidential. For example, for years, the names of juvenile offenders were kept strictly confidential. Now the victim and the victim's family have the right to know the name of the juvenile offender. They have the right to attend the hearing where the judge makes a decision about the disposition of the juvenile's case, and to speak at the hearing about the impact that the juvenile's actions have had on their lives.

K. Statement: Anyone 15½ years old is treated as an adult under Missouri's traffic laws.

True. The juvenile court does not have jurisdiction over juveniles who violate traffic laws. The state of Missouri decided that anyone 15½ years old is responsible enough to drive. Therefore, for the purposes of all laws related to driving, anyone over 15½ years old is considered an adult and will appear in regular traffic court, see Section 211.031. However, if a juvenile is charged with a felony related to driving, such as vehicular manslaughter, the juvenile will be referred to the juvenile court.

L. Statement: Having a switchblade handy under your car seat is a crime.

True. Under Section 571.030, RSMo 1994, having a weapon—something capable of lethal use—on your person or having items readily available, such as under your car seat, in a glove box or in a console, constitutes the crime of unlawful use of a weapon.

M. Statement: Skipping school may make my parents angry, but it is not against the law.

False. Children between the ages of 7 and 16 must be in school. See Chapter 167 RSMo 1994. If a juvenile is caught skipping school, the juvenile may be charged with the status crime of truancy.

N. Statement: A judge may not place a juvenile offender in a juvenile detention center the first time the juvenile commits a crime.

False. No one who commits a crime is entitled to "one bite of the apple." If a judge determines that a juvenile would benefit from being placed in a detention center, even if the juvenile has never been in trouble before, the judge has the discretion to do so.

Lesson 2:
When Juveniles Are Treated as Adults

1. This lesson is about **certification**, the process whereby a judge determines if a juvenile should stand trial as an adult. If anyone under age 17 is charged with a crime, the case begins in the juvenile court. The juvenile judge will determine if a juvenile should be "certified" to stand trial as an adult.

2. As a class, read the following section on Age Limits for Certification.

3. Discuss the serious implications of a juvenile being certified to stand trial as an adult.
   Some of the most serious are:
   A. If convicted, the juvenile will have a record of criminal conviction for the rest of his or her life;
   B. If convicted, the juvenile can be sent to adult prisons; *and*
   C. If convicted and if the juvenile commits further offenses he or she will always be considered an adult.

4. Explore together the many factors a judge considers in the certification process.

5. Students should now divide into four groups. Distribute one case to each group to read and discuss. Each group should discuss its case and list reasons for and against certification. Each group should then choose a person to play a judge, a bailiff, a lawyer who argues for certification, and a lawyer who argues against certification.

   Each group should then hold a certification hearing on its case for the entire class. At the end of the hearing, the judge should "retire" to consider the case, out of the hearing of the rest of the class. While the judge is considering the case, the class should discuss how they would rule. The judge should then render his or her decision and give the reasons for the decision. The class should compare and contrast their decision with that of the judge.

Age Limits for Certification

You may be tried as an adult for any crime convicted at age 17 or older. If you commit an offense at age 16 or younger, the police will refer your case to the juvenile court. At any age, if you are alleged to have committed a serious offense such as murder, sale of drugs, robbery, rape or assault, or if you are a repeat offender, the juvenile court may certify you as an adult and transfer you to the adult criminal system. At age 12, the juvenile court can also certify you as an adult for other serious crimes, such as stealing a car, drug possession and carrying a weapon.

(See Section 211.071 RSMo. Supp. 1995)

Factors that a Judge Considers in a Certification Hearing

1. The seriousness of the offense and whether the community needs protection from the juvenile offender.

2. Whether the alleged offense involved viciousness, force or violence.

3. Whether the alleged offense was against people or against property. If the offense was against people and the people were injured, there is a greater chance that the juvenile offender will be certified as an adult.

4. Whether the alleged offense is part of a repetitive pattern that indicates the juvenile offender cannot be rehabilitated by the juvenile justice system. In other words, the court will look at whether the juvenile offender has committed these same kinds of crimes before, and if he or she has, the judge will carefully consider whether the juvenile offender can really be helped in the juvenile system.

5. The record and history of the juvenile offender, including past experiences with the juvenile justice system. In other words, does the juvenile have a history of trouble with the law?

6. The sophistication and maturity of the juvenile offender. Does the juvenile offender appear and act as an adult in most situations? Does the juvenile offender understand the difference between right and wrong?

7. The age of the juvenile offender.

8. The program and facilities available to the juvenile court. Does the juvenile justice system have a place suitable to house the juvenile offender? Does the juvenile offender need the more restricted atmosphere of an adult corrections facility or a prison?

9. Whether or not the juvenile offender can really benefit from the treatment or rehab programs available in the juvenile justice system. Has the juvenile offender already demonstrated that he or she does not benefit from these programs?

(See Section 211.071 RSMo Supp. 1995)

Cases for Certification Exercise

Case 1

While driving without a license, Jenny, almost age 17, hits a nine-year-old girl playing in the street in front of her house. The little girl is seriously injured and may be permanently disabled. Jenny's blood alcohol level at the time was 0.13. As a result of a previous incident, Jenny has had her license suspended for driving while intoxicated.

Jenny is an above average student in school. She lives with both of her parents. Jenny's mother is an alcoholic and has occasionally beaten her daughter. Jenny likes school but hates her home life.

Should Jenny stand trial as an adult for second-degree assault?

See Section 565.060(3) RSMo 1994—A person commits second-degree assault if he or she causes physical injury to someone while operating a motor vehicle in an intoxicated condition.

Case 2

Julie, age 15, runs away with her boyfriend, Jack, age 16. They travel to Missouri from Illinois. Julie and Jack have a hard time making a living. They have both dropped out of school. Jack finds minimum wage work at McDonald's. Julie has to stay with the baby girl that she and Jack had shortly after moving from Illinois. Jack suggests that they give up their baby because they cannot afford a child. After a long discussion, Jack and Julie decide to leave the child, wrapped in a blanket on the steps of a church.

During the night, the baby becomes cold and ill. When the minister finds the baby, he rushes her to the hospital. Shortly after being admitted to the hospital, the baby dies of pneumonia.

The police are able to trace the baby back to Julie and Jack. They admit to abandoning their baby. Julie has a record of being a runaway. Jack has no record.

Should Julie be certified to stand trial as an adult for the death of their child? Should Jack?

Case 3

Jim, age 14, and a group of guys he hangs out with break into Central High School one night. Some of the guys are 18. Jim is the youngest in the group, although he acts older than his age. The guys vandalize the science lab and some of them start taking computers and VCRs out of the school.

The night janitor sees the boys and chases them. Jim is almost caught by the janitor, but just as the janitor reaches Jim, the janitor slips and hits his head hard. The boys manage to get away, taking the computers and VCRs with them. The janitor is able to get to a telephone and call the police. The janitor identifies Jim because he remembers how nice Jim usually is in school and recalls that Jim was a finalist in the Citizen Bee Contest.

The police take Jim into custody. Jim lives with his mother and four other brothers and sisters. Jim's mother and father are divorced. His mother works two jobs. Jim has been in juvenile court twice before for illegal possession of alcohol.

Should Jim be tried as an adult for burglary and stealing?

Case 4

Bill, a 15-year-old high school student, has been diagnosed as hyperactive. Bill has had this condition for several years and doctors have prescribed a special medicine to control his behavior. When Bill does not take his medication, he sometimes loses control and becomes aggressive. This has happened to Bill a couple of times and although no one was hurt, he was once suspended from school for fighting. Bill admitted to his mother that he had stopped taking his medication on these occasions. Bill's mother warned him that he must take his medication and reminded him that he must act responsibly. Some of Bill's friends dared him to stop taking his medicine. They also talked Bill into trying marijuana. Unknown to Bill, the marijuana had been dipped into PCP. Under the influence of the drugs, Bill picked up a bat and severely beat a classmate who had been teasing him, fracturing his skull and cracking several ribs. The police take Bill into custody.

Should Bill be tried as an adult for possession of illegal drugs? For assault?

Real Life Results

All four of the previous examples were based on actual Missouri cases but with fictitious names and locations. The results of the actual cases are as follows:

Case 1—Jenny was not certified. The judge ordered her into an institution for alcohol counseling.

Case 2—Julie was not certified and was placed in a juvenile detention center. Jack was certified, found guilty of endangering the welfare of his child and given five years' probation.

Case 3—Jim was not certified. He was placed on probation for four years. Jim is now in his mid-20s, and is a college graduate who gives inspirational talks to young people about getting a second chance.

Case 4—Bill was not certified. He was placed on probation. The major component of his probation was that he come to the school nurse's office every morning and every noon to take his medicine in front of the nurse.

Lesson 3:
You Be the Judge!

1. This lesson outlines the various ways a judge can deal with juvenile offenders and those convicted of adult crimes. It will also explore the factors that judges look at when deciding what to do with a juvenile offender or an adult criminal.

2. Have you heard the phrase, "Let the punishment fit the crime"? That is a challenge that juvenile and trial court judges have with every conviction. In juvenile court, the judge determines the sentence since there are no juries. In Missouri, the trial court judge is the final sentencer and the jury's sentence is actually only a recommendation. See Section 557.036 RSMo 1994. The judge often follows the jury's recommendation but may reduce the sentence.

3. Have you ever wondered why two people who have committed the same crime are not given the same punishment? This lesson will clarify this issue by examining the various factors involved in making a sentencing decision.

4. Read the Sentencing Options, Sentencing Factors, and Probation Guidelines on the following pages. Note that serious crimes such as first- and second-degree murder, forcible rape and robbery usually require a prison sentence regardless of the offender's background.

In-Class Activity

Divide the class into five groups. Assign each group a juvenile case and an adult case from the following pages. Discuss the cases and explore various sentencing options. Based on the following pages, consider the minimum and maximum sentence.

Then each group should choose a person to play a judge, a bailiff, a lawyer arguing for maximum sentencing and a lawyer arguing for minimum sentencing.

Each group should hold a sentencing hearing on its case for the class. At the end of the hearing, the judge should "retire" to consider the case, out of earshot of the class. While the judge considers the case, the class should discuss how they would rule. The judge should then render his or her decision and the reasons why. Compare and contrast the decisions.

Sentencing Options

Juveniles

1. Community service
2. Counseling
3. Foster home
4. Juvenile detention center for a short time
5. Juvenile detention for an extended period of time
6. Probation—supervised
7. Probation—unsupervised
8. Commitment to a mental health institution

Adults

1. Community service
2. Counseling
3. Probation—supervised
4. Probation—unsupervised
5. Restitution
6. Fine
7. Fine and up to one year in the county jail
8. Imprisonment
9. Commitment to a mental health institution

Sentencing Factors

1. The Crime—Did the crime involve bodily harm to another person? Harm to another person's property?

2. The Offender's Actions—Were the offender's actions brutal, dangerous and callous, or were they unintentional and restrained?

3. The Victim—Was the victim also involved in criminal activity and aggressive, or was the victim caught unaware, possibly even vulnerable mentally or physically?

4. Weapon—Did the offense involve a weapon of some sort?

5. Offender's Participation—Did the offender act alone, was he the leader of a group committing crime, or was he a follower in a group that committed the crime?

6. Criminal Record—Has the offender been convicted of other crimes? How serious were the prior convictions?

7. Psychological State—Was the offender deliberate and calculating? Was the offender provoked or under stress?

8. Age—Is the offender either very young or very old?

9. Offender's Attitude—Is the offender hostile and defiant or does the offender admit guilt and show remorse?

10. Public Attitude—How will the public and law enforcement community react to the sentence?

Other factors that may be considered are the offender's reputation, contributions and position in the community, and character.

Probation Guidelines

1. Did the offender cause or threaten serious harm?

2. Did the offender intend to cause or threaten serious harm?

3. Did the offender act under strong provocation from someone else?

4. Are there other factors that tend to excuse or justify the criminal conduct?

5. Did the victim contribute in some way to the crime?

6. Did the offender agree to compensate the victim?

7. Is this the offender's first offense?

8. Was the criminal conduct the result of circumstances not likely to happen again?

9. Does the offender's attitude and character show that he or she is unlikely to commit another crime?

10. Will the offender benefit from probationary treatment, such as drug counseling, alcohol rehabilitation, counseling for the ill effects of an abusive relationship, and so on?

11. Would imprisonment cause excessive hardship to the offender or his or her family?

12. Would the community benefit more from the offender's probationary community service than it would from imprisonment of the offender?

13. Does the offender have a good family and/or friends who will help him or her stay out of trouble?

14. Is the offender willing to further his or her education?

Juvenile Case #1

Name: Mary Carrell

Age: 16

Offense: Minor in possession of alcohol

Education: A junior in high school.

Prior Record: One previous minor in possession of alcohol and one previous shoplifting charge.

Comments: Mary is an average student, maybe slightly above. Her school attendance record is good. She lives at home with her father who is a banker, her mother who is a housewife, and two older brothers who have had two speeding tickets in the last year.

The offense of minor in possession is a misdemeanor punishable by up to one year imprisonment and/or a fine of not less than $50 and not more than $1,000. See Sections 311.325 and 311.380.

Juvenile Case #2

Name: Henry Johnson

Age: 15

Offense: Minor in possession of alcohol, stealing an automobile, possession of cocaine, tampering with an automobile.

Education: A sophomore in high school.

Prior Record: None.

Comments: Henry confessed to stealing an automobile belonging to his neighbor. When the automobile was found, the tires were slashed, the compact disc player removed, spray painted obscenities covered the car, and there were empty beer cans in the back seat. When the police picked Henry up, he had a small amount of cocaine in his jacket pocket. Henry is an honor student, on the basketball team, and belongs to Young Republicans. He lives with his father, a state representative. His mother, who is divorced from his father and remarried, lives in South Dakota.

If Henry had been certified as an adult, the following punishments would have applied: The offense of minor in possession is a misdemeanor punishable by up to one year imprisonment and/or a fine of not less than $50 and not more than $1,000 (Sections 311.325 and 311.380). Considering the damage to the car, the charge would be tampering in the first degree, which is a Class C felony (Section 569.080, RSMo 1994) and punishable by a sentence of imprisonment for up to 7 years (Section 558,011, RSMo 1994) and/or a fine of up to $5,000 (Section 560.011, RSMo 1994). Possession of cocaine is also a Class C felony (Section 195.202, RSMo 1994).

Juvenile Case #3

Name: Wendy Potts

Age: 16

Offense: Burglary and vandalism.

Education: Dropped out of school during her sophomore year.

Prior Record: Possession of marijuana, and burglary of an elementary school.

Comments: Wendy broke into her old high school with another friend. They spray painted about twenty lockers and used permanent magic marker to write obscenities on the principal's office door. Wendy is currently not enrolled in school. She lives with her mother who works from 11 p.m. until 7 a.m. as a nurse's aide at the local hospital. Wendy was involved in a lot of fights at school and did not get along well with her teachers.

If Wendy had been certified as an adult and found guilty, she would have been subject to the following punishments: Possession of marijuana is a Class A misdemeanor which is punishable by a fine of up to $1,000 and/or imprisonment up to 1 year (Sections 195.202, 558.011 and 560.016, RSMo 1994). Damaging property is a Class B misdemeanor which is punishable by up to six months in prison and/or a fine of up to $500.

Juvenile Case #4

Name: Andy Wax

Age: 14

Offense: Murder and robbery.

Education: Freshman in high school.

Prior Record: Four prior encounters with the law: one for driving without a license and being underage for driving, one for minor in possession of alcohol, one for being a runaway and one for vandalizing a neighbor's property.

Comments: Andy shot and killed an elderly woman when she refused to give him her purse during a robbery at a local grocery store. Andy was living on the street since running away from home again. His father died three years ago, and Andy has eight brothers and sisters and a mother who began abusing alcohol when his father died.

If Andy had been certified to stand trial as an adult and was convicted on these charges, he would have been subject to the following punishments. Second-degree murder is a Class A felony punishable by a prison sentence of not less than 10 years and not more than 30 years (Sections 565.021 and 558.011, RSMo 1994). Robbery is also a Class A felony (Section 569.020, RSMo 1994).

Juvenile Case #5

Name: Sarah Jackson

Age: 16

Offense: Selling marijuana on school grounds.

Education: Junior in high school.

Prior Record: Four prior encounters with the law: one for public nudity (mooning the student body while playing in the band during a school assembly), one for minor in possession of alcohol, one for tampering with a vehicle, and one for selling marijuana to elementary students.

Comments: Allegedly has been selling drugs for almost three years; violent temper; and "D" grade average. Sarah lives with her father who is an attorney and her mother who is a college professor. She has three older brothers, one who is a professional football player, one who is studying to be a doctor, and one who is studying to be a priest. Her parents have had her in counseling for two years.

If Sarah had been certified as an adult, she would be subject to the following punishment: Selling marijuana on school grounds is a Class A felony punishable by not less than 10 years in prison and not more than 30 years (Sections 195.214 and 558.011, RSMo 1994).

Adult Case #1

Name: Jean Polson

Age: 23

Current Case: Following her escape from Fulton State Mental Hospital, Jean was put in the local county jail until personnel from the hospital could transport her back to Fulton. While she was incarcerated, she stabbed another inmate with a fork, injuring her severely. As the paramedics took the injured inmate away, Jean said, "I wish I had killed her." She was convicted of first-degree assault.

Prior Record:

Crime	Action Taken
Soliciting prostitution	One year probation
Automobile theft	One year probation
Shoplifting	Counseling
Shoplifting	One year probation
Burglary	Three years probation
Stealing	Probation continued

Comments: Jean Polson is one of ten children from a broken family. She never knew her father, and has a poor emotional relationship with her mother. She cannot read or write and is borderline retarded. She has no employment skills and has a long history of drug abuse. She has attempted suicide, had three children by two different fathers, and is currently married. Her husband is incarcerated for assault and selling drugs. Her children live with a relative. Since age 11 she has been in and out of mental institutions for emotional problems and drug use.

First-degree assault where serious injury results is a Class A felony punishable by not less than ten years imprisonment and not more than 30 years (Sections 565.050 and 558.011, RSMo 1994).

Adult Case #2

Name: Paul Harrison

Age: 25

Current Case: One year after being paroled for assaulting a police officer, Paul was arrested for armed robbery and automobile theft. He pleaded guilty to the crime of auto theft but claimed he needed the car to get back and forth to work. He also claims it was not an armed robbery because he was only pointing his finger through his shirt at the victim. No gun was found at the scene of the crime or on Paul at the time of his arrest. He was convicted of automobile theft and robbery in the second degree.

Prior Record:

Crime	Action Taken
Possession of heroin	One year probation
DWI	Counseling
Possession of cocaine	County jail—1 year plus three years probation
Burglary	County jail—30 days and probation continued
Assault	Three years imprisonment

Comments: Paul is the oldest of six children. His father is an alcoholic and compulsive gambler. His parents were divorced when he was 10. Paul dropped out of school his junior year in high school due to failing grades and excessive absenteeism. Paul does have an average IQ. He has been unable to hold a job due to his numerous arrests.

Automobile theft is a Class C felony punishable by a sentence of imprisonment for up to seven years (Sections 570.030 and 558,011, RSMo 1994) and/or a fine of up to $5,000 (Section 560.011, RSMo 1994). Robbery in the second degree is a Class B felony punishable by not less than five years and not more than 15 years imprisonment.

Adult Case #3

Name: Frederick Frawley

Age: 31

Current Case: Frederick and his partner rented police uniforms, stole a police car and then robbed a liquor store. The pair tried the same thing two days later but were caught. Frederick immediately confessed to the crimes, saying he needed the money because his catering business was failing. He pled guilty to impersonating a police officer, stealing a police car, and robbing the liquor store.

Prior Record:

Crime	Action Taken
Receiving stolen property	Case dismissed for lack of evidence
DWI	County jail—10 days & fine
Selling four stolen stereos	County jail—6 months Sentence suspended

Comments: Frederick comes from a two-parent family and has an above average IQ. He graduated from junior college and is married with one child, age four.

Impersonating a police officer is a Class A misdemeanor (Section 575.120, RSMo 1994) which is punishable by a fine of up to $1,000 and/or imprisonment up to one year (Sections 558.011 and 560.016, RSMo 1994). Stealing a car is a Class C felony punishable by a sentence of imprisonment for up to seven years (Sections 570.030 and 558,011, RSMo 1994) and/or a fine of up to $5,000 (Section 560.011, RSMo 1994). Robbery in the second degree is a Class B felony punishable by not less than five years and not more than 15 years imprisonment.

Adult Case #4

Name: Marvin Valcome

Age: 18

Current Case: Marvin was out on parole for stealing an automobile. Ten days after being paroled, he robbed and stabbed a 21-year-old pizza delivery man, inflicting serious injuries. When the pizza man arrived at Marvin's house, Marvin put his arm around the deliveryman's neck and pointed the knife at his throat. Marvin confessed that the man begged Marvin not to hurt him. Marvin stabbed him numerous times and admitted that the man continued to beg for his life until he passed out from the stab wounds. He confessed to the crime of first-degree assault to police.

Prior Record:

Crime	Action Taken
Stealing (age 8)	Counseling & released to mother
Burglary (age 9)	Placed in a home for emotionally disturbed boys; placed in several similar institutions from ages 9 to 15. Expelled at age 15 for hitting another boy with a rock.
Auto theft (age 16)	Certified to stand trial as an adult; sentenced to three years imprisonment; paroled after 18 months.

Comments: Marvin has a long history of very unstable behavior. At birth the doctors believed he had suffered brain damage. He was a behavior problem at school and at home. Marvin never knew his father, who was imprisoned when Marvin was a baby for first-degree robbery and was killed by another inmate. His mother lived with several other men during Marvin's childhood, none of whom took any interest in Marvin. He has always had trouble relating to his peers. His schoolwork and attendance were very poor.

First-degree assault where serious injury to the victim has occurred is a Class A felony (Section 565.050, RSMo 1994) and is punishable by imprisonment of 10 to 30 years (Section 558.011, RSMo 1994).

Adult Case #5

Name: John Mitchell

Age: 61

Current Case: John Mitchell was charged with four others in President Nixon's administration with five counts of obstruction of justice. In addition, Mitchell was charged with perjury before a grand jury and the Senate Watergate Committee and conspiracy to obstruct justice. Specifically, Mitchell was accused of approving the original Watergate Hotel break-in, ordering destruction of evidence, and encouraging the payment of hush money to those arrested for the break-in. Mitchell was found guilty on all counts.

Prior Record: None.

Comments: John Mitchell is a college and law school graduate, a corporate lawyer and U.S Attorney General—the highest law enforcement officer in the nation, appointed by President Nixon.

Perjury in Missouri is a Class C felony (Section 575.040, RSMo 1994). A Class C felony is punishable by a sentence of imprisonment for up to seven years (Section 558,011, RSMo 1994) and a fine of up to $5,000 (Section 560.011, RSMo 1994). Conspiracy to obstruct justice in this case would be a Class C felony since Mitchell conspired to burglarize the Watergate Hotel (Section 564.016, RSMo 1994).

Chapter 7
Juvenile Justice in Missouri

End of Chapter Questions

Use the text along with outside material to answer the following questions. Be sure to review the key terms and concepts from the beginning of the chapter before you start.

1. What are the strengths and weaknesses of Missouri's juvenile laws?

2. What did you find surprising or difficult about the certification process?

3. What surprised you or what did you find difficult to understand in the sentencing process?

End of Chapter Activities

Use the text along with outside material to complete the following activities.

1. Make suggestions as to what changes you would make in the law and send your ideas to your state legislators.

2. Invite a legislator who has sponsored juvenile law legislation to speak to your class.

Out of Class Activity

As a class, visit the General Assembly while juvenile laws are being debated.

Note: Brochures containing the "Juveniles and the Law" material in this chapter may be obtained by writing The Missouri Bar, P.O. Box 119, Jefferson City, MO 65102.

Chapter

Local Government: Organization & Practice

Key Terms & Concepts

alderman

city-administrator form of government

commission form of government

constitutional charter

council-manager form of government

county

general purpose government

home rule

mayor-council form of government

municipality

parish

school district

special charter cities

special district

special purpose government

township

Introduction to Local Government

Local governments are really "where the rubber meets the road," as the saying goes. The most familiar governmental services are provided at this level, although national and state issues are often considered more exciting by the media, and receive more air time.

Education, law enforcement, fire protection, planning and zoning, and a variety of other services are performed by local government units. As of the mid-1990s, Missouri ranked eighth in the United States in the total number of local governments, higher by far than its ranking in population.

Governance would be extremely difficult—indeed impossible—without local governments. There are two basic types of local government: (1) general and (2) special purpose governments. As might be suspected, the **general purpose government** has broader powers and provides more services. They are more familiar and include (1) counties, (2) cities, (3) villages, and (4) townships, in certain counties. They are often created for law enforcement purposes, but there are many other motivating reasons as well. Sometimes, their creation is to avoid annexation by a nearby municipality, to raise tax dollars for roads or other desired public projects, and to gain planning and zoning powers to prevent undesirable development.

Special purpose governments, on the other hand, have limited powers and usually perform only one function, such as education, water supply, fire protection and ambulance service. There are almost as many special purpose governments as there are governmental functions. Special or single purpose governments or districts are important because they can operate in other jurisdictions—the only local government that can do so—and are found in both rural and metropolitan areas. The boundaries of special purpose governments can even include several counties in a metropolitan area, and can even cross state boundaries with state and congressional approval.

It is often difficult for the average citizen to know in which political jurisdictions he or she resides. People living just outside a city's limit often assume they are part of the city, which legally they are not. Others are not familiar with all of the jurisdictions that tax them (state, county, city, school district, and perhaps a hospital, ambulance and library district, to mention only a few).

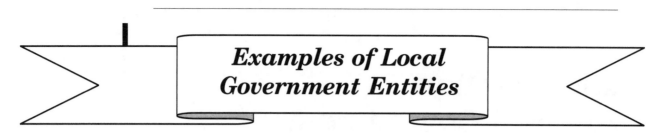

Examples of Local Government Entities

Municipalities

A municipality is an incorporated local government, meaning it is organized with corporate and governmental characteristics. Cities, villages and incorporated towns are considered municipalities. Municipalities are classified on the basis of their population.

Townships

A township is a sub-administrative unit of county government with very limited powers. Usually, the main function of a township is road maintenance. There are 23 counties in Missouri with township government, mostly located in the northwest.

Counties

Counties are sub-administrative units of state government. Counties carry out crucial state functions such as taxation and law enforcement. There are 114 counties in Missouri. In the state of Louisiana, a county is called a **parish**. Counties are classified based on their assessed property value.

Special Districts

A special district is usually a one-service local government. It can overlay other local entities. The most common special districts provide fire protection, road maintenance and water supply.

School Districts

School districts administer and provide for public education within recognized governmental systems. In Missouri, they function under dual control of local and state governmental influences or mandates.

Frankenstein, Missouri, population 30, is the only town in the country with this unique name. Its name was selected by early German settlers. In 1999, the townspeople decided to have some fun and generate some publicity at the same time. Twenty-five skydivers dressed up as Frankenstein sky-dived into the local ballpark to promote the re-release of Mel Brooks' movie "Young Frankenstein." The town was also renamed "Young Frankenstein" for a day.

Examples of Local Government

Municipalities

A municipality is an incorporated local government, meaning it is organized with corporate and governmental characteristics. Cities, villages and incorporated towns are considered municipalities. Municipalities are classified on the basis of population.

Incorporation, which defines a municipality, means that a community has followed the necessary state legal procedures to become a local government (and public corporation). The Missouri Constitution outlines the procedure for a community to incorporate. It should be noted that all local governments are completely subordinate to the state, even though the home rule movement to provide local autonomy has tried to change this relationship. With incorporation, boundaries are established, a form of government is chosen, and a municipality is given the ability to tax. State laws limit the options for governance in each classification.

Almost three-fourths of the U.S. population lives in municipalities. Missouri is less urbanized than the nation as a whole, with only two out of three citizens living in municipalities.

Villages

Villages are generally the smallest population units and have the simplest form of government. They have governmental authority to tax and perform some other services, but do not have as much authority as cities. They are ideal, though, for communities with small populations that need only basic governmental services. There are approximately 260 villages in Missouri. They are governed by boards of trustees.

Towns & Townships

A town, which is a generic term applying to all urban communities, may be incorporated or just a population without a government. In the Midwest there are also townships, which are basically sub-units of county government. In New England, early towns of varying geographic sizes acted as counties. Later, many were incorporated and added urban services. Originally, they were governed by selectmen who were elected at an annual town meeting. This was and still is considered the epitome of direct democracy, with all eligible voters able to take part in decision-making at the annual town meeting. However, many townships have mutated into a more modern form because of urban pressures.

Cities

Cities are the most numerous of municipalities. In Missouri, they range in population from the city of Lakeside, in Miller County, which has a population of 38, to Kansas City with a population of 434,829, according to the 1990 census.

There are approximately 550 third- and fourth-class cities in Missouri. Cities must have at least 400 inhabitants to incorporate (or only 200 if they are already a village). Very small population cities are usually products of hard times, left with the name of a city but not the population. Economic factors may lead

The Boone County Courthouse in Columbia.

The St. Louis Arch, riverfront and skyline have become symbols for the evolution of St. Louis from a simple trading post to a thriving center for national and international commerce.

to population increases or declines, but state law does not require cities to change their status, unless desired and approved by a vote of the people. In some instances cities have disappeared—their populations having died off or moved away. To disincorporate requires a vote of the people. But if there were no population left to do this, it complicates matters even further.

Classification of cities based on population is permitted by the Missouri Constitution. There are presently five general classes. These include third and fourth classes, villages, special and constitutional charter cities. The statutes for first- and second-class cities were repealed in 1975, because no cities were using them. **Special charter cities** are those that received individual tailor-made charters from the General Assembly before 1875 (the 1875 constitution prohibited such special acts). **Constitutional charters** are those developed by the cities themselves, through a special process.

Example of Local Government: Columbia, Missouri

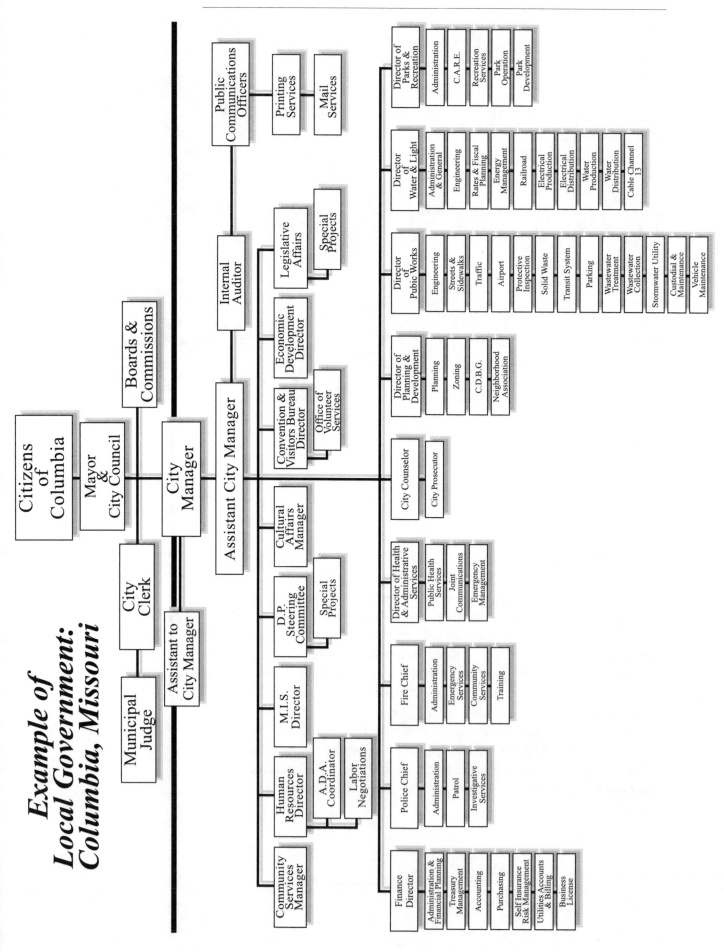

Classification is important because different laws pertain to different classes, such as those specifying the forms of government to be used. The form refers to the type of governmental organization, such as mayor-council, commission, or other. Classification has also led to abuses of power. Some laws are disguised as general, broad acts, but when analyzed, the laws obviously apply to only one city. Although special laws have been prohibited since 1875, there have been relatively few challenges to them and the Missouri Supreme Court has only occasionally enforced the prohibition.

Forms of Government

The **mayor-council form of government** is the oldest and most used in Missouri, with council members, or **aldermen**, elected by wards (either one or two members per ward, depending on the class). There is also a mayor elected at large who has some authority, but not as much, for example, as a city manager. The mayor's duties are restricted to carrying out the ordinances decided by the council. The organization is somewhat decentralized with several department heads sometimes elected by the people.

Rep. Tim Harlan, center, addresses the audience during a forum with area legislators, including Ken Jacob, left, and Steve Gaw, right, at the Columbia Public Library in 1995. At right, Bob Dietiker of Columbia addresses the legislators about public schools issues.

Support for planning and zoning is strongest in urban areas. Almost every county in or near a large city has planning and zoning. In contrast, few rural counties have adopted planning and zoning. The main exceptions include three tourism-impacted counties in southwest Missouri and a half-dozen counties in northwest Missouri. In total, 29 counties have adopted zoning, and 85 counties have not.

The **council-manager form of government** has council members elected city-wide, and in the pure form, no mayor (a member of the council acts as mayor). The model for the organization is the business corporation, with a highly centralized structure under the chief executive officer. In the council-manager plan, the council hires a non-partisan city manager (usually professionally trained) to act as the chief executive officer of the city. The city manager in turn appoints all department heads, much as a chief executive officer would do in a private business. This model is a product of the reform movement to "take politics out of government," and run it like a business. It is very similar to school district organization, with a school board and superintendent.

The **city-administrator form of government** is a compromise between old and new. Some fast-growing cities desire professionally trained chief executives but do not want a city manager. These fast-growing cities believe a city manager has too much authority. Instead, the city wants to keep the mayor and ward elections. So a city council will compromise by hiring a city administrator who can be assigned some of the mayor's powers and be on the job full-time. The city administrator is a helpful addition to local government, since mayors, except in large cities, are part-time elected officials. Many cities in Missouri have adopted a city-administrator form of local government, since it tends to offer a more diffused political climate, which is still controlled primarily by the mayor, as opposed to the centralized power that comes with a city-manager form, which has no mayoral position.

The **commission form of government** is a more traditional, highly decentralized form of local government. It is comprised of an elected committee with each of its commissioners serving one or more departments. The commissioners perform both legislative and executive functions. A product of reform in the early 1900s, the commission form has lately declined in popularity. It does not have a chief executive, which has been cited as a real weakness.

Forms of Municipal Government

Strong Mayor-Council Form

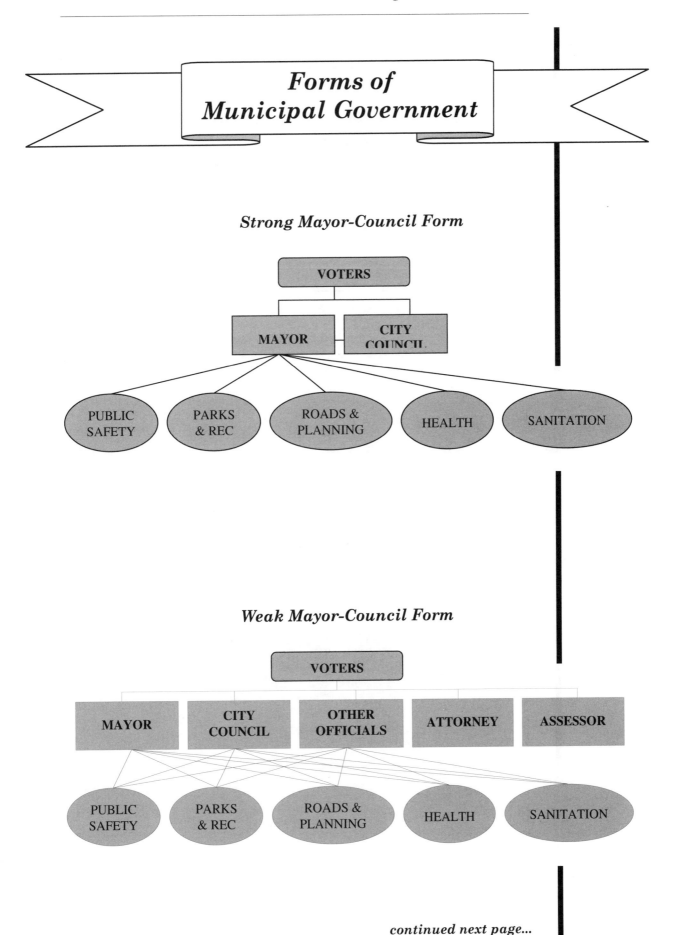

Weak Mayor-Council Form

continued next page...

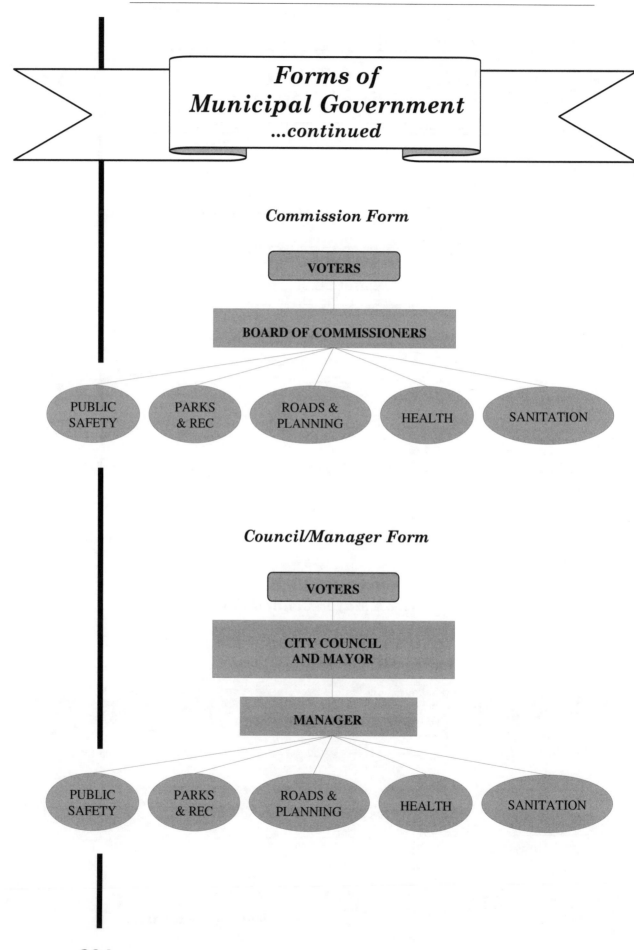

Forms of Municipal Government
...continued

Commission Form

VOTERS

BOARD OF COMMISSIONERS

PUBLIC SAFETY | PARKS & REC | ROADS & PLANNING | HEALTH | SANITATION

Council/Manager Form

VOTERS

CITY COUNCIL AND MAYOR

MANAGER

PUBLIC SAFETY | PARKS & REC | ROADS & PLANNING | HEALTH | SANITATION

Home Rule

Home rule is the epitome of local self-government. It is a process allowing a local population to create its own form of governmental organization. If desired by enough voters, a charter commission is elected and has a year to develop a charter or local constitution. Voters then adopt or reject the charter. The charter establishes the form of government, which can be anything except a monarchy or a dictatorship. There is great flexibility with this process, but not many eligible cities (those with over 5,000 people) in Missouri have taken this option. There appears to be some fear that charters will call for reform structures, most often a council-manager form, and eliminate many elected officials. This diminishes democracy, in the opinion of those opposed to it, and has led many communities to reject home rule. Still, some cities in Missouri have adopted home-rule charters for greater flexibility and more autonomy from the General Assembly. Missouri, it should be noted, was the first state to authorize constitutional home rule, in 1875.

Thomas Pendergast (1872-1945)
Kansas City Alderman, 1911, Political Boss

Pendergast was the most infamous name in Kansas City politics in the first part of the 20th century. Pendergast entered the family business of political machinery and faction-building under the wing of his brother Jim. By the time the older Pendergast died in 1911, Tom had established a name for himself. Tom filled Jim's seat on the city council and learned to play local politics with a masterful touch. After defeat by Republicans in 1920, Pendergast supported Harry Truman for Jackson County judge in 1922. The fact that Truman showed no loyalty to the Pendergast machinery in return ironically served only to strengthen the political boss by giving him legitimacy.

Pendergast mastered Kansas City politics using this same philosophy of masking corruption with the face of respectability. When anti-corruption activists attempted to clean up the administration of Kansas City, Pendergast courted them and effectively gained control of the body charged with ridding the city of graft and corruption.

The Pendergast machine was built on a system of political favors. The year 1932 was a great one for Pendergast. His man Lloyd Stark won the gubernatorial seat in Missouri and Franklin Roosevelt came to power in Washingon. The federal New Deal programs sent great amounts of money out across the country and Pendergast controlled its distribution in Missouri. However, after Stark was elected governor, he immediately turned reformer against Pendergast. By the mid-1930s, the boss was indicted on a series of charges, ranging from election fraud to tax evasion. After serving time in prison, Pendergast died on January 26, 1945.

Counties

A county seat is the center of county government, where the county courthouse is located.

Macon is the county seat of Macon County. Macon was originally called Bloomington. In 1862, federal militia general Lewis Merrill ordered the county seat of Bloomington burned to drive out the families of southern sympathizers living there. However, one of Merrill's staff found a way to replace Bloomington without leveling it. He wrote a bill changing the county seat name to Macon City. The word "City" was dropped in 1863.

Nicknamed "The City of Maples," the courthouse stands in the midst of old trees given by a taxpayer in lieu of taxes.

County government impacts everyone. There are 114 counties plus the city-county of St. Louis, which overlay the entire state. Both city and non-city populations are within their jurisdiction, and county governments preside over an increasingly non-urban population (those living outside of municipalities). Many individuals have moved to the countryside for the open spaces and to avoid city taxes. Consequently, many growing counties have had to increase their responsibilities and add services.

The history of county government is actually quite ancient. Counties were used in England as early as 603 A.D. They were originally called shires and were administrative areas of the crown. A representative of the king was assigned to deal with local problems. Following the Norman invasion of 1066, shires became known as "contes" or counties. By around 1300, county officials began to be elected rather than appointed.

When Missouri became a territory in 1812, five counties were established, and by statehood in 1821, the number of counties had reached 25. Counties are assigned to one of four classes by the constitution, based upon their assessed property value. The county assessor computes this figure, representing a percentage of all tangible property. Counties must move to the next higher classification if their assessed value reaches the required threshold and remains there for five years.

The reason for classification, as noted, is to apply different laws to different sized counties. Obviously, St. Louis County with its more than one million people needs different laws than the county of Worth, with just a bit more than two thousand inhabitants. The laws reflect the varying problems and needs of each county.

When Missouri became a territory in 1812, five counties were established. By statehood in 1821 the number of counties had reached 25.

Missouri Counties

ATCHISON
NODAWAY
WORTH
HARRISON
MERCER
PUTNAM
SCHUYLER
SCOTLAND
CLARK
HOLT
ANDREW
GENTRY
GRUNDY
SULLIVAN
ADAIR
KNOX
LEWIS
DE KALB
DAVIESS
LINN
MACON
SHELBY
MARION
BUCHANAN
CLINTON
CALDWELL
LIVINGSTON
CHARITON
RANDOLPH
MONROE
RALLS
PLATTE
CLAY
RAY
CARROLL
PIKE
AUDRAIN
HOWARD
SALINE
BOONE
LINCOLN
JACKSON
LAFAYETTE
MONTGOMERY
COOPER
CALLAWAY
WARREN
ST. CHARLES
ST. LOUIS CITY
CASS
JOHNSON
PETTIS
MONITEAU
ST. LOUIS
COLE
OSAGE
GASCONADE
FRANKLIN
HENRY
MORGAN
JEFFERSON
BATES
BENTON
MILLER
MARIES
ST. CLAIR
CAMDEN
CRAWFORD
WASHINGTON
STE. GENEVIEVE
HICKORY
PHELPS
VERNON
PULASKI
ST. FRANCOIS
PERRY
CEDAR
DALLAS
LACLEDE
DENT
IRON
POLK
BOLLINGER
MADISON
CAPE GIRARDEAU
BARTON
DADE
REYNOLDS
WEBSTER
TEXAS
WRIGHT
JASPER
SHANNON
LAWRENCE
GREENE
WAYNE
SCOTT
MISSISSIPPI
CARTER
CHRISTIAN
DOUGLAS
STODDARD
NEWTON
HOWELL
BUTLER
STONE
OREGON
RIPLEY
BARRY
TANEY
OZARK
NEW MADRID
McDONALD
© Pebble Publishing, Inc.
PEMISCOT
DUNKLIN

Gasconade County government provides many services, such as road repairs near Hermann.

Local government in Cole County provides students at Moreau Heights Elementary School in Jefferson City transportation to and from school.

Special Districts

Special districts are governments that serve a limited purpose. They are different from general purpose governments, such as municipalities and counties, in that special districts usually perform only one service. For example, most cities provide drinkable water, sewer service, fire and police protection, and build and maintain streets and roads. In contrast, the most common special district provides for fire protection only.

There are several reasons for the creation of special districts. One is ideological. Since many Missourians dislike big government, they prefer creating new, small governments rather than making existing governments larger and more powerful. This is consistent with Thomas Jefferson's philosophy, with its fear that individual liberty might be threatened by increased public power. Better to separate powers and decentralize than risk concentrated power, Jeffersonians would argue. This ideology is reflected in the state legislature's preference to create local governments. Many counties have seen increases in population outside of cities and villages, but the state is reluctant to "unleash" county governments by allowing them to provide needed urban services. Counties are

C.J. Lexow has been a fire engineer for Station One, Columbia Fire Department, for ten years. She operates Ladder One, the station's largest engine, which has a 100-foot aerial ladder.

"The ability of zoning battles to turn ordinarily reasonable people into wide-eyed fanatics is a never-ending source of amazement."

— Clan Crawford

considered to be sub-administrative units of state government, responsible for only traditional and limited services that the state wants performed.

Federal policies have also been responsible for creating special districts. Dust bowl conditions in the 1930s led the federal government to push soil conservation districts. Similarly, central city problems led to some housing and urban redevelopment authorities. Federal policy also helped suburbanization following World War II. The additional cities and villages meant there was no entity capable of providing area-wide services, because of local "sovereignty." A city or village cannot provide a service in another governmental jurisdiction. Only special districts can provide a service across boundary lines.

Still another reason for the creation of a special district is the desire to separate an activity from city hall or the county courthouse. The seats of local government are often considered "too political" to be allowed to provide important services. Engineers, school administrators, teachers and

Alfonso Cervantes (1920-1983)
St. Louis Board of Aldermen, 1949
St. Louis mayor, 1965

Alfonso Cervantes began life as the son of poor second-generation Spanish immigrants in St. Louis in 1920. He had an entrepreneurial spirit even as a young boy. At age 15, he left high school to live in California. He started his first business, a rhumba club, and was living comfortably before World War II broke out. After serving his country in the merchant marine, he returned to St. Louis where he started an insurance business. As he became more successful in the business community, he began a tenure on the Board of Aldermen in 1949.

He became mayor of St. Louis in 1965. His energies were focused on reducing racial discrimination, fighting crime in the city, and beginning the effort to rebuild downtown St. Louis and the riverfront. The Council on Human Rights and the Commission on Crime and Law Enforcement were two of the committees to which his administration gave impetus. However, he is most remembered for the renovation of downtown St. Louis, which he oversaw. One of his greatest achievements was the construction of the Gateway Convention Center. After serving two terms as mayor, he spent his last years in various business activities until his death in 1983.

others push for an independent government for their pet function—independent, at least in theory, from local politics. The rationale for this position is that certain functions are so important they "must be taken out of politics." The result, though, is only a different kind of politics.

Economics also plays a role in special districts. Some areas do not have a large enough tax base to provide a given service. A water district, for example, can require a large capital expenditure and annual expenditures for maintenance. However, serving a larger area may provide sufficient revenues to meet both needs. On another front, in metropolitan areas with many local governments, a special district may be the only way to provide a much-needed area-wide service.

However, creating a special district is similar to dedicating revenues to a single function, something public administrators try to avoid. Their concern is that government loses flexibility when revenues are "earmarked" or dedicated. If there is an emergency in another sector, the government cannot use the earmarked revenues, even though there may be a surplus in that particular fund. With special districts, a new government is created that in effect dedicates revenues to only one function.

There is an amazing variety of special district governments in Missouri and throughout the country. In Missouri, the most numerous include roads, fire protection, water, libraries, drainage, soil conservation, ambulance, sewers, health, and nursing homes. More exotic types of special district governments include Johnson Grass (a noxious weed) eradication and street light maintenance. The state of Minnesota even has mosquito abatement districts.

School districts are often independent governments as well, although in some eastern cities they are part of city government. Education was one of the earliest functions to be split off for special treatment, probably because of its high esteem, and the successful efforts of school administrators and teachers in pushing for independent status.

The Man Behind the Badge:
Ted Boehm, Boone County Sheriff

By Hugh Curran, editor of *The Columbia Business Times*

Ted Boehm knows that when most citizens think of the Boone County Sheriff's Department, they think of the tall, imposing guys who pull you over when you're speeding outside the city limits. The image is accurate, but the Boone County Sheriff hopes Boone Countians realize the department does a lot more than just that.

"Sheriff departments have more responsibilities than other law enforcement agencies in the state," Boehm said. "Law enforcement is a big part of it, but we also have civil papers to serve, adult orders of protection, warrants for arrest, we have to collect all the bond receipts and get them to the circuit clerks, and of course we have to run the jail, which is a 24-hour, seven-day-a-week commitment."

On top of the department's responsibilities are added the county's population growth and the parallel growth in the department that Boehm has seen since first being elected sheriff 15 years ago.

In 1985, Boehm inherited an enforcement department with 18 officers, 14 staff members, and a budget of $795,000. Today, he oversees a $2.8 million annual budget, 39 officers and 16 support staff. In 1985, the department received 14,000 calls for service from a population of 35,000 under the department jurisdiction. This year, the department estimates it will receive up to 54,000 calls from a population of 50,000 people.

The numbers have also gone up at the Boone County Jail.

In 1985, the jail had an annual budget of $538,000 and held 50 inmates watched over by a staff of 18. Today, the prison has a budget of $3 million annually and holds 207 inmates monitored by a staff of 43. Watching over it all is Boehm, age 54, who describes his job as "100 percent administrative."

"I deal with budgets, promotions, demotions, personnel issues for 110 employees, policies and procedures," Boehm said. "Everyday is something of an unknown. Within 30 minutes of getting to work, I don't know what direction I'll be moving in."

This year, Boehm must also run for reelection to his office against court marshal Fred Baer in the Democratic primary August 8. Baer accuses Boehm of stripping him of his credentials after running against Boehm four years ago.

And then there's the matter of how to raise the estimated $11 million to build an extension to the Boone County Jail.

"The key is going to be in educating the public to the need for it," Boehm said. "If there's any one of the options I hear negative comments on, it's the raising of property taxes to fund it. It sounds like a sales tax or bonds would have more of a chance."

Despite it all, Boehm wants to stay right where he's at.

"I am still very motivated with this job and I feel there's still a lot to do," Boehm said. "Building phase two of the prison is one example of the challenges still facing this department. We've got staffing and salary studies going on, training issues, computerized technology moving into place and that we'll be using more and more. During my time as sheriff we've raised $1.6 million in federal grant money, we've decentralized the department with substations out in the community where the officer has a computer and phone and filing cabinet so he doesn't have to come running back here, we've set up bicycle patrols to get the officers out where the people are and talking to them. There's now a canine program thanks to asking for money from not-for-profits. It's cut our search of a building from four hours tying up our personnel to only 30 minutes with a canine. I'm proud of what I've accomplished, but of course, there's always room for improvement."

Summary & Conclusions

Although special districts have been termed phantom governments because of their low visibility in the public eye, they are often the only way to provide certain services. When a problem is severe enough, a special district may have to be created to cope with it. If the problems of special districts in turn become a major concern, it is perhaps then that comprehensive reorganization of all local governments will become an item on the public agenda.

In 1999, Kenny Hulshof, U.S. Representative for the 9th District, confers with Almeta Crayton, Columbia's first ward councilwoman.

Chapter 8
Local Government: Organization and Practice

End of Chapter Questions

Use the text along with outside material to answer the following questions. Be sure to review the key terms and concepts from the beginning of the chapter before you start.

1. Why does the author say that local government is "where the rubber meets the road"?

2. What are some of the primary services performed by local governments? Why are these services not provided for at the state or national level?

3. List some of the special districts in Missouri and their primary functions. Can you identify any special districts that directly affect you?

4. What is one of the primary reasons that municipalities incorporate?

5. In terms of its government, do you live in a town, township, village or city? How does this classification probably determine the type of local government you experience?

6. Why is the correct classification of local governments so important?

7. What are the four different types of local government? How does each of these differ from the others?

8. Why has the city-administrator form of local government become more popular? What advantages does it have over the more traditional mayor-council arrangement?

9. According to the author, the home rule charter represents the "epitome of local self-government." What does the author mean?

10. What are two of the major advantages of local governments adopting home-rule charters?

11. Why has the number of counties in Missouri increased from five in 1821 to more than 114 today?

12. What is the importance of "taxable assessed value" and how is it related to county government?

13. What are special districts and what are some of the primary reasons for their creation?

End of Chapter Activities

Use the text along with outside material to complete the following activities.

1. Outline the characteristics of (1) villages, (2) towns and townships, and (3) cities. What are some of their similarities? What are some of their differences?

2. Identify the type of local government where you live. Also, show how the type or classification of your local government affects its operations.

3. Make a list of some of the special districts in Missouri. Briefly explain some of their purposes and possible reasons for their creation. Why do you think these issues were not handled by state or county governments?

Chapter

Overview of Jefferson City: Missouri Capital

Missouri's State Capitol.

Key Terms

capital
capitol

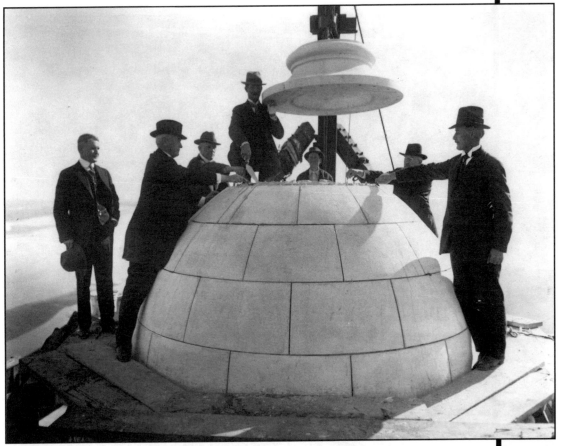

Capitol commissioners at the dome capstone ceremony on December 5, 1916.

History of the Missouri Capitol

Missouri's first legislators wrote in the constitution that the state's capital must be located on the Missouri River on a site within 40 miles of the mouth of the Osage River. They wanted a capital that was centrally located in the state, but no sizable settlements existed in the specified area. Competition for the capital was fierce, but finally the legislature decided in 1821 to design the City of Jefferson, named in honor of Thomas Jefferson, from the ground up to be Missouri's capital city. "Missouriopolis" was another name proposed for the capital. The choice of location was a controversial one and would remain so for years. Residents of St. Louis were certain that their already-established city was a better candidate, and some critics suspected that land speculators had influenced the decision.

Speculative drawing of the first Jefferson City capitol, based on descriptions. No contemporary plans or prints of this building survive.

Throughout this chapter you will see two similar words: "capital" and "capitol." The word **capital** is used to signify the city in which a central government is located—in this case Jefferson City. The word **capitol** is used to signify the domed building in which the Missouri state legislature meets.

While Jefferson City was being developed, a temporary capitol was maintained at St. Charles from 1821 to 1826. Missouri's legislators met on the top floor of a two-story brick building owned by three St. Charles merchants who kept their residences on the first floor. This site was fully restored in 1970, and today provides visitors with an instructive look back into Missouri's early history.

The second capitol was located in Jefferson City near the present site of the governor's mansion. It measured only 40 by 60 feet, and contained both houses of the legislature and the governor's quarters. Although the slow growth of Jefferson City fueled doubts about its suitability to be the capital city, the legislature authorized the building of a penitentiary and a governor's residence there in

*The Missouri Capitol and Lohman's Landing (now called Jefferson City),
as seen from the east, circa 1840-1850.*

1833. The state government eventually outgrew the building, but
before it could be enlarged, it was destroyed by fire in 1837. The
government was temporarily moved to the Cole County courthouse.

The third and much larger capitol, located on the grounds of
the present one, was erected in 1840. Modeled after Pennsylvania's
capitol building and built largely with prison labor, it measured
approximately 200 by 80 feet and was topped by a 130-foot-high
dome. Its construction was remarkable, considering that Jefferson
City's population was only 1,174 at the time. While the building
was greatly admired, it ran so far over budget that it would not be
fully finished for 10 years, at a total cost of about $400,000. During
the Civil War, Missouri's confederate government-in-exile made
its own capital in Marshall, Texas.

In 1871, a new governor's mansion was erected, and it is still
the one in use today. In 1887 the capitol was greatly enlarged,
with new north and south wings for the legislature and a 200-
foot-high dome, but even this structure was soon outgrown.

Throughout the period other cities kept agitating to have the
capital moved, with Boonville and Sedalia being the most
prominent voices, but in an 1896 statewide ballot, Missourians
declined to change the capital city.

Above, the Missouri Capitol after 1887-1899 expansion and renovation.

At right, the capitol building engulfed in flames on the night of February 5, 1911.

This capitol was also destroyed by fire, when lightning struck the dome on the evening of February 5, 1911. Again, St. Louis urged moving the capital, but to no avail. Later that same year, Missourians approved a bond issue of $3.5 million to construct a new state capitol and a competition was held to select the building's design. In the meantime, a temporary capitol building was erected in Jefferson City and used from 1913 to 1917.

The current capitol under construction. April 15, 1915.

The current capitol, completed in 1918.

The present capitol was constructed between 1913 and 1918. It is built of white crystalline limestone from Carthage and it is 10 times larger than the previous capitol. The building is 437 feet long and 300 feet wide at the center. The dome towers 262 feet above ground level.

A scene from Thomas Hart Benton's painting, "A Social History of the State of Missouri," located in the Missouri State Capitol.

Upon completion of the building, the government created the Capitol Decoration Commission to design interior and exterior artwork for it. A $1 million surplus left after all construction costs provided funding. Above is a section of the most well-known painting in the capitol, a mural by Thomas Hart Benton entitled "A Social History of the State of Missouri." It was considered scandalous at the time for its depictions of drunkenness and diaper changing, among many other aspects of life. Perhaps the politicians of the day had hoped for a more conservative piece of artwork.

Today Benton's work is a powerful reflection of the many facets of early Missouri life. Benton's murals can be viewed by appointment at the capitol building. Many other paintings of historical events, such as Lewis and Clark's expedition, bronze statues of famous Missourians, a Missouri Museum, amazing architectural highlights, as well as ornate stained glass ceilings permeate the capitol with a heightened sense of purpose.

For additional history on Missouri's capitols, read Marian Ohman's book, *The History of Missouri Capitols,* published by the University of Missouri-Columbia, Extension Division in 1982.

A Walking Tour of the Capitol Grounds

A short walk around the capitol grounds offers students a first-hand look at Missouri government in action. The grounds of the Capitol also offer students a series of interesting statues and tributes to the veterans of Missouri, law enforcement agents, our forebears, the earth and even the seasons that sustain Missouri's bountiful harvest.

A walk around the capitol is like a quick walk through Missouri. Take the time to read the walking tour on the next few pages, and on your next visit to Jefferson City spend a few moments reflecting on all the hard work, planning, determination and sacrifice that allow us to enjoy today's Missouri.

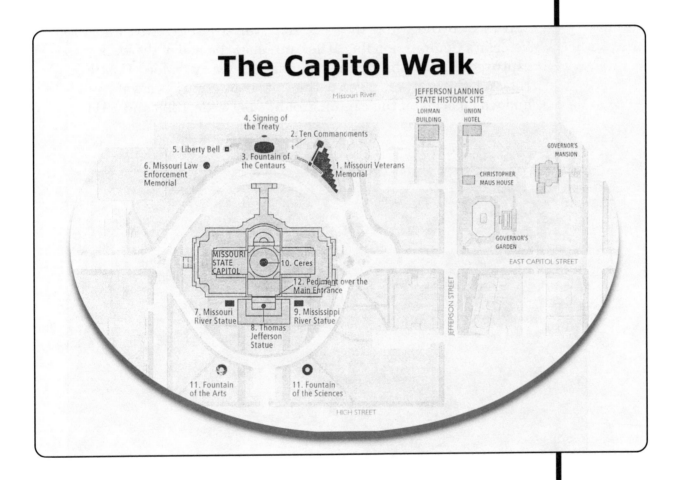

The Capitol Walk

1. Missouri Veterans Memorial

This tribute to all of Missouri's veterans was dedicated on November 11, 1991. The jets of water in the fountain symbolize the turmoil of war and a single arc of water shoots over the jets to symbolize peace.

The 24 steps along the waterfall honor Missouri's entrance into the Union as the 24th state. "Missouri Veterans—Guardians of Liberty" is inscribed in the reflecting pool at the end of the fountain. The five bays of the colonnade overlooking the river are a reminder of the five branches of the armed forces: Army, Navy, Air Force, Marines, and the Coast Guard. Each of the eight black granite posts along the walk represent a war that has been fought since Missouri became a state. The wars include the Mexican-American, Civil War, Spanish-American, World War I, World War II, Korean, Vietnam, and Persian Gulf. Three flags guard the entrance to the walk: the U.S. flag, the Missouri flag, and the Veteran's Commission flag. The cannon at the end of the walk was captured during the Spanish-American War at Moro Castle in Havana, Cuba. It was given to the state of Missouri as a war trophy and was placed on the capitol grounds between 1898 and 1911.

This cannon, from the Spanish-American war, is on display at the Missouri Veterans Memorial.

"Missouri Veterans: Guardians of Liberty."
The Missouri Veterans Memorial was dedicated
November 11, 1991.

2. The Ten Commandments

This stone marker was presented to the state by the Missouri State Aerie Fraternal Order of Eagles on June 28, 1958.

3. The Fountain of the Centaurs

This fountain was designed by Adolph Alexander Weinman. The large figures in this fountain are mythological half-animal, half-human creatures known as centaurs. They are seen wrestling with serpents and giant fish to represent the wildness of the West. The smaller, boyish figures are sea urchins. They are spraying water on the centaurs with their fish to represent the playfulness of the small animals of the West.

4. *The Signing of the Treaty*

This sculpture was designed by Karl Bitter for the 1904 St. Louis World's Fair. It depicts Robert Livingston standing, James Monroe seated, and François Barbé-Marbois signing the treaty by which the United States acquired the Louisiana Territory from France in 1803. Missouri became the second state formed from the Louisiana Purchase.

President Thomas Jefferson wanted control of New Orleans, the major trading port on the Mississippi River. To accomplish this he sent Robert Livingston and James Monroe to France to negotiate the purchase of that city. Napoleon Bonaparte, ruler of France, was in need of money because England was about to declare war on his country.

Marbois, Napoleon's treasurer, urged him to sell the United States not only New Orleans, but the entire Louisiana Territory. Marbois reasoned that France needed the money and if England declared war, the first thing they would take would be France's holdings in the New World. France sold the entire Louisiana Territory to the United States for $15 million. This averages out to approximately three cents per acre.

5. The Liberty Bell

This is a reproduction of the Liberty Bell that rang in 1776 declaring our nation's independence. It was presented to the people of Missouri by John W. Snyder, the U.S. Secretary of the Treasury. This bell is one of 53 that were cast in France in 1950 and given to the U.S. government by patriotic donors.

6. The Missouri Law Enforcement Memorial

This tribute to all Missouri law enforcement officers killed in the line of duty was dedicated on June 17, 1994. Plaques on the walls give their name, position, city or town, and the date they died.

7. *The Missouri River Statue*

This statue was designed by Robert Aitken. The female figure crowned with cattails represents the Missouri River. Her left arm rests upon a cornucopia of fruit while she holds a stalk of corn in her left hand and a bundle of wheat in her right hand. The turtle by her knee is one of the many small creatures dependent upon the river, and the catfish and four smaller fish behind her symbolize the river as a resource for fishing and recreation. The ox skull is a symbol of the loss of life and property due to flooding and drought.

The four panels beneath the statue portray different aspects of water. On the front long panel, the Sun God stands in the middle before the sun and its life-giving rays with the sacred serpent wrapped around his waist. Nature's forces opening rocks to form new streams of water are to the left, and the figures with long, streaming hair to the right of the Sun God personify the melting snows. The long panel on the back of the statue also portrays the Sun God and to the left are figures depicting the storm winds, lightning and rain. The rising mists and vapors are represented by the figures to the right of the Sun God. The side panels also depict aspects of water. One of the panels is entitled "Water Is Power" and the other "Water Is Life."

8. The Thomas Jefferson Statue *(see preceding full-page photo)*

The man for whom our capital city was named, Thomas Jefferson, rightfully stands upon the front steps of the capitol. Jefferson was an accomplished writer, architect and scholar. As the third president of the United States, he was primarily responsible for the Louisiana Purchase. This 13-foot statue was designed by James Earl Fraser and is one of the finest statues of Jefferson in existence.

9. The Mississippi River Statue

The Mississippi River statue was also designed by Robert Aitken. The male figure represents the Mississippi River, often called the "Father of the Waters." In his left hand he holds the rudder of commerce and the anchor of a steamboat signifying river trade. The caduceus in his right hand was the magic wand of Hermes, the god of travelers and commerce. He rests upon a cornucopia, which symbolizes agriculture. The alligator by his knee is a reminder of what life is like on the southern portion of the river. The dolphin behind him is a symbol of good luck to travelers on the river and the three small fish represent the river as a resource for fishing and recreation. The four panels on the base of this statue are the same as those on the Missouri River statue, only reversed.

10. Ceres

Standing more than 400 feet above the river on top of the capitol dome is a statue of Ceres designed by Sherry Fry. Ceres is the Roman goddess of grain and agriculture and was selected as the patron goddess of Missouri. Her left hand holds a sheaf of grain and she extends her right hand forward in perpetual blessing over the state.

11. The Fountains of the Arts and Sciences

These fountains, designed by Robert Aitken, are characterized by their dignity and simplicity. The fountain on the southeast side of the capitol is the Fountain of the Sciences; to the southwest is the Fountain of the Arts. Aitken believed that the Arts and Sciences were the guardians of the welfare of the state. So these two fountains stand as sentinels on either side of the capitol entrance.

The Fountain of the Arts

Four figures are positioned around the central pillar of this fountain. Architecture, a male, is the father of all arts. His hands are resting on a Greek pillar. Sculptor, a male, has his chisel and hammer to free his idea from the rock. Painting, a female, has her palette and brush. Music, a female, holds her musical instrument as she listens for the strains of harps in the distance.

The Fountain of the Sciences

Four figures are positioned around the central pillar of this fountain as well. Geometry, a male, is the oldest and noblest of the sciences. He holds his compass and sphere. Geology, a male, is studying the crystals that he has broken from a ledge. Chemistry, a female, holds her lamp of investigation as she studies the contents of her test tube. Astrology, a female, holds her astrolabe while gazing into the distant stars to read the horoscope of humanity.

12. Pediment over the Main Entrance

These sculptures are symbolic of the state's aspirations. The central figure of an enthroned woman represents Missouri. Her left arm rests on a shield bearing the state's coat of arms. At her right stands a boy with a winged globe, the Spirit of Progress. To the right of this central group is Agriculture, represented by a man driving a yoke of oxen and a youth bearing a sheaf of grain. This group is followed by a female teaching a youth, Learning, and a female figure leaning upon a capital supporting a harp representing Art. On the left of the central group is Commerce, the god Hermes guiding the Steeds of Industry. These are followed by a reclining male figure, Law, contemplating enscribed tablets of the Ten Commandments. Next is a reclining woman representing Order. She is crushing the serpent of anarchy. The figure at left represents the Genius of Justice. The figure at the extreme right represents the Genius of Light.

Tour Information

The Missouri State Capitol

The Missouri State Museum is located on the first floor of the capitol. Visit the History Hall to see exhibits of Missouri's past and present—from early Native American inhabitants to the modern day. Visit the Resources Hall to learn about Missouri's natural resources, its people and the development of the state. Be sure to take the tour and enjoy Thomas Hart Benton's famous mural "A Social History of the State of Missouri," painted in 1936.

The Missouri State Capitol is open from 8 a.m. to 5 p.m. daily, except January 1, Easter, Thanksgiving and Christmas. Tours are available from 8 a.m. to 11 a.m. and from 1 p.m. to 4 p.m. every hour. Reservations for group tours are required and can be made by calling (573) 751-4127. Walk-in visitors are welcome.

Other Places of Interest in Jefferson City

Jefferson Landing State Historic Site

This site preserves the hub of Jefferson City's riverfront commerce from the mid-1800s. This is a complex of three restored buildings, the Christopher Maus House, the Lohman Building visitor center, and the Union Hotel gallery, located a block from the capitol at the foot of Jefferson Street. Tours are available by reservation at the Lohman Building and the Union Hotel from 10 a.m. to 4 p.m. daily. The tours last 30 minutes and include a 12-minute slide show. Call (573) 751-3475.

Governor's Mansion

The Governor's Mansion, home of Missouri's first families since the 1870s, is located just east of Jefferson Landing. Tours are offered free of charge. Traditional Christmas Candlelight Tours are held during the holiday season. The mansion is accessible for persons with disabilities. Reservations are required for groups of 10 or more, and are strongly recommended for smaller groups. For tour information and reservations, call (573) 751-7929.

Supreme Court Building

Reservations are required. Call (573) 751-3839.

Cole County Historical Society

Cole County Historical Society Museum, located across the street from the Governor's Mansion, is open to the public. Admission for tours. For information and tour reservations, call (573) 635-1850.

Runge Conservation Nature Center

Features a hands-on exhibit hall, a large fish aquarium and hiking trails. Open daily. Call (573) 526-5544 for more information.

Highway Patrol Safety Education Center & Museum

Open weekdays. Call (573) 526-6419 for more information.

North Jefferson Katy Trail State Park Access

North of Jefferson City, just across the Missouri River Bridge, be sure and take a detour a quarter mile west of the clover leaf to visit the large shelter and trailhead of the Jefferson City Spur Trail, which connects the North Jefferson area to the Katy Trail State Park approximately one mile away.

Not in Jefferson City . . . But Worth the Visit

The First Missouri State Capitol

The First Missouri State Capitol State Historic Site in St. Charles offers tours, displays and living history presentations. Call (636) 946-9282 for more information.

Chapter

Summary of the Missouri State Constitution

Introduction to the Missouri Constitution

Missouri has been governed by four constitutions since becoming a state. The first, adopted in 1820, was required to be presented to the U.S. Congress before Missouri was granted statehood. The second constitution was drafted and adopted in 1865 at the close of the Civil War. The U.S. Supreme Court declared it unconstitutional 10 years later, creating a new constitution in 1875. That constitution served the people until our current constitution was adopted in 1945. Since then, it has been amended many times as Missourians seek to improve their government and the rules it operates under.

Government is obligated to the people, but the people determine how government works best through citizen participation, education and other efforts. Each of us can better fulfill that reponsibility by understanding the basic framework of state government. The Missouri Constitution is that framework, and it exists to help you be an effective citizen participating in Missouri's government. Excerpts of the Missouri Constitution can be found through this book where they pertain to the subject matter. A brief overview is also included in this chapter.

The Missouri Constitution is published by the secretary of state. Order a copy free of charge by writing: Secretary of State, Publications Division, P.O. Box 1767, Room 168, James C. Kirpatrick State Information Center, Jefferson City, MO 65102. Or call (573) 751-1813.

The Missouri Constitution

PREAMBLE

We, the people of Missouri, with profound reverence for the Supreme Ruler of the Universe, and grateful for His goodness, do establish this constitution for the better government of the state.

Article I
BILL OF RIGHTS

In order to assert our rights, acknowledge our duties, and proclaim the principles on which our government is founded, we declare:

Section 1: Source of political power–origin, basis and aim of government—That all political power is vested in and derived from the people; that all government of right originates from the people, is founded upon their will only, and is instituted solely for the good of the whole.

Section 2: Promotion of general welfare–natural rights of persons–equality under the law–purpose of government— That all constitutional government is intended to promote the general welfare of the people; that all persons have a natural right to life, liberty, the pursuit of happiness and the enjoyment of the gains of their own industry; that all persons are created equal and are entitled to equal rights and opportunity under the law; that to give security to these things is the principal office of government, and that when government does not confer this security, it fails in its chief design.

Section 3: Powers of the people over internal affairs, constitution and form of government—That the people of this state have the inherent, sole and exclusive right to regulate the internal government and police thereof, and to alter and abolish their constitution and form of government whenever they may deem it necessary to their safety and happiness, provided such change be not repugnant to the U.S. Constitution.

Section 4: Independence of Missouri–submission of certain amendments to Constitution of the United States—That Missouri is a free and independent state, subject only to the U.S. Constitution; that all proposed amendments to the Constitution of the United States qualifying or affecting the individual liberties of the people or which in any wise may impair the right of local self-government belonging to the people of this state, should be submitted to conventions of the people.

Section 5: Religious freedom–liberty of conscience and belief–limitations—That all men have a natural and indefeasible right to worship Almighty God according to the dictates of their own consciences; that no human authority can control or interfere with the rights of conscience; that no person shall, on account of his religious persuasion or belief, be rendered ineligible to any public office or trust or profit in this state, be disqualified from testifying or serving as a juror, or be molested in his person or estate; but this section shall not be construed to excuse acts of licentiousness, nor to justify practices inconsistent with the good order, peace or safety of the state, or with others rights.

Section 6: Practice and support of religion not compulsory–contracts therefore enforceable—That no person can be compelled to erect, support or attend any place or system of worship, or to maintain or support any priest, minister, preacher or teacher of any sect, church, creed or denomination of religion; but if any person shall voluntarily make a contract for any such object, he shall be held to the performance of the same.

Section 7: Public aid for religious purposes–preferences and discriminations on religious grounds—That no money shall ever be taken from the public treasury, directly or indirectly, in aid of any church, sect or denomination of religion, or in aid of any priest, preacher, minister or teacher thereof, as such; and that no preference shall be given to nor any discrimination made against any church, sect or creed of religion, or any form of religious faith or worship.

Section 8: Freedom of speech–evidence of truth in defamation actions–province of jury—That no law shall be passed impairing the freedom of speech, no matter by what means communicated: that every person shall be free to say, write or publish, or otherwise communicate whatever he will on any subject, being responsible for all abuses of that liberty; and that in all suits and prosecutions for libel or slander the truth thereof may be given in evidence; and in suits and prosecutions for libel the jury, under the direction of the court, shall determine the law and the facts.

Section 9: Rights of peaceable assembly and petition—That the people have the right peaceably to assemble for their common good, and to apply to those invested with the powers of government for redress of grievances by petition or remonstrance.

Section 10: Due process of law—That no person shall be deprived of life, liberty or property without due process of law.

Section 11: Imprisonment for debt—That no person shall be imprisoned for debt, except for nonpayment of fines and penalties imposed by law.

Section 12: Habeas corpus—That the privilege of the writ of habeas corpus shall never be suspended.

Section 13: Ex post facto laws–impairment of contracts–irrevocable privileges—That no ex post facto law, nor law impairing the obligation of contracts, or retrospective in its operation, or making any irrevocable grant of special privileges or immunities, can be enacted.

Section 14: Open courts–certain remedies–justice without sale, denial or delay—That the courts of justice shall be open to every person, and certain remedy afforded for every injury to person, property or character, and that right and justice shall be administered without sale, denial or delay.

Section 15: Unreasonable search and seizure prohibited–contents and basis of warrants—That the people shall be secure in their persons, papers, homes and effects, from unreasonable searches and seizures; and no warrant to search any place, or seize any person or thing, shall issue without describing the place to be searched, or the person or thing to be seized, as nearly as may be; nor without probable cause, supported by written oath or affirmation.

Section 16: Grand juries–composition–jurisdiction to convene–powers—That a grand jury shall consist of twelve citizens, any nine of whom concurring may find an indictment or a true bill: Provided, that no grand jury shall be convened except upon an order of a judge of a court having the power to try and determine felonies; but when so assembled such grand jury shall have power to investigate and return indictments for all character and grades of crime; and that the power of grand juries to inquire into the willful misconduct in office of public officers, and to find indictments in connection therewith, shall never be suspended.

Section 17: Indictments and information in criminal cases–exceptions—That no person shall be prosecuted criminally for felony or misdemeanor otherwise than by indictment or information, which shall be concurrent remedies, but this shall not be applied to cases arising in the land or naval forces or in the militia when in actual service in time of war or public danger, nor to prevent arrests and preliminary examination in any criminal case.

Section 18(a): Rights of accused in criminal prosecutions—That in criminal prosecutions the accused shall have the right to appear and defend, in person and by counsel; to demand the nature and cause of the accusation; to meet the witnesses against him face to face; to have process to compel the attendance of witnesses in his behalf; and a speedy public trial by an impartial jury of the county.

Section 18(b): Depositions in felony cases—Upon a hearing and finding by the circuit court in any case wherein the accused is charged with a felony, that it is necessary to take the deposition of any witness within the state, other than defendant and spouse, in order to preserve the testimony, and on condition that the court make such orders as will fully protect the rights of personal confrontation and cross-examination of the witness by defendant, the state may take the deposition of such witness and either party may use the same at the trial, as in civil cases, provided there has been substantial compliance with such orders. The reasonable personal and traveling expenses of defendant and his counsel shall be paid by the state or county as provided by law.

Section 19: Self-incrimination and double jeopardy—That no person shall be compelled to testify against himself in a criminal cause, nor shall any person be put again in jeopardy of life or liberty for the same offense, after being once acquitted by a jury; but if the jury fail to render a verdict the court may, in its discretion, discharge the jury and commit or bail the prisoner for trial at the same or next term of court; and if judgment be arrested after a verdict of guilty on a defective indictment or information, or if judgment on a verdict of guilty be reversed for error in law, the prisoner may be tried anew on a proper indictment or information, or according to the law.

Section 20: Bail guaranteed–exceptions—That all persons shall be bailable by sufficient sureties, except for capital offenses, when the proof is evident or the presumption great.

Section 21: Excessive bail and fines–cruel and unusual punishment—That excessive bail shall not be required, nor excessive fines imposed, nor cruel and unusual punishment inflicted.

Section 22(a): Right of trial by jury–qualification of jurors–two-thirds verdict—That the right of trial by jury as heretofore enjoyed shall remain inviolate; provided that a jury for the trial of criminal and civil cases in courts not of record may consist of less than twelve citizens as may be prescribed by law, and a two-thirds majority of such number concurring may render a verdict in all civil cases; that in all civil cases in courts of record, three-fourths of the members of the jury concurring may render a verdict; and that in every criminal case any defendant may, with the assent of the court, waive a jury trial and submit the trial of such case to the court, whose finding shall have the force and effect of a verdict of a jury.

Section 22(b): Female jurors–optional exemption—No citizen shall be disqualified from jury service because of sex, but the court shall excuse any woman who requests exemption therefrom before being sworn as a juror.

Section 23: Right to keep and bear arms–exception—That the right of every citizen to keep and bear arms in defense of his home, person and property, or when lawfully summoned in aid of the civil power, shall not be questioned; but this shall not justify the wearing of concealed weapons.

Section 24: Subordination of military to civil power–quartering soldiers—That the military shall be always in strict subordination to the civil power; that no soldier shall be quartered in any house without the consent of the owner in time of peace, nor in time of war, except as prescribed by law.

Section 25: Elections and right of suffrage—That all elections shall be free and open; and no power, civil or military, shall at any time interfere to prevent the free exercise of the right of suffrage.

Section 26: Compensation for property taken by eminent domain–condemnation juries–payment–railroad property—That private property shall not be taken or damaged for public use without just compensation. Such compensation shall be ascertained by a jury or board of commissioners of not less than three freeholders, in such manner as may be provided by law; and until the same shall be paid to the owner, or into court for the owner, the property shall not be disturbed or the proprietary rights of the owner therein divested. The fee of land taken for railroad purposes without consent of the owner thereof shall remain in such owner subject to the use for which it is taken.

Section 27: Acquisition of excess property by eminent domain–disposition under restrictions—That in such manner and under such limitations as may be provided by law, the state, or any county or city may acquire by eminent domain such property, or rights in property, in excess of that actually to be occupied by the public improvement or used in connection therewith, as may be reasonably necessary to effectuate the purposes intended, and may be vested with the fee simple title thereto, or the control of the use thereof, and may sell such excess property with such restrictions as shall be appropriate to preserve the improvements made.

Section 28: Limitation on taking of private property for private use–exceptions–public use a judicial question—That private property shall not be taken for private use with or without compensation, unless by consent of the owner, except for private ways of necessity, and except for drains and ditches across the lands of others for agricultural and sanitary purposes, in the manner prescribed by law; and that when an attempt is made to take private property for a use alleged to be public, the question whether the contemplated use be public shall be judicially determined without regard to any legislative declaration that the use is public.

Section 29: Organized labor and collective bargaining—That employees shall have the right to organize and to bargain collectively through representatives of their own choosing.

Section 30: Treason–attainder–corruption of blood and forfeitures–estate of suicides–death by casualty—That treason against the state can consist only in levying war against it, or in adhering to its enemies, giving them aid and comfort; that no person can be convicted of treason, unless on the testimony of two witnesses to the same overt act, or on his confession in open court; that no person can be attainted of treason or felony by the general assembly; that no conviction can work corruption of blood or forfeiture of estate; that the estates of such persons as may destroy their own lives shall descend or vest as in cases of natural death; and when any person shall be killed by casualty, there shall be no forfeiture by reason thereof.

Section 31: Fines or imprisonments fixed by administrative agencies—That no law shall delegate to any commission, bureau, board or other administrative agency authority to make any rule fixing a fine or imprisonment as punishment for its violation.

Section 32: Crime victims' rights—Crime victims, as defined by law, shall have the following rights, as defined by law: (1) The right to be present at all criminal justice proceedings at which the defendant has such right, including juvenile proceedings where the offense would have been a felony if committed by an adult; (2) Upon request of the victim, the right to be informed of and heard at guilty pleas, bail hearings, sentencings, probation revocation hearings, and parole hearings, unless in the determination of the court the interests of justice require otherwise; (3) The right to be informed of trials and preliminary hearings; (4) The right to restitution, which shall be enforceable in the same manner as any other civil cause of action, or as otherwise provided by law; (5) The right to the speedy disposition and appellate review of their cases, provided that nothing in this subdivision shall prevent the defendant from having sufficient time to prepare his defense; (6) The right to reasonable protection from the defendant or any person acting on behalf of the defendant; (7) The right to information concerning the escape of an accused from custody or confinement, the defendant's release and scheduling of the defendant's release from incarceration; and (8) The right to information about how the criminal justice system works, the rights and the availability of services, and upon request of the victim the right to information about the crime.

Articles II — XIV

II. .... The Distribution of Powers
III. ...... Legislative Department, Legislative Proceedings, Limitation of Legislative Power, State Lottery, Initiative & Referendum
IV. .... Executive Department, Revenue, Highways & Transportation, Agriculture, Economic Development, Insurance, Social Services, Mental Health, Conservation, Natural Resources, Public Safety, Labor & Industrial Relations, Office of Administration, Appointment of Administrative Heads, Higher Ed., Nondiscrimination in Appointments
V. .... Judicial Department, Schedule
VI. ...... Local Government, Special Charters, Local Government, Finances, City & County of St. Louis, City of St. Louis
VII. ..... Public Officers
VIII. ... Suffrage & Elections
IX. ...... Education
X. .... Taxation
XI. ...... Corporations, Railroads, Banks
XII. ..... Amending the Constitution, Schedule
XIII. ... Public Employees
XIV. .... Schedule

Even with the Missouri Constitution, the Only Constant Is Change

Even with the Missouri Constitution, there is constant change and revision taking place. The previous articles have many addenda citing precedent-setting court cases. On the previous pages, these addenda have been excluded due to space limitations. But they are listed in their entirety in the official Constitution of the State of Missouri, published by the secretary of state. A sample article is included below to show how, over time, various court cases continue to mold and strengthen the Missouri state constitution.

Section 26: Compensation for property taken by eminent domain–condemnation juries–payment–railroad property—

That private property shall not be taken or damaged for public use without just compensation. Such compensation shall be ascertained by a jury or board of commissioners of not less than three freeholders, in such manner as may be provided by law; and until the same shall be paid to the owner, or into court for the owner, the property shall not be disturbed or the proprietary rights of the owner therein divested. The fee of land taken for railroad purposes without consent of the owner thereof shall remain subject to the use for which it is taken. *Source: Const. of 1875, Art. II, § 21.*

(1954) Contention that condemnation procedure authorized by charter of the city of St. Louis violated equal protection provision of federal constitution held waived by failure to raise same in court below. City of St. Louis v. Gruss (Mo.), 263 S.W.2d 387. (1955) The measure of damages for the taking of land is determined as of the time of taking and from the point of view of what the owner has lost, not what the condemnor has gained so that uses to which property may be put under city zoning regulations may be considered by jury in determining damages. In re Armory Site in Kansas City (Mo.), 282 S.W.2d 464. (1956) In action to condemn lands for gas storage under §§ 393.410 to 393.510, owners of lands adjoining those sought to be condemned did not have right to intervene because only damage they could suffer would result from use of condemned lands and not from condemnation. Laclede Gas Co. v. Abrahamson (Mo.), 296 S.W.2d 100. (1956) Damage to land from water overflow which allegedly would result from highway construction ruled consequential damage, no claim for which would arise prior to infliction and claimants were therefore not aggrieved by plaintiffs' voluntary dismissal of condemnation action as to them and had no right of appeal. State ex rel. State Highway Comm. v. Lynch (Mo.), 297 S.W.2d 400. (1957) Where landowner was advised by state highway department that it planned to construct highway through his property and began negotiations with him for acquisition of right-of-way, and as a result he changed his subdivision development plans, there was no "taking" or "damaging" within the constitutional provision. Hamer v. State Highway Comm. (Mo.), 304 S.W.2d 869. (1957) Abutting owners have an easement of access to a highway which is a property right and interest in land and the only way to estinguish such right is by the exercise of the power of eminent domain. State ex rel. Highway Dept. v. Green (Mo.), 305 S.W.2d 688. (1957) A trial court has no power to add any amount (such as interest) to the sum fixed by the jury in condemnation action (Ark. Mo. Pow. Co. v. Hamlin (A.), 288 S.W.2d 14, and State ex rel. State Highway Comm. v Galloway (A.), 292 S.W.2d 904 to the contrary, in effect overruled). State ex rel. Highway Dept. v. Green (Mo.), 305 S.W.2d 688. (1959) Where power to take property by eminent domain exists, the condemnor may determine the location and route of the improvement and the land or easement to be taken for it. State ex rel. N.W. Electric Power Coop. v. Waggoner (A.), 319 S.W.2d 930. (1959) Where amount of judgment for damages in condemnation suit exceeded commissioner's award which was paid into court, property owner was entitled to interest on excess. St. Louis Housing Authority v. Mafagas (Mo.), 324 S.W.2d 697. (1959) Where city appropriated private sewer without complying with statutory procedure, its action would amount to taking private property for public use without just compensation. Gunn v. City of Versailles (A.), 330 S.W.2d 257. (1960) This provision of the constitution requires an allowance of compensation to the landowner for the loss of the use of the amount of money by which the circuit court judgment exceeds the award of the commissioners from the time of taking or appropriation until the entry of judgment fixing the amount of damages. City of St. Louis v. Vasquez (Mo.), 341 S.W.2d 839. (1961) Evidence held sufficient to sustain judgment against city because of injury to property resulting from discharge of sewage into stream running through such property. Lewis v. City of Potosi (A.), 348 S.W.2d 577. (1961) A provision of an ordinance in the City of St. Louis which provided that damages should be assessed as of the date of the ordinance directing the condemnation held invalid. The date on which the money is paid into the registry of the court is the date on which the value of the property is to be fixed. City of St. Louis v. International Harvester Company (Mo.), 350 S.W.2d 782. (1962) Highway commission had authority to condemn easement to provide a substitute location for pipelines which was necessary for interstate highway construction as the taking was for public purpose and was not in violation of Article III, § 38(a) since state received compensation in surrender of existing right-of-way. State ex rel. State Highway Commission v. Eakin (Mo.), 357 S.W.2d 129. (1963) Assuming that telephone company had a certificate of convenience and necessity to serve a certain area, public service commission's orders directing another company to provide service to the area did not constitute a taking of telephone company's property in violation of this constitutional provision. State ex rel. Doniphan Telephone Co. v. Public Service Commission (Mo.), 369 S.W.2d 572. (1963) Fact of taking of property constitutes a prima facie case thus giving rise to right to have the value determined by a jury, and although owners produced no evidence to prove value of damages, jury under proper instruction could have found damages within reasonable limits of their own experience and observation and giving of instruction which foreclosed landowners from jury determination of damages was error. State ex rel. State Highway Commission v. Cady (A.), 372 S.W.2d 639. (1964) Trial court properly limited evidence and instructing as to valuation of property as of the date condemnor paid amount of commissioners' award into court and deterioration of value of property as result of announcement of proposed housing project and institution of condemnation action was not an item of just compensation within the meaning of this constitutional provision. St. Louis Housing Authority v. Barnes (Mo.), 375 S.W.2d 144. (1964) Although metropolitan sewer district was immune to action in tort for damages resulting from negligent operation of drainage ditch, this provision of constitution is binding upon state as well as others having power of eminent domain and its self-enforcing and court suggested plaintiff might proceed under procedure known as condemnation in reverse or inverse condemnation where facts alleged in petition indicated plaintiff's property was taken (or damages) for public use. Page v. Metropolitan St. Louis Sewer District (Mo.), 377 S.W.2d 348. (1964) The admission of evidence in condemnation case by owner of land zoned for agricultural purposes as to value of land for industrial use was error in absence of showing of reasonable probability of change in zoning restriction in reasonably near future and fact that land was being taken for electric power plant did not establish reasonable probability that zoning restriction would be changed in reasonably near future to permit industrial use generally. Union Electric v. Saale (Mo.), 377 S.W.2d 427. (1964) In proceedings to condemn property by city for construction and maintenance of sanitary sewers evidence justified finding that special benefits equalled or exceeded the damages and owners were not entitled to awards. Thomson v. Kansas City (A.), 379 S.W.2d 194. (1967) If property is taken or damaged without agreement or legal proceedings, one of several remedies of the owner is that he may waive the tort and sue for the compensatory damages to which he would have been entitled if condemnation proceedings had been instituted prior to the entry. Twiehaus v. Wright City (Mo.), 412 S.W.2d 450. (1967) Expenses of litigation paid by landowners before termination of of condemnation proceedings did not constitute taking or damaging his property for public use without just compensation. Dietrich v. St. Louis County (Mo.), 415 S.W.2d 777. (1969) Section 88.673, RSMo, does not prevent recovery of damages under Art. I, § 26, of the constitution, for private property taken or damaged for public use. Lange v. City of Jackson (A.), 440 S.W.2d 758. (1973) This provision declared to be self-enforcing. Wells v. State Highway Commission (Mo.), 503 S.W.2d 689. (1986) Section 64.090, RSMo, was held to violate section 26 of Article I of the Missouri Constitution insofar as it attempted to give certain counties the power to zone out existing uses of property. People Tags, Inc., v. Jackson County Legislature, 636 F.Supp. 1345 (W.D. Mo. 1986). (1987) Eminent domain statutes are narrowly construed, and an activity conducted beyond the scope of such statute, such as a "soil survey", may be enough of an intrusion to constitute a taking. Missouri Highway and Transportation Commission v. Eilers, 729 S.W.2d 471 (Mo.App. 1987). (1993) When, as result of public works project, private property is damaged by an unreasonable diversion of surface waters, whether by design or by mistake, or when private property is damaged by nuisance operated by an entity having power of eminent domain, proper remedy is an action in inverse condemnation. Heins Implement v. Mo. Highway & Transportation Commission, 859 S.W.2d 681 (Mo. en banc).

Missouri Government: On-Line Resources

Learn About State Government on the Internet

Missouri residents and non-residents can keep on top of all areas of state government with only a few clicks of their mouse. Fortunately, the state of Missouri has made its websites as user-friendly as possible. All sites related to Missouri can be entered through the main home page or through more direct routes by requesting searches on specific subjects. Here are but a few websites within the Missouri government web pages with their addresses so that one can enter directly.

Missouri State Government Home Page   http://www.state.mo.us/

This home page is the only address necessary to keep abreast of state government in Jefferson City and the rest of the state. It serves as a true gateway, allowing one to enter the pages of all branches of state government and departments, check the Missouri Constitution and Statutes, review job listings, look up e-mail addresses and phone numbers of state employees, and keep informed of board and commission meetings, as well as search through all of the state government web sites for specific information. There is even a kids' page to teach Missouri's future voters about government, and up-to-the-minute lottery results. All of the following listings can be accessed through this website, except for the Missouri Bar Association.

Missouri Governor's Office   http://www.gov.state.mo.us/index.htm

The governor's home page is a way for the governor to communicate his or her current and past achievements, speeches, legislative action, plans and constituent services to the citizens of Missouri and elsewhere. Additionally, there is a page about the governor's family entitled "Mansion Happenings," a biography of the governor and even the governor's own page directed to Missouri's children.

Missouri Secretary of State's Office   http://mosl.sos.state.mo.us/

The secretary of state's basic responsibility is to inform the citizens of Missouri about what is happening in Missouri government. This site is an excellent source for anyone curious about information on elections, business services, the state library system, Missouri archives, or administrative services. *The Official Manual of the State of Missouri* or *Blue Book*, as it is commonly called, can be found on-line through the secretary of state's home page. The *Blue Book* contains information on all political figures in the three branches of state government, general information about the state and a listing of all state personnel. The secretary of state home page is also the source for up-to-the-minute information concerning current federal and state elections.

Missouri Judiciary Home Page   http://www.osca.state.mo.us/

Through the Supreme Court of Missouri, one can access full-text opinions, docket summaries, judicial biographies and even Bar Exam results. Lower court sites also allow all interested parties to stay current with specific cases.

Missouri General Assembly   http://www.moga.state.mo.us/

Of main interest here are all joint bills and committees and real audio debates from the Missouri house and senate. The Missouri Constitution can also be viewed here. Copies of the constitution, along with its statutes, can be ordered through this site as well.

Missouri State Senate   http://www.senate.state.mo.us/

This site is invaluable for keeping abreast of the actions of the Missouri Senate, including past and current legislation, senate leadership and committees, rules of the senate, and various addresses, among them: the governor's State of the State on real audio, the president pro tem's opening address, and the State of the Judiciary address. This page has a lot of information in common with the house of representatives' page, specifically calendars, journals, and hearings for both houses; an explanation of the legislative process; and a further source for the Missouri Constitution and Revised Statutes. A Missouri citizen can find out who represents them in the senate or the house of representatives at this website using a simplified search program that uses one's zip code, also available at the website listed below.

Missouri House of Representatives   http://www.house.state.mo.us/home.htm

This page shares a lot of information with the Senate page. A few items are specific to the actions of the House, such as House committees and House bills along with past and current House action. Other unique features include lobbyist information, employment opportunities, as well as public information sites. A Hall of Famous Missourians and information about tours of the Capitol in Jefferson City are included in the public information pages.

Representative & Senator Search   http://www.house.state.mo.us/searchzp.htm

This is the direct Internet address for residents of Missouri to find out who represents them in the General Assembly simply by entering their zip code. Once the names of the legislators appear, one only needs to click on the name of the representative or senator to enter that member's home page. These pages include mailing, phone and e-mail information. Other information given includes party affiliation, terms in the Assembly, county or counties represented, and committees in which they participate. There are also links to biographical information and current legislation sponsored by that representative or senator.

Missouri State Employment Opportunities   http://www.oa.state.mo.us/stjobs.htm

This page not only allows one to check vacancies at all state agencies, but also openings at the University of Missouri system, Southeast Missouri State University, and federal jobs in Missouri. There are also links to national job listings and employment in Kansas City and St. Louis.

Missouri Department of Conservation   http://www.conservation.state.mo.us/

Missouri is home to a diverse and rich array of natural resources. This page is the authoritative source for anyone interested in fishing and hunting, forestry, state parks and other recreational areas, and Missouri nature in general.

Missouri Bar   http://www.mobar.org/

Law and legal resources for the public, educators, lawyers and the media. Learn about the state bar and its resources that help the public. Public information topics cover everything from how to find a lawyer to family legal issues such as adoption, divorce, wills and probate.

Bibliography / Recommended Reading

Abrams, Jim. *"Court to Rule on Campaign Spending."* Yahoo! News, Associated Press Page: Politics Headlines. 25 January 2000. 2 February 2000 http://dailynews.yahoo.com/h/ap/20000125/pl/congree_contributions_2.html

Aulbur, Millie. *Juvenile Justice in Missouri Hand-Out.* Jefferson City: Missouri Bar, 1999.

Anderson, Susan. *"The Safe Schools Act Protects Missouri Students."* Journal of the Missouri Bar vol. 55, no. 5. Jefferson City: Missouri Bar.

Blunt, Roy D. *Official Manual: State of Missouri, 1985-1986.* Edited by Steven N. Ahrens. Jefferson City: Secretary of State, 1986.

The Brookings Institution. *"Contribution & Spending Limits: Supreme Court to Hear Challenge to Contribution Limits."* Recent Developments in Campaign Finance Regulation: Contribution Limits. 25 January 1999. 2 February 2000. http://www.brook.edu/gs/campaign/updates/shrink/htm

Carelli, Richard. *"Court Backs States on Contributions."* Yahoo! News, Associated Press Page: Politics Headlines. 24 January 2000. 2 February 2000 http://dailynews.yahoo.com/h/ap/20000124/pl/scotus_contributions_7.html

Carnahan, Jean. *If Walls Could Talk: The Story of Missouri's First Families.* Jefferson City: MMPI, 1998.

Christensen, Lawrence O., et al., eds. *Dictionary of Missouri Biography.* Columbia: University of Missouri Press, 1999.

Cook, Rebecca McDowell. *Constitution State of Missouri.* Jefferson City: Secretary of State, 1997.

——. *General Assembly Roster.* Jefferson City: Secretary of State, 1999.

——. *1999-2000 Missouri Roster.* Jefferson City: Secretary of State, 1999.

——. *Official Manual: State of Missouri, 1999-2000.* Edited by Julius Johnson. Jefferson City: Secretary of State, 1999.

"Court automation Plan for Missouri on track." *Columbia Daily Tribune,* April 6, 1997, p. 6C.

Dohm, Richard R. Article published in *Government Affairs Newsletter.* Columbia: University of Missouri-Columbia Extension Division, October 1981, p. 1.

Dunne, Gerald T. *The Missouri Supreme Court: From Dred Scott to Nancy Cruzan.* Columbia: University of Missouri Press, 1993.

Foley, William, and Perry McCandless. *Democracy in Action: Missouri's Constitution and Its Government.* Davenport, Iowa: Lindsay Industries, 1987.

Gaw, Steve. *1821. An Introduction to Missouri Government, Citizenship and History.* Jefferson City: Missouri House of Representatives, n.d.

Gaw, Steve, and Dick Franklin. *Missouri House of Representatives Budget Fast Facts 1999, Fiscal Year 2000.* Jefferson City: Missouri House of Representatives, 1999.

Hardy, Richard J., Richard R. Dohm, and David A. Leuthold, eds. *Missouri Government and Politics.* Columbia: University of Missouri Press.

Hearnes Center Facts. University of Missouri Home Page. 3 February 2000 http://www.hearnescenter.com/about.html

——. *"In Shrink PAC vs. Nixon, Supreme Court to Hear Challenge to Contribution Limits."* Recent Developments in Campaign Finance Regulation: contribution Limits. 3 February 2000 http://www.brook.edu/gs/cf/headlines/shrink/htm

Lurie, Leonard. *Party Policies: Why We Have Poor Presidents.* New York: Stein and Day, 1980.

Karsch, Robert. *Missouri Under the Constitution.* Columbia, Mo.: Lucas Brothers, 1968.

Kestenbaum, Lawrence. *The Political Graveyard: Shriner Politicians in Missouri.* 2 February 2000 http://politicalgraveyard.com/group/shriners/MO.html

McDowell Cook, Rebecca. *See* Cook, Rebecca McDowell

Meyer, Duane G. *The Heritage of Missouri.* Springfield, Mo.: Emden Press, 1982.

Missouri Department of Elementary and Secondary Education. *Missouri's Framework for Curriculum Development in Social Studies,* p. viii.

Missouri House of Representatives. *"Missouri Revised Statutes, Chapter 130: Campaign Finance Disclosure Law, Section 130.032."* Missouri Revised Statutes. 28 August 1999. 7 February 2000 http://www.moga.state.mo.us/statutes/c100-199/1300032.htm

——. *Missouri 1821*. Jefferson City: 1988.

——. *Missouri 90th General Assembly Legislative Roster 1999-2000*. Jefferson City: Association of Missouri Electric Cooperatives, 1999.

——. *Official Manual: State of Missouri 1995-1996*. Edited by Steven N. Ahrens. Jefferson City: Secretary of State, 1996.

Missouri Governor's Office: Governor's Biography. Missouri State Government Web Page. 2 February 2000 http://www.gov.state.mo.us/bio.htm

The Missouri Quick Fact-Book. Topeka, Ks.: Capper Press, 1991.

Nixon, Attorney General of Missouri, et al. vs. Shrink Missouri Government PAC et al. *No. 98-963 (US January 24, 2000)* 2 February 2000 <javascript:MakeNewWindow ('supct.law.cornell.edu/supct/html/98-963.ZO.html')

Ohman, Marian M. *Encyclopedia of Missouri Courthouses*. Columbia: University of Missouri Extension, 1981.

——. *The History of Missouri Capitols*. Columbia: University of Missouri Extension, n.d.

——. *A History of Missouri's Counties, County Seats, and Courthouse Squares*. Columbia: University of Missouri Extension, 1983.

Parrish, William E., Charles T. Jones Jr., and Lawrence O. Christensen. *Missouri: The Heart of the Nation*. 2nd edition. Wheeling, Ill.: Harlan Davidson, 1992.

Quick, Edward, and Senate Appropriations Staff. *Missouri Senate Appropriations Committee 1999 Annual Fiscal Report, Fiscal Year 2000*. Jefferson City: Senate Appropriations Staff, 1999.

Riekes, Linda, Melissa Hellstern, Joyce Cheney, and Sharon Slane. *Missouri Citizens: Then, Now and the Future,* St Louis: N.p., 1996.

Rose, Forrest. *"1-800-Elect Me: Shady Operators Are Standing By!"* Columbia Daily Tribune Online. 1 February 2000. 2 February 2000 http://archive.showmenews.com/tribonline/comment/2000020109.html

Schmidt, Chris S. *Our Federal Constitution, Our Missouri Constitution*. Merrill, Wisc.: R.J.S. Publications, n.d.

Self-Guided Outdoor Walk of the Capitol. Jefferson City: Department of Natural Resources, n.d.

Senator John Ashcroft. United States Senate Home Pages. 2 February 2000 http://www.senate.gov/~ashcroft/aboutjda.htm

Shafritz, Jay M. *The Dorsey Dictionary of American Government and Politics*. Chicago: Dorsey Press, 1988.

——. *The HarperCollins Dictionary of American Government and Politics*. New York: Harper Perennial, 1993.

Stacy, Darryl, and Dr. James D. Bimes. *Missouri Studies: Government & Constitution*. Phoenix, Ariz.: Cloud Publishing, 1989.

——. *"Supreme Court Upholds Missouri Law Limiting Contributions, Strongly Reaffirms Buckley Contribution Limits 'To Prevent Corruption and Appearance of Corruption.'"* Recent Developments: Supreme Court Ruling in Nixon vs. Shrink Missouri Government PAC. 2 February 2000 http://www.brook.edu/gs/cf/headlines/2000013001.htm

Waters, Henry. *"Campaign Donation Caps: US Supreme Court OKs State Law."* Columbia Missouri Tribune Online. 30 January 2000. 2 February 2000 http://archive.showmenews.com/archive/2000/jan/30/comment/20000013001.html

Webber, David. *"Ruling Breathes New Life Into Campaign Reforms."* Columbia Missouri Tribune Online. 31 January 2000. 2 February 2000 http://archive.showmenews.com/archive/2000/jan/31/comment/20000013105.html

Photo Credits

Many thanks to all of the photographers and sources who provided reprint permission. Photo credits are listed below. Where possible, individual photographers are cited.

Barbara Baird: 197; Angie Blume: 100, 208(2); Margo Carroll: 103; *Columbia Daily Tribune:* Lisa Finger: 74, 201(2). Sean Meyers: 75, 214. Patty Roksten: 116. Schiappa: 129. Mike Stewart: 62, 128. Michael Vosburg: 72. Photographer not cited: 41, 201; Brett Dufur: ii, viii, xii, 198, 209, 224, 226, 227, 228(2), 229, 230(2), 231, 232, 233, 234, 236(2), 238, inside back cover author photo; John Knight, photo illustrations pp. i and 256. Photos appear courtesy Missouri State Archives and *Columbia Daily Tribune;* Missouri Division of Tourism: 199; Missouri State Archives, Laura Jolley, photo editor. Photos taken by Gerald Massie and others: 14, 16, 17, 20, 22, 23, 24, 25, 35, 37, 38, 48, 52, 63, 69, 85, 89, 90, 91, 93, 96, 113, 117, 119, 121, 160, 210, 217, 219, 220, 221, 222, 223, 239; L.G. Patterson, courtesy *The Columbia Business Times:* 212.

Index

Note: A page number followed by an (s) means the indexed subject appears in the sidebar on that page.

Abuse and Lose It Law, Missouri, 169
Advisory Committee on Evidence Rules, 160
affirmative action, 73
African Americans, 35, 49, 155, 158
Aitken, Robert, 232, 233, 235
Anheuser Busch, Inc., St. Louis, 24
Arrow Rock, 21
Articles of Confederation, 31
Ashcroft, John, 39, 73, 83, 86, 92, 95
attorney general, 67, 82, 98
Austin, Moses, 155
automation, 160

Baer, Fred, 213
Baker, Sam, 95
Barbé-Marbois, François, 229
Barnes, Jim, 128
Bates, Frederick, 19, 95
Battle of Pea Ridge, the, 20
Battle of Wilson's Creek, the, 18
Benton, Duane, 138, 139
Benton, Senator Thomas Hart (senator), 20, 69
Benton, Thomas Hart (muralist), 102, 224
Berlin Wall, in Missouri, 21
Bingham, George Caleb, 102
Bitter, Karl, 229
Blair, James Jr., 95
Blunt, Roy, 39
Board of Fund Commissioners, 96, 99
Boehm, Ted, 212-13
Boggs, Lilburn, 95, 156
Bonaparte, Napoleon, 16, 229
Bond, Christopher S. (Kit), 39, 83, 85, 93, 95, 96
Boone County Sheriff's Department, 212-13
Boonville, 18, 221
Bradley, General Omar N., 21
Brown vs. Board of Education of Topeka, 49
Brown, Benjamin, 95
Buckley vs. Valeo, 66-68
Burden vs. Hornsby, 157
Burden, Charles, 157

Calloway, Deverne Lee, 117
Camden County, 71s
campaign finance, 66
Cape Girardeau, 24, 46
Capitol Decoration Commission, 224
Carnahan, Mel, 73, 82, 83, 88-89, 95
Carthage, 18, 223
Caulfield, Henry, 95
Cervantes, Alfonso, 210
Charitable Choice provision, 73

charter commission, 205
Chevalier vs. Chouteau, 155
child support, 153
child welfare laws, 92
Churchill, Sir Winston, 21
circuit courts, 37, 136, 137, 140-43, 149; and campaign funding, 67-68; judicial, 64-65
cities, 197-98; special charter, 199
City of Columbia Industrial Revenue Bond Authority, 160
civil rights, 35, 73, 113, 156
Civil War, 27, 69, 102, 138 s, 156; and Missouri, 18, 50, 221; veterans, 226
Clark, James Beauchamp (Champ), 43
Clark, William, 26, 85; Fort, 16
Clay, William, 39
Cleveland, Grover, 94
Cole County: courthouse, 221; Historical Society, 238
College Republicans, 62
Commission on Crime and Law Enforcement, 210
Commission on Retirement, Removal and Discipline, 151
Conference of Chief Justices of the United States, 160
conservatism, 45, 50-51
constitutional charters, 199
Contract with America, 42, 61
Cook, Rebecca McDowell, 82
Council on Human Rights, 210
Court Reform and Revision Act, 135
courts, 98, 136, 142, 148, 165. *See also* Circuit courts; Missouri Court of Appeals
Covington, Ann, 139, 160
Cozad, Woody, 92
Crayton, Almeta, 214
Crittenden, Thomas, 95
Cruzan vs. Harmon, 158
Cruzan, Nancy, 158

Dalton, John, 95
Danner, Pat, 39
Democratic party, 61, 71, 149; Leadership Group, 42
Dierker, Robert H. Jr., 159
Dietiker, Bob., 201
Dockery, Alexander, 95
Donnell vs. Osburn, 158
Donnell, Forrest, 95, 158
Donnelly, Phil, 85, 95
Doolittle, James H., 21
Drake, Charles, 27
Dred Scott case, 138 s, 156
Dun and Bradstreet, 52
Dunklin, Daniel, 95

Eagleton, Thomas, 96
Edwards, John, 95
elections, 64-66, 76; city, 70; of judges, 65, 149; mail-in, 75; non-partisan, 69, 76; senatorial, 112
electoral college, 65, 76
Ellis Fischel Cancer Center, 89
Emerson, Jo Ann, 39
Entrepreneur magazine, 52

environmental interests, 54
Equal Protection Clause, 67
Excellence in Education Act, 93

Family and Medical Leave Act, 40
Family Care Safety Registry, 73
Federal Housing Association (FHA), 49
Fisher, Mike, 119
flag etiquette, 56
Fletcher, Thomas, 95
Folk, Joseph, 92, 95
Fort Osage, 16, 26
Francis, David, 94, 95
Frankenstein, Missouri, 197
Fraser, James Earl, 233
Fredman, Zev David, 67
French, the, 16, 27, 155
Fry, Sherry, 234

Gamble, Hamilton Rowan, 95, 102
Gardner, Frederick, 95
Gaw, Steve, 201
General Motors, 24, 53
Gephardt, Richard, 39, 42, 64
GI loans, 49
Gingrich, Newt, 42, 66
government: confederal system of, 31; county, 65,
         196, 206; federal, 31-34; different forms
         of, 201-2; general purpose, 195
Governor's Committee on Interstate Cooperation, 99
Governor's Mansion, Jefferson City, 237
Graham, Chuck, 72
Grant, Ulysses S., 27
Great Seal of Missouri, the, 97
Griffin, Robert, 119
gun control, 73

Hadley, Herbert, 95
Hall, Willard, 95
Hallmark, Inc., 24
Hancock Amendment, 51, 152s
Hancock, Mel, 51
Hardin, Charles Henry, 95, 102
Harlan, Tim, 201
health care, 73, 104
Hearnes, Warren, 85, 88, 90-92, 95
Highway Patrol Safety Education Center, 238
Highway Patrol. *See* Missouri State Highway Patrol
Holden, Bob, 68, 82
Holstein, John, 139, 152
home loans, 48-49
Hornsby, Leonidas, 157
Hulshof, Kenny, 39, 214
Hyde, Arthur, 95

Independent party, 149
International Brotherhood of Sleeping Car Porters, 113
Internet, 47 s, 73; voting, 75
Irene Emerson vs. Dred Scott, 156

Jackson, Andrew, 69
Jackson, Claiborne Fox, 20, 95

Jackson, Hancock, 95
Jacob, Ken, 201
Jefferson, Thomas, 16, 33, 209, 229; statue of, 233
Jefferson Landing State Historic Site, 237
Jefferson Women's Democratic Clubs, 62
Joliet, Louis, 15
judges, 65, 136, 139, 149, 150-51
Juvenile Justice Advisory Board, 160
juvenile law, 142, 165, 153

Kansas City, 16, 21, 24, 46, 52, 72, 87, 140
Kelly, Margaret, 83
King, Austin, 95
Kraemer vs. Shelley, 158
Kraemer, Louis and Fern, 158

la Salle, Robert Cavalier Sieur de, 15
Law Library, St Louis, 27
lawmaking, 73, 74, 92, 94, 122, 125, 158-59, 169
Legislative Council, Missouri, 17
Legislative Intern Program, 128
Lewis, Meriwether, 19, 26
Lewis and Clark Expedition, 16, 19
liberals, 45
Libertarian party, 62
lieutenant governor, 67, 82, 84, 96, 113
Limbaugh, Stephen Jr., 139
Lincoln, Abraham,
line item veto, 89
Livingston, Robert, 229
lobbyists, 52, 55, 129-30
"log rolling," 88
Lohman's Landing, 221
Louisiana Purchase, 19, 27, 94, 229, 233
Louisiana Territorial Militia, Clark and, 26
Louisiana Territory, 16, 19, 155

Major, Elliot, 95
Marmaduke, John, 95
Marmaduke, Meredith, 95
Marquette, Father John, 15
Marshall Plan, 35
McCarthy, Karen, 39
McCaskill, Claire, 82
McClurg, Joseph, 95
McDonnell-Douglas Corporation, St Louis, 24, 53
McGovern, George, 96
McNair, Alexander, 85, 95
McNeal, Theodore, 113
merit system, 70, 76
Merrill, Lewis, 206
Mid-American Dairymen, Inc., Springfield, 24
Mid-Missouri Legal Services Corporation, 160
Miller, John, 95
Milligan, Maurice, 89
Minor vs. Happersett, 156
Minor, Virginia, 156
Miranda rights, 169
Missouri, 18, 21, 52, 93, 207; executive branch
         (flowchart), 81, 82; facts, 22-23;
         government, 36-37; political regions of,
         64s-65s; ranking, 26, 50-53, 195; Show
         Me State, 15, 51

Missouri Bar, 135
Missouri Compromise, 18, 27, 69
Missouri Constitution, 81, 85, 136 s, 197, 246-47;
        amendments to, 89; Article I, 241-46;
        Article IV, 87s; Article V, 135s; first, 18;
        preamble of, 37 s, 241
Missouri Council of the Arts, 90
Missouri Court Automation Committee, 152
Missouri Court of Appeals, 37, 137, 140
Missouri Cultural Trust, 98
Missouri Department of Agriculture, 26, 71, 100
Missouri Department of Conservation, 26, 100, 105
Missouri Department of Economic Development,
        26, 52, 101
Missouri Department of Natural Resources, 26
Missouri Department of Public Safety, 87, 103
Missouri Department of Revenue, 26, 71, 104
Missouri Department of Tourism, 26
Missouri Federated Republican Women, 62
Missouri General Assembly, 18, 37; and Ashcroft,
        86; and budget, 123; and business, 52; and
        campaign funding, 67; description of, 111-
        12; 80th, 116; governor and, 106; parties
        and, 62, 71, 91; and presidential primaries,
        64; rating of, 130; and reapportionment,
        120-21; referendums called by, 90; 73rd,
        19; and speaker, 119; and State of the
        State Address, 81s; structure of, 129; and
        U.S. Constitution, 124
Missouri Missouri Highway Reciprocity
        Commission, 99
Missouri House of Representatives: districts, 118;
        standing committees, 120; terms of office,
        39
Missouri Housing Development Commission,
        96, 98
Missouri-Illinois Bridge Company, 89
Missouri Investment Trust, 98
Missouri Plan, 151
Missouri Senate: facts, 116; standing committees,
        115; terms of office, 39
Missouri Southern State College, 121
Missouri State Employees Retirement System, 98
Missouri State Highway Patrol, 71, 87, 168
Missouri Supreme Court, 37, 98, 136-39, 139 s,
        151, 156, 158, 201
Missouri Supreme Court Library, 138s
Missouri Territory, 19
Monroe, James, 229
Monsanto, St. Louis, 24
Moreau Heights Elementary School, 208
Morehouse, Albert, 95
Mormons, 156
Moseley, Joe, 115
"motor-voter" law, 74
Muleskinners, the, 63
municipalities, 196-97

NAFTA. *See* North American Free Trade
        Agreement (NAFTA)
Napoleon. *See* Bonaparte, Napoleon
Native Americans, 13, 15, 155

NATO. *See* North Atlantic Treaty Organization
        (NATO)
New Deal, 205
Nickolaus, Charles, 72
Nixon, Jeremiah (Jay), 82
North American Free Trade Agreement
        (NAFTA), 42
North Atlantic Treaty Organization (NATO),
        Truman and, 35
North Jefferson Katy Trail State Park, 238

Office of Administration, 86, 99
Office of State Courts Administrator (OSCA),
        138, 152, 159
Oregon Trail, 47
Osburn, Morris, 158
OSCA. *See* Office of State Courts Administrator
        (OSCA)
Outstanding Schools Act, 88
Ozark Mountains, 50
Ozark Products Company, Bellefontaine, 25

Pachyderms, the, 62-63
PACs, 127
PACs. *See* Politican Action Committees (PACs)
Parents As Teachers (PAT) program, 40, 88
Park, Guy, 95
PAT. *See* Parents As Teachers (PAT) program
patronage system, 70-71, 76
Pendergast, Thomas, 35, 68, 72, 89, 119, 205
Pendergast, Jim, 205
Perot, Ross, 65, 68
Pershing, John J., 21
Peterson, Mary, 74
Phelps, John, 95
Phelps, William, 103
Phillips, Micah, 75
planning and zoning, 53-55, 143, 195, 202 s, 210 s
Platte Purchase, 13
pledge of allegiance, 56
political parties, 71-74, 91; adjunct organizations,
        62-63; committees, 76; platforms, 68, 72;
        primaries, 63-64. *See also* Democratic
        party; Independent party; Libertarian
        party; Reform party; Republican party
Political Action Committees (PACs), 66
Polk, Trusten V., 69, 95
Pony Express, 21
Pratt, Charles, earl of Camden, 71s
president pro tem, 71, 113, 115, 123
Price, Sterling, 95
Price, William Ray, 139
privatization, 45-46
Procter & Gamble Paper, Cape Girardeau, 24
Progressive Era, 43

racism, 49, 73
railroads, 24, 46; regulation of, 92, 94
Rapp, Bill, 72
reapportionment, 120-21
Red Tape Reduction Act, 40
Reform Movement, 68

Reform party, 65
Reorganization Act of 1974, 83
Republican party, 61; and election of judges, 149;
        fundraising, 66; and General Assembly,
        71; pro-business stance of, 73;
Revised Statutes of Missouri, 97
Reynolds, Thomas, 95
Rollins, James Sydney, 102
Roosevelt, Franklin, 35, 89, 92; death of, 21;
        mentioned, 205
Runge Conseervation Nature Center, 238

Safe Schools Act, 124
Sappington, John S., 20
Schock, Bevis, 67
school districts, 196, 211
schools, 49, 88-89, 93
Scypion, Marie Jean, 155
secretary of state, 67, 97, 82, 83
Sedalia, 221
Shear, Sue, 128
Shelley, J.D. and Ethel, 158
Shrink Missouri Government PAC, 67
Skelton, Ike, 39
small claims court, 143-47
Smith, Forrest, 95
Smith T, John, 155
Snyder, John W., 230
Souter, David, 67
Spanish Conquistadores, 15
speaker of the house, 119, 123
speaker pro tem, 119
special districts, 196, 209
special interest groups, 123, 127
split-ticket voting, 70
Springfield, 24, 52, 140
St. Charles, 16, 26, 220
St. Joseph, 21, 46
St. Louis, 16, 20, 24, 46, 50, 52, 69, 140; and 1904
        World's Fair, 94, 229; population, 49
St. Louis Arch, 199
St. Louis Board of Aldermen, 210
St. Louis Board of Police Commissioners, 87,
        113, 159
St. Louis Enquirer, 69
St. Louis Gateway Convention Center, 210
St. Louis Missouri Fur Company, 26
St. Louis Post-Dispatch, 159
Stark, Lloyd, 89, 95, 205
Stark Brothers Nursery, 89
state auditor, 67, 82, 83, 97,
state committee, 65, 76
state militia, 87
State of the Judiciary Address, 138
State of the State Address, 81 s, 88
state treasurer, 67, 82, 98
State vs. Joseph Smith, 156
status crime, 168
statutes, 63
Ste Genevieve, 16, 155
Stephens, Lon, 95
Stewart, Robert, 95

Stone, William, 95
straight-ticket voting, 69
Sublett, Roy, 74
suburbanization, 48-49
Sunshine Law, 159
Supreme Court Building, Jefferson City, 238

Talent, James, 39, 68
tax base, 53-54, 55
taxes, 53, 73, 93, 104, 106, 152 s
Teasdale, Joseph, 83, 85, 95
Territorial House of Representatives, Missouri, 17
Territory of Missouri, 17
Thomas vs. Austin, 155
tobacco industry, 73
Tourism Commission, 96
townships, 64, 196-97
truancy, 172
Truman, Harry S, 21, 35, 89, 205
Truman Doctrine, 35

United States vs. Ouipinicaka, 155
University of Missouri Board of Curators, 92,
        87, 113
U.S. Congress, 17, 38
U.S. Constitution, 32, 33; Article I, 37; Article IV,
        33 s, 83; First Amendment, 67, 127; 14th
        Amendment, 67, 156; 10th Amendment,
        31 s, 33 s
U.S. Supreme Court, 67, 70, 156
U.S.S. *Missouri,* 21

Van Buren, Martin, 71s
Vandiver, Willard D., 15
Vest, George Graham, 157
video: arraignments, 152; -conferencing, 47 s
veterans memorial, 226
villages, 197
voters, 61, 64, 74, 76

War of 1812: mentioned, 69, 85
Watergate, 66
Webster, Richard, 121
Weinman, Adolph Alexander, 228
Westminster College, Fulton, 21
White, Ronnie, 139
Williams, Abraham, 95
Wilson, Roger, 82
Wolff, Michael, 139
Woods, Harriet, 83, 115
Woodson, Silas, 95
workers' fraud, 103
World War II, 35, 226
writs, 136

Young Democrats, 62

zoning. *See* Planning and zoning